Tales from the Left Coast

True Stories of Hollywood Stars and Their Outrageous Politics

JAMES HIRSEN

With NewsMax.com

THREE RIVERS PRESS
NEW YORK

For Margaret,
who has given me a preview
of heaven . . . by faith, in hope,
with love.

Published by Three Rivers Press, New York, New York.
Member of the Crown Publishing Group, a division of Random House, Inc.
www.crownpublishing.com

THREE RIVERS PRESS and the Tugboat design are trademarks of Random House, Inc.

Originally published in hardcover by Crown Forum, a division of Random House, Inc., in 2003.

Printed in the United States of America

Library of Congress Cataloging-in-Publication Data
Hirsen, James L.
Tales from the left coast : true stories of Hollywood stars and their outrageous politics / James Hirsen with NewsMax.com.—1st ed.
p.   cm.
     Includes bibliographical references and index.
     1. Motion picture actors and actresses—United States—Political activity—History—20th century. I. NewsMax.com. II. Title.
PN1998.2.H59   2003
791.43'028'092273—dc21
2003006919

ISBN 1-4000-5305-6

10 9 8 7 6 5 4 3 2 1

First Paperback Edition

791,43
Hir

095680

Contents

Why Hollywood Leans Left

1. The San Andreas Fault has caused the continental plate located under Hollywood to buckle left.

2. Extraterrestrials have bombarded the West Coast area with brain-wave projections that are capable of turning minds into macaroni and cheese.

3. Going from waiting on tables to waiting to board private jets has created an epidemic of "afluenza" in Tinseltown, the side effects of which are pangs of liberal guilt.

4. Most Hollywood actors graduated from the Chairman Mao School of Acting.

5. Followers of Timothy Leary have been seeding the water with psychedelics for almost four decades.

6. Tinseltown folks smoke their Vietnamese pot using recycled paper.

7. Plastic surgeons are implanting "L" chips into the residents of Hollywood with each procedure performed.

8. The entire town is secretly under the total control of Barbra Streisand.

9. Almost all of the inhabitants of La La Land have completed the Anthony Robbins seminar "Awaken the Liberal Within."

10. The entertainment capital's essential coffee table book is *It Takes a Village*.

11. Hollywood locals religiously attend services each Sunday at the Yoga, Tai Chi, Buddhist, Hindu, Bahai, Scientology, Raelian Chanting Center.

12. Tinseltown dwellers have developed a deep empathy for the working class, after spending long hours supervising servants, gardeners, personal assistants, cooks, drivers, hairdressers, valets, TV remote pushers, nannies, and pet walkers.

13. Green rooms have been serving too many M&Ms with red dye #2.

14. Psychiatrists in Hollywood routinely induce patients into a sleeplike trance by playing the audio version of Al Gore's *Earth in the Balance*.

15. Hollywood hipsters have witnessed a rash of cars with Bush-Cheney bumper stickers being unceremoniously towed away.

16. The liberal thought police have used crop dusters to blanket the Tinseltown landscape with *Right-Be-Gone*.

17. Folks in La La Land believe that they really do have a rich uncle with an endless supply of money who goes by the name of Uncle Sam.

Those who make their home in Tinseltown quickly find out that when it comes to the A-list, you're either left or you're left out.

The Politics of Fame

There's a sort of "group think" in Hollywood. Ask anyone who's lived there, worked there, or played there. The whole crazy, intriguing town leans decidedly to the left.

A lot of theories have been floated to try and explain the phenomenon. Some suspect the condition is caused by a rare virus that lies dormant in overly groomed poodles. Others think it comes from Botox needle sharing. Oh heck, maybe it's the sushi. Like the veritable fish in water, residents of Tinseltown are generally unaware of the left-churning whirlpool they're soaking in.

But the most obvious sign of their cockeyed mentality is seen whenever a star decides to speak out on a political or social issue. Pick any topic from the last 30 years. Chances are if a celebrity commented on it, his or her take was, more often than not, unmistakably liberal.

When Julia Roberts, Barbra Streisand, and Alec Baldwin open their mouths in public, cameras rush in. The press is there to capture their every word. Things like accuracy and merit don't seem to matter much. The celebrity status of the speaker is what counts.

Now not all star speech is the same, but it's basically treated that way. Whether the individual is talking about mundane matters of life (like where to live, which servants to hire, what clothes to shoplift, or what color to paint the yacht) or about monumental issues (like foreign policy or federal procedure), the patter is likely to get equal attention.

Because of our preoccupation with celebrity standing, every bit of information about the famous somehow seems newsworthy. The public wants to know who they're dating, who their plumber is dating, and who their plumber's second cousin, twice removed, is thinking of dating.

There's a sort of "group think" in Hollywood. The whole crazy, intriguing town leans decidedly to the left.

The public's hunger for an account of the life struggles, courtships, marriages, tragedies, and deaths of prominent personalities is insatiable. It's fed by both the entertainment and information media outlets. And these days it's getting increasingly tough to tell the two apart. A typical news teaser nowadays has listeners hearing something like "Hollywood doctor reveals how star clients lower their cholesterol and achieve normal regularity—Details on Eyeball News at 11."

There's a formula that underlies the sort of muddled mess we're seeing. Take the right amount of controversy and slap it up against an attention-grabbing public figure. The result is media attention to the max. Bill Clinton's escapades, Robert Downey Jr.'s rehab, Robert Blake's courtroom capers, and Brad Pitt's facial hair are all cases in point. Each managed to overshadow most of the other news of the day. If the trend continues, we can expect the evening news to have a celebrity link for every story: "Rioting in Rio—Catherine Zeta-Jones forced to change vacation plans."

Still, we all need someone to look up to. We yearn for excitement, glamour, and beauty in our own lives, especially if things seem a tad boring in our neck of the woods. Not that a nine-to-five routine, irritable-kid syndrome, and income taxes aren't exciting. But we do seem to need a little acknowledgment for our existence. Each of us seeks a sense of acceptance, some proof that we belong to something that's larger than ourselves. This explains, in part, why we're so fascinated with the famous.

Celebrity fever has spread just about everywhere. It's no surprise since TV delivers stars right into our living rooms. Although we'd sometimes prefer not to have people barging in unannounced, stars are usually the exception. Viewers fall in love with movie, sitcom, and drama characters. There's a feeling that they're part of an extended family. And all the new technology only serves to narrow the distance between us and them.

The media explosion that's going on is propelling fresh faces into the celebrity spotlight each and every day. Reality show participants are suddenly recognized everywhere they go, regardless of how many weird things they're willing to eat on cue. Extras on music video productions land their own contracts. And personalities like Cindy Margolis expand existing fame to extraordinary heights thanks to the Internet peep show.

Technology is actually causing an increase in the overall celebrity population. And that's a godsend for oddities like *Celebrity Boxing, Celebrity Fear Factor,* and *Celebrity Booty Camp.* Naturally, the more celebrities there are, the more press coverage that's needed.

Over the past several years, reporting on celebrities has grown into a massive industry. From nonstop TV updates to entertainment sections of virtually every newspaper, tracking the stars has become big business. The enormous success of tabloids and television entertainment shows provides living proof. Remember, it wasn't so long ago that *Entertainment Tonight* was pretty much the only show devoted exclusively to celebrity news. Now we have the 24-hour cable channel E! and a host of other shows, like *Extra, Inside Edition, Where Are They Now?, Where Have They Been?,* and *What Are They Doing on This Cheesy Nostalgia Show?,* just to name a few.

Technology is actually causing an increase in the overall celebrity population. And that's a god-send for oddities like *Celebrity Boxing, Celebrity Fear Factor,* and *Celebrity Booty Camp.*

Still, there is the matter of the personal investment that takes place on the part of fans. Because of the amount of energy expended, people start to assume that they're entitled to know everything about a public figure. Print, radio, television, and film media try to satisfy the marketplace by giving the public as much information as possible. Naturally, celebrities want to withhold certain details about themselves, like whether they wear boxers, briefs, or plus-sized thongs, but this only makes the public more curious. What happens, in the end, is one heck of an info battle.

When we look at the relationship between celebrities and fans, we realize how unique it is. In a peculiar way, it's an involvement where both sides win, or lose, depending on how you look at it.

Fans identify with celebrities they admire. They often imitate their behavior, thinking, manner of dress, and lifestyle. Those who feel a bit ordinary themselves can latch onto a grander image. It's their chance to mentally connect with someone who has a more sophisticated edge and understated flair, like Marilyn Manson. Fans even come to believe that they actually know celebrities intimately. Despite the fact that stars are likely to be distant strangers, folks feel as if they're truly personal friends.

At the same time, stars desire, and desperately need, their fans. They need the steady stream of what money isn't always the best at getting—publicity. So a quiet tug-of-war wages on each day. Those in charge of publicity try to get favorable information into the public square. At the same time, they try to keep the more unflattering stuff out. This explains why so many paparazzi end up with cameras stuck in places that were never designed to accommodate wide, angular objects.

Because of the exaggerated interest, many stars develop an inflated sense of their own importance. Not that flying in a private jet or buying a medieval castle is necessarily going to change a person. But stars often find themselves living in a different world than most other people. As their status grows, they're slowly wrapped up in a kind of a cocoon. It's a physical barrier of private transportation, private clubs, and private rooms in macrobiotic restaurants, far away from admiring throngs. Phone calls are screened, appointments selected, appearances restricted, public contact limited, homes secured, and workplaces guarded.

Eventually they end up surrounded by a human buffer. For some, the hoopla feels tremendous. They're so esteemed. For others, it's suffocating. But that doesn't make them any more eager to give up the perks.

Regardless of perspective, for almost all celebrities, there's one question that haunts them, wherever they go, whatever they do. And that is, How do others see me? With the kind of constant pressure this question brings, it's sometimes difficult to maintain reality. And hovering about is the image created through PR, the media, and recent arrest records. It can all literally take on a life of its own.

Star status involves lots of illusion. Whenever the paparazzi catch a star in pre-hair-waxed condition and Wal-Mart attire, the results can be out and out shocking. Sometimes the star's individual identity is swallowed up by the image molded by the media. The star emerges as a product to be sold rather than a person. But fame doesn't ever remain static. It's like the life cycle of a human being. The star is born, grows, matures, has 7,003 plastic surgeries, and ultimately fades away. As a result, careers are in a perpetual state of flux. Fame is either increasing or decreasing, depending on one's stage in the cycle.

Like fear of death, the famous often experience anxiety about the inevitable loss of their celebrity cachet. Competition is intense, and so is the knowledge that fame will someday dwindle. Otherwise the names of the actors from *Gilligan's Island* would still be on the tip of everyone's tongue. It's because of the drive to remain in the public eye, and to have some sort of meaning beyond the show business world, that activism draws some stars like a magnet.

In so many instances, the nature of the actor's, writer's, and musician's work is fictional. In the case of Oliver Stone, it's the consequence of paranoia. Anyway, it all fuels a desire to impact the real world. It stands to reason that a good number of people in the creative arts long to be taken seriously when they step offstage. For some, like Pee-Wee Herman, this may be enormously difficult. But what could be better than to have continued publicity and credibility and maybe even have an impact on society? When you look at it from this angle, political activism begins to become downright alluring.

Now some people say, Who cares what stars think, say, or do on the political front? Why should it matter if celebrities make fatuous statements or take up any number of goofy causes? Well, there's one little old word that explains why it matters. It's called *influence*.

In this town, influence comes in three flavors: money, power, and merchandise. When it comes to money, success often brings massive wealth to a chosen few, and the windfall can happen in two shakes of a silicone lamb's tail.

Hollywood heavyweights then throw large amounts of star-soaked personal and corporate cash at half-baked causes and liberal political candidates. This gives certain celebs the kind of power that can make a Speaker of the House sit up and beg and may even get a president or two to roll over.

Then there's the merchandise. We're talking about the actual products being shipped out of the Left Coast: music, television shows, films, documentaries, and the like. If you start to pay attention, more and more you'll notice there's a commonality to the banality.

This is where celebrity influence starts to get real serious. Why? Because the kind of influence we're talking about ends up affecting the beliefs, morals, dreams, and directions of an entire society.

Right now, Hollywood is pretty much in liberal lockstep, politically speaking. It has been for a number

> The kind of influence we're talking about ends up affecting the beliefs, morals, dreams, and directions of an entire society.

of decades. We can't get away from the fact that what the stars say and do on the political front matters. Their words and actions carry tremendous weight in all-day spas, Pilates circles, and society at large. They carry tremendous weight in Washington, D.C. And more and more their ideas are infiltrating our minds in the sneakiest way possible—through our entertainment.

Americans seem to go through phases where they wonder why so much of what they see and hear feels out of touch with their own thinking. Long-held values are ridiculed, and the most extreme kind of liberal behavior is portrayed as commonplace.

Then something happens. After having been mentally massaged by the "group think," the culture takes a leap. How we should act, what we should believe, and how we should view the world simply changes.

When we look at this kind of influence through the lens of politics we see that, in the end, it can affect how people reason, what view of the world eventually wins out, and, ultimately, the kind of society we end up with.

You Know You're a Closet Conservative ...

- If you have to hide in the bathroom until your gagging subsides after someone suggests Hillary's going to make a great president.

- If you wrap up your copy of *National Review* in the latest issue of *Mother Jones*.

- If during an election season, with a flick of a switch, the Republican sign on your front lawn changes into a "Save the Planet" poster.

- If you get into your SUV, park it a mile away from work, and pull out your folding bicycle to take you the rest of the way there.

- If when a co-worker insults Ronald Reagan, you have to pretend that crushing his foot with the desk chair was just an accident.

- If you have lost all feeling in your tooth-marked tongue and have to have it treated for calluses.

- If you drive 50 miles outside of town to get a steak sandwich for lunch.

- If you tell your colleagues that you were at a Maya Angelou poetry reading when you were really at the firing range putting bullet holes in a paper Osama.

- If you listen to Charlie Daniels through your headphones while you're mouthing the words of the latest Rage Against the Machine tune.

- If you pretend you enjoyed last night's episode of *The West Wing* when you were really glued to *The O'Reilly Factor.*

- If you wear sunglasses to the Joe Lieberman rally so no one notices your eyelids are shut.

- If your partners at work want to go see the latest Michael Moore flick and you give them directions to the Nixon Library.

- If you sneak into the commissary with your magic marker and blacken the front teeth on the Slick Willie photo.

CHAPTER ONE

Baa Baa Blacklist

It seems that some people are always trying to come up with new ways to defend the media. When you're operating in this mode, you typically do what the guardians of the mainstream media have always done—deny that liberal bias exists.

Sorry, but that fib won't fly. To believe it you'd have to be living in a basement in Kankakee, Illinois. And be wearing several blindfolds. And maybe be using heavy-duty earmuffs, like the guys who wave in the planes on aircraft carriers. That's about the only way to avoid knowing about the left-leaning favoritism that exists in the media.

But oftentimes libs in Hollywood manage to move even further askew than their partners in the press. One example of the entertainment industry's extreme tip to the left can be seen in a recent decision made by the producers of NBC's *The West Wing*.

To begin with, this TV program idealizes a liberal Democrat administration and is careful to strip Republican characters of any trace of humanity, intelligence, or modern clothing. Well, after four seasons the show decided to do something really bent-headed. It fired all of its GOP-type consultants. It may have been in response to sagging ratings, but in any case, the incident demonstrates the deep-rooted Tinseltown tendencies.

The scenario played out this way. Former Press Secretary Marlin Fitzwater, pollster Frank Luntz, and former Reagan speechwriter Peggy Noonan woke up one morning to discover that their consultant jobs had come to a brisk end. For some reason, their Democrat counterparts received different treatment. Kept were the services of former Clinton administration enablers Dee Dee Myers and Gene Sperling.

Fitzwater commented to the *Federal Paper,* "They dropped us because they decided they didn't want a conservative viewpoint anymore."

Another NBC foray into broadcast subjectivity was originally touted as a *Mr. Smith Goes to Washington*–type series. It's called *Mister Sterling.* In it, Barbra Streisand's stepson Josh Brolin plays a reluctant politician who's supposedly an independent, compassionate, stand-up guy who ends up in the U.S. Senate.

It turns out that the series has a strong connection with *The West Wing.* Lawrence O'Donnell, producer and writer for the fictional Pennsylvania Ave. drama, is billed as executive producer and creator of *Mister Sterling.* According to the *Boston Globe,* O'Donnell is "the heart and mind behind this television tale of an idealistic freshman California senator, William Sterling, Jr. (Brolin), a compassionate political independent thrust into office when he is appointed to replace a recently deceased Democratic senior senator." Word has it that O'Donnell writes every episode of the show.

A little reminder: O'Donnell was a top advisor to the late Senator Daniel Patrick Moynihan and, at a later date, chief of staff of the Senate Committee on Environment and Public Works. Perfect political credentials for Tinseltown.

Okay, let's see. Babs's husband, James Brolin, guested on *The West Wing,* and stepson Josh Brolin stars in *Mister Sterling.* Will we be seeing *Yentl on the Potomac* anytime soon?

There is another question that needs to be asked here. Did NBC care more about publicizing the TV show than it did about duping the electorate? Well, a week before the 2002 midterm elections, the network ran a series of spots that were indistinguishable from real campaign ads. The fake campaign for the *Mister Sterling* drama was apparently an attempt to lure in politically minded viewers. But in retrospect, it looks as though it was just another sneaky way of promoting a program that's designed to give the Hollywood take on what politics ought to be.

It's no wonder some viewers think the network's slogan should be changed to Must Flee TV.

It's no wonder some viewers think the network's slogan should be changed to Must Flee TV. What is it about conservative viewpoints that makes the Hollywood community so nervous? This is a bunch that supposedly lives and breathes to champion free speech and tolerance. Why are they so, well, intolerant?

Does a TV show about a house in D.C., which tells the adventurous tales of roommate Senators Schumer and Durbin and Congressmen Delahunt and Miller, sound interesting to you? Apparently, it's extremely appealing to *Saturday Night Live* alumnus Al Franken. He's been working on a television sitcom called *Little House on the Hill.*

Franken, author of a book that slammed radio talk-show megastar Rush Limbaugh, dreams of filling our homes with seemingly hilarious programming about four middle-aged Democrat roomies who share a passion for expanding government and raising taxes. Doesn't sound like *Friends* has anything to be nervous about.

It brings up a question that's been asked a gazillion times by average folks who don't understand why one very visible and otherwise impressive group is so uniform in its thinking and expression. Why is such a large segment of Hollywood so liberal in its politics? Part of the explanation can be found in a Hollywood tale. It's one that's been passed down from one starlit generation to the next.

Kicked in the Kazan

We're pretty used to seeing the entertainment industry throw self-congratulatory parties and host galas on TV for the whole world's amusement. Let's face it. We're bursting at the seams with awards shows. There are so many going on it won't be long before we'll need a dedicated awards cable channel. It'll feature the Oscars, the Emmys, the Tonys, the Golden Globes, the Ozzys, and the Best Power Lunches on Sunset Awards.

One awards show a few years back had something very strange happen right smack in the middle of the program. A legendary director was receiving an honor for his life's work. Many of the stars in attendance actually refused to applaud or cheer for the man. In fact, most of the celebrities present sat in stony silence, posing like exhibits from the Hollywood Wax Museum. Nick Nolte and Ed Harris were among the frozen figures. The award being given was the 1999 Honorary Award from the Academy of Motion Picture Arts and Sciences. The director was Elia Kazan.

Outside of the awards venue, protesters held banners saying "Kazan: Snitch" and "Elia Kazan: Benedict Arnold." Elia

Kazan may just as well have been a serial killer, a terrorist, or an Enron auditor.

Kazan has a long list of prominent classic films under his belt. This didn't matter a whit. He was treated like a reject. Why would anyone in the room act this way toward an Oscar winner and director of such masterpieces as *On the Waterfront, East of Eden,* and *A Streetcar Named Desire*? Why all the venom for this guy?

The reason for the demonstration of loathing goes back to 1952, when Kazan gave testimony to a congressional committee. His capital crime? He disclosed the names of a number of his Hollywood colleagues who had been members of the Communist Party.

Elia Kazan gave testimony before the House Un-American Activities Committee (HUAC) twice. The first time was in January 1952. Kazan answered all the questions posed but refused to reveal the names of people he knew who were members of the Communist Party.

At a second installment of testimony—brace yourself for this one—Kazan named some names. He said that he had been wrong in refusing to give the committee the names "because secrecy serves the Communists and is exactly what they want."[1]

The day after Kazan testified, he took out a full-page ad in the April 12, 1952, *New York Times* to explain the reasons for his actions. Here's the text:

> In the past weeks intolerable rumors about my political position have been circulating in New York and Hollywood. I want to make my stand clear:
>
> I believe that Communist activities confront the people of this country with an unprecedented and exceptionally tough problem. That is, how to protect ourselves

from a dangerous and alien conspiracy and still keep the free, open, healthy way of life that gives us self-respect.

I believe that the American people can solve this problem wisely only if they have the facts about Communism. All the facts.

Now, I believe that any American who is in possession of such facts has the obligation to make them known, either to the public or to the appropriate Government agency.

Whatever hysteria exists—and there is some, particularly in Hollywood—is inflamed by mystery, suspicion and secrecy. Hard and exact facts will cool it.

The facts I have are sixteen years out of date, but they supply a small piece of background to the graver picture of Communism today.

I have placed these facts before the House Committee on Un-American Activities without reserve and I now place them before the public and before my co-workers in motion pictures and in the theatre.

Seventeen and a half years ago I was a twenty-four-year-old stage manager and bit actor, making $40 a week, when I worked.

At that time nearly all of us felt menaced by two things: The depression and the ever growing power of Hitler. The streets were full of unemployed and shaken men. I was taken in by the Hard Times version of what might be called the Communists' advertising or recruiting technique. They claimed to have a cure for depressions and a cure for Naziism and Fascism.

I joined the Communist Party late in the summer of 1934. I got out a year and a half later.

I have no spy stories to tell, because I saw no spies. Nor did I understand, at that time, any opposition between

American and Russian national interest. It was not even clear to me in 1936, that the American Communist Party was abjectly taking its orders from the Kremlin.

What I learned was the minimum that anyone must learn who puts his head into the noose of party "discipline." The Communists automatically violated the daily practices of democracy to which I was accustomed. They attempted to control thought and to suppress personal opinion. They tried to dictate personal conduct. They habitually distorted and disregarded and violated the truth. All this was crudely opposite of their claims of "democracy" and "the scientific approach."

To be a member of the Communist Party is to have a taste of the police state. It is a diluted taste but it is bitter and unforgettable. It is diluted because you can walk out.

I got out in the spring of 1936.

The question will be asked why I did not tell this story sooner. I was held back, primarily, by concern for the reputations and employment of people who may, like myself, have left the party many years ago.

I was held back by a piece of specious reasoning which has silenced many liberals. It goes like this: "You may hate the Communists, but you must not attack or expose them, because if you do you are attacking the right to hold unpopular opinions and you are joining the people who attack civil liberties."

I have thought soberly about this. It is, simply, a lie.

Secrecy serves the Communists. At the other pole, it serves those who are interested in silencing liberal voices. The employment of a lot of good liberals is threatened because they have allowed themselves to become associated with or silenced by the Communists.

Liberals must speak out.

I think it is useful that certain of us had this kind of experience with the Communists, for if we had not we should not know them so well. Today, when all the world fears war and they scream peace, we know how much their professions are worth. We know tomorrow they will have a new slogan.

Firsthand experience of dictatorship and thought control left me with an abiding hatred of these. It left me with an abiding hatred of Communist philosophy and methods and the conviction that these must be resisted always.

It also left me with the passionate conviction that we must never let the Communists get away with the pretense that they stand for the very things which they kill in their own countries.

I am talking about free speech, a free press, the rights of property, the rights of labor, racial equality and, above all, individual rights. I value these things. I take them seriously. I value peace, too, when it is not bought at the price of fundamental decencies.

I believe these things must be fought for wherever they are not fully honored and protected whenever they are threatened.

The motion pictures I have made and the plays I have chosen to direct represent my convictions.

I expect to continue to make the same kinds of pictures and to direct the same kinds of plays.

It's a pretty good bet that Kazan never expected his Hollywood colleagues to hold the grudge for decades. But hang on they did, with a vengeance. The chip on Hollywood's shoulder grew bigger and bigger with each turn of the page. And with theatrical flair, the players made sure they passed on the tale to each new Hollywood generation.

Legendary anchorman, journalist, and talk-radio icon George Putnam remembers the period well. Putnam told me that when he was working in New York, he noticed that the union was motivated by "left-wing issues" and "Soviet favoritism." When he came to Los Angeles, some big-name actors informed him that fellow actors and actresses were actually "in bed with the Communists."[2]

Enduring glamour girl and actress Jane Russell told me that, at that time, the studio system had lenience and acceptance of liberal Democrats. She said, "They just wanted to discourage communists." Maybe it was because, as Russell recalls, during the blacklist era there were "people sitting around on sets reading communist newspapers."[3]

Movies like *The Front* (1976), *Julia* (1977), *Guilty by Suspicion* (1991), and *The Majestic* (2001) only served to fatten up the Hollywood fable. Stacks of books on the subject were written, too. They were usually penned by relatives of those who were blacklisted and tended to focus on abuses that victims had to endure. Inevitably, bad guys were portrayed as jingoistic, flag-waving maniacs. And Hollywood was happily populated with tons of good-looking and talented Dudley and Daisy Do-Rights.

Robert Redford recently invoked the name that silences a Hollywood gathering faster than a subpoena from a divorce attorney. The actor-director compared the actions of the Bush administration to those of—Joseph McCarthy.

Practicing some left-handed slaps at the president, Redford stirred the latent fears of creative pros by bringing up censorship. At his own personal film festival, Sundance, Redford said, "The early signs are this administration could go further, shutting down information, not allowing certain truths to get out." Then he added, "And all you've got to do is look at history to see what that led to. The McCarthy era." So reports MSNBC.com.

Guess Redford forgot about all of the communist infiltration that was confirmed by Russian documents after the fall of the Soviet Union.

Maybe it was Redford's pattern of Bush-bashing that motivated a group of people to heckle him and throw snowballs in his direction during a TV interview on the balcony of his Riverhorse Cafe. The *New York Daily News* reported that the police had to come and disperse the crowd. Hey, maybe the heckling and snowball thing will catch on.

Somehow the name *McCarthy* or *McCarthyism* always seems to creep into the text of Tinseltown projects. The *M* word may be coyly placed in the title, or it may just pop up unexpectedly with a line like "These McCarthy-like shoes are killing me."

In a film, it may breezily surface in the dialogue.

TODD: Do you remember Charlie McCarthy?

CHLOE: No, but I voted for Eugene McCarthy.

TODD: Was he related to Jenny McCarthy?

CHLOE: Could've been. Did you catch her in *Singled Out*?

TODD: You mean that documentary on McCarthyism?

Most people know Hollywood is a place that thrives on fiction. Invented stories are the lifeblood of movies, TV shows, and scores of celebrity alibis. Unfortunately, some of the imaginary tales are pawned off as fact.

Actors, directors, and writers know better than anyone that half-truths are merely lies in disguise. If you're only aware of one side of the story, you don't know the real deal. Residents of Tinseltown have made it their mission to promote only "side A" of the Hollywood blacklist record. Their version goes something like this:

Blacklisted and Blue

A long time ago, even before color TV and DVDs, a crazed committee of evil, sexually repressed politicians came after some noble Hollywood writers. These politicians were led by a wild-eyed man named Joseph McCarthy. McCarthy appeared to be just an average, ordinary U.S. senator. But this monster from Wisconsin turned out to be nothing of the sort. His name would eventually become synonymous with "Satan of the Senate."

The brutish politician set out to make a speech. It was one with an evil design in mind. You see, the crafty ogre had brewed up a nasty pot of words. The concoction was meant to terrify the nation.

> If you're only aware of one side of the story, you don't know the real deal. Residents of Tinseltown have made it their mission to promote only "side A" of the Hollywood blacklist record.

One day the senator grabbed his linguistic potion and took it to a gathering in Wheeling, West Virginia. With fiendish fury, he splattered the verbiage on an unsuspecting crowd. Outrageous claims like "The communists have gained access to the U.S. State Department" singed the tender ears of the audience. Listeners were transfixed. By the time McCarthy finished talking, every mind in the place had been altered.

McCarthy went back to Capitol Hill and got his buddies to take part in the all-out assault on Hollywood. Politicians everywhere went after writers, actors, and other creative geniuses. Soon there was havoc in the entertainment streets. Celebrities were attacked mercilessly.

G-men armed with subpoenas shamelessly assaulted frail Woody Allen look-alikes. Poor souls who were minding their own moviemaking business were suddenly overtaken by reptiles in horn-rimmed glasses. Freedom of speech was quickly disintegrating.

Sadly, some studio bosses buckled under the pressure. They began to fire anyone who was thought to be a member of the Communist Party. Some individuals were able to survive the ordeal by selling their scripts under false names. They used what was called a front. Others weren't as clever or lucky. Those who were canned or denied work, based on the wild charges, were said to have been— *BLACKLISTED!*

Eventually, some high-drama congressional hearings on the matter were held in Washington, D.C. The whole scene was an inquisition, with people pointing fingers, shaking fists, and scaring folks out of their wits.

One group, though, stood tall through the grilling and refused to talk. Real champs, they were. They were so stalwart, they became legendary. They even had a cool-sounding nickname added to their credits. They were the heroic Hollywood Ten.

By the time madman McCarthy was done with his dastardly deeds, the reputations of many of the poor folks in Tinseltown lay mangled in the streets. It would take many years to recover from that horrible Fed reign of terror.

Yes, what had occurred could only be called a West Coast witch-hunt.

"How could this have happened?" the folks in Hollywood exclaimed. "We possess the power. We tell the story. We write the scripts," they shouted in unison.

"We will never forgive," they chanted. "And we will never, ever forget."

The End

Well, now you know the Hollywood version of the blacklist story. It's still being spun today. But what about the flip side of that Hollywood hit single?

If Broadway Joe Stalin was forced to take an injection of truth serum, his version might sound a wee bit different.

The Making of a Blacklist Blockbuster

Joe Stalin here, the Runt of Steel. Had to change my name from Vissarionovich Dzhugashvili to "Steel" in Russian. Hey, a guy's gotta have a stage name if he's going to take over a bunch of nations and commit mass murder.

I was pretty successful at what I did, collecting countries like a bunch of marbles. But of all the countries in the world, the one I really wanted was the U.S. It would be my crown jewel of conquests. Way back then, though, the Communist Party wasn't a real force in America. My goal was to change all that.

Contrary to what you've been told, Joseph McCarthy had zip to do with the whole Hollywood investigation thing. Toadies in Tinseltown just liked hurling his name around like an evil incantation.

Back in the days when I was struggling to be the king of the world, folks in the U.S. were all bent out of shape about commies. They thought we were hiding out everywhere—government offices, schools, parks, churches, campuses, movie theaters. Heck, they were checking under their beds. They were suffering from something called the Red Scare.

The paranoids were kind of right about the hiding out stuff. Well, actually they were dead on target. Except in Hollywood. La La locals marched to their own bongo drums, which meant they were pretty much dumb as stumps. They thought people with the Red Scare were delusional. They believed the Communist Party U.S.A. was a harmless group of caring people with the best intentions at heart. The idea that some of them were working for us and plotting evil against the United States was just plain absurd to them.

In fact, the Hollywood community and its fellow libs believed that McCarthy was a crackpot, the investigation into communist activities was a partisan ploy meant to mess up Roosevelt's New Deal, and Alger Hiss was actually innocent. What a bunch of saps.

Rather than some right-wing flight of imagination, Senator Joseph McCarthy, horns, tail, and all, was actually right.[4] My minions were secretly working in the federal government during the 1930s, '40s, and '50s. And Moscow was giving dough to the Communist Party in the U.S.

Yeah, we had American agents in the State Department and the Treasury Department. We had agents in a lot of the New Deal agencies. We had agents on the War Production Board. And we had good ol' Lauchlin Currie, advisor to FDR, right inside the White House itself.

So despite what you've been led to believe, McCarthy's basic premise was on the button. There were commies in America. They operated in secret. They were intentionally working to help enemies of the U.S. And they were beholden to an evil murderous regime—mine.

Truth is we burrowed deep into Hollywood. The Party dominated the politics, creative projects, and pocketbooks of the faithful. The rights that Kazan talked about in his ad—free speech, free press, property rights, labor rights, racial equality—we really *did* want to subvert those rights.

The HUAC bunch actually started a formal investigation of the motion picture pros around 1947. When they did, they found 41 people in Hollywood they identified as "friendly witnesses." Hollywood wouldn't be so palsywalsy with these folks in the future, that's for sure.

The friendly witnesses named names of individuals who could be members of the Communist Party. The 10 named—Dalton Trumbo, Edward Dmytryk, Herbert Biberman, Lester Cole, Albert Maltz, Adrian Scott, Samuel Ornitz, Ring Lardner Jr., John Howard Lawson, and Alvah Bessie—claimed that your First Amendment thing gave them the right to refuse to answer the HUAC questions. Too bad the courts didn't buy their line of reasoning. All 10 of them went to jail for six months to a year.

Friendly witnesses like Elia Kazan and Edward Dmytryk got theirs, though. They were slandered, booed, and slighted when it came to praise, recognition, and awards. The old guard in Tinseltown knew how to carry a good grudge, and they taught every new kid coming in exactly how to practice the fine art of snubbing.

They got the most ticked at one group in particular, though—the spotlight-seeking bureaucrats. They thought the politicos had caused innocent people to suffer. But here's the rub. We had more than just a handful of not-so-innocent people operating in Hollywood at the time. Like I said, they were saps.

I had big plans back then, plans to break into the theater arts, music, and television. No, I didn't want to be a movie star myself. Not that I wouldn't have made a great leading man. What I wanted was an agent. Actually, I wanted a lot of agents.

I got some assistance from Willi Munzenberg. Willi just happened to be one of the founders of Communist International. And he was also one of my very own envoys in the U.S. Willi had already organized and promoted art exhibits, magazines, radio programs, benefit concerts, propaganda theaters, and motion pictures in Germany. His MO was to go after the well educated rather than the working stiff. He set up front groups he called Innocents Clubs. Charming.

Willi hooked up with a gal named Babette Gross. They were too tight in my opinion. She was a real snoop. Babette saw up close what all the ardent, paranoid, commie haters had suspected—that we had a plan to pose as idealists in order to convince the entertainment community that our handpicked political activists were harmless. In other words, our agitators would stay mum on the Soviet party line. Instead, they'd talk about how to stop fascism, racism, oppression of workers, and war.

Babette knew about Willi's approach to getting key players in Hollywood. The instructions were, Don't call yourself a communist. Don't declare your love for the regime. And don't call on people to support the Soviets!

And Babette figured out what I, Joe Stalin, really wanted to do in Tinseltown. I didn't want to make Stalinist movies. I wanted to get at the American glamour culture.

Babette knew about how Moscow had a hand in the formation of the Screen Writers Guild, too. Willi had developed his Hollywood networks during the 1930s, first from offices in Berlin and Paris and then from New York. His key man in Hollywood was Otto Katz. Katz went by the name of Rudolph Breda and pretended to be anti-fascist. The guy was so smooth, he ended up working with a bunch of the Hollywood Ten.[5]

Another character in our commie cast was John Howard Lawson. He handled the Hollywood talent guilds and was a big-time networker. He'd go around urging writers to sneak things into their scripts. Scripts would come into the studios putting down business and clergy and glorifying workers and the poor.

All of a sudden some studio execs began to take notice, like Jack Warner of Warner Bros. He gave testimony to HUAC about how he suspected that some of my buddies had infiltrated the studio that he ran as far back as 1936. Once Warner got wind of a commie-loving writer, the dude's contract wasn't renewed. What a jerk. ,

Warner said that the writers put down capitalism. He brought up the example of a screenplay, where the rich man was always the bad guy. Hey, that's the truth!

Warner found the treatment of capitalism strange because the guys writing the scripts were getting paid big hunks of money. Guess he couldn't have known that they were just an early form of limousine lefties. Commie haters just weren't getting the writing jobs. Thank goodness that was the kind of blacklisting no one talked about.

Warner quit renewing contracts for commie-loving writers. He named the writers that were cut loose. Seven of the Hollywood Ten made the list. Rats!

Still, things stuck pretty close to my playbook overall. The first communist organization in Hollywood called itself the Hollywood Anti-Nazi League. We picked the name because it sounded good. Even back in my time, image was important. And for some reason, fighting fascists and Nazis went over better than supporting commie dictators. Imagine that.

Soon it became clear to almost everyone that this Hollywood group wasn't all that hot on fighting communism.

The league ran into a teensy problem in 1939. I got into a deal with my fascist friend Adolf Hitler. We put our tyrannical heads together and made a pact. Suddenly, the Tinseltown group needed a name change real badly. With some quick thinking and sleight of syllables, the Hollywood Anti-Nazi League transformed itself into the Hollywood League for Democratic Action. That did the trick.

Some of the members still knew that, rather than being devoted to fighting Nazis, these folks were basically suckers—for me, that is. The organization survived anyway. But things would be different. The newly named Hollywood League for Democratic Action would put down U.S. involvement in World War II. Neutrality and peace would be the new buzzwords. And FDR would be a friend no longer. He'd be called a warmonger.

It helped to have loyal fans in Hollywood. They stayed devoted to me even while I was cleansing my country of wrong-thinking scum. I let around 10 million Ukrainian peasants starve to death, and I had to knock off 10 million others, but hey, it was for all the right reasons. Some of the undesirables were executed. Others got sent off to camp for a permanent vacation.

You know, Lenin was right when he talked about useful idiots. And just think—he'd never even been to Hollywood!

The End[6]

Now that you've heard Joe's midnight confessions, you know that there's more to the tale than meets the Hollywood eye. And it goes a long way in explaining how there could be so many gripping stories that never made it to the big or little screen.

Tales They Won't Tell

Writers, producers, and directors claim to be curious. They profess to be true explorers of the human condition. But their explorations seem to ignore one of the most compelling stories of our time. No, it's not the mystery of who's really throwing Anna Nicole's voice or the enigma of how a guy like Tony Soprano could get hooked on therapy. It's the long-running, highly intense, true-life drama about the communist clash with democracy. So why does Tinseltown avoid the issue like the plague of cellulite?

There is, after all, a wellspring of material surrounding the forbidden subject out there, so the collective dodge makes no sense. The theme is tailor-made for anyone who dreams of making cinematic magic. It contains all that a mogul or mogulette could ever want—heroes, villains, mystery, suspense, hope, despair, joy, misery, triumph, and tragedy. But for some reason Hollywood won't touch the topic. It's the unwanted child of the stage and screen.

When you think about it, scoundrels like Stalin, Mao, Pol Pot, and Castro offer the kind of despicable characters you know actors would give up their right abs to play. Couldn't you just see Joe Pesci as a tortured tyrant, ruddy-faced and slightly paunchy, being followed around by a band of bootlickers, sadists, and socialist climbers? Makes you think a certain ex-president would be perfect for the part.

Leftists in Hollywood were skilled at squelching material that would expose the truth about communism. An organization called the Story Analysts Guild was established to weed out ideas that might be perceived as negative for communism.

Story analysts acted like filters for the studios. They were the ones who said whether to go forward with a given script or pass on it. By placing friendly story analysts in the right positions, films that exposed the dark side of communism could conveniently be shelved.

Hollywood Ten teammate Dalton Trumbo once bragged that the Left had been successful in blocking anti-Red scripts from consideration. Included in the cast-offs were works by Arthur Koestler and Victor Kravchenko, who had the gall to express their love for freedom.

Leftists in Hollywood were skilled at squelching material that would expose the truth about communism.

Koestler's *Darkness at Noon*[7] is one of the greatest novels of the 20th century. It lent itself well to celluloid. But for some reason, the Hollywood community passed on it. You see, Koestler was a repentant Red. He'd been exiled from Hungary. He'd seen firsthand the Stalin show trials of the late 1930s. *Darkness at Noon* was written when Joseph Stalin had a death grip going on the Soviet Union. As was the practice then and now, with paranoid power-mongers, rivals faced swift eradication.

Koestler's preface spells out the purpose of his work:

The characters in this book are fictitious. The historical circumstances which determined their actions are real. The life of the man N.S. Rubashov is a synthesis of the lives of a number of men who were victims of the so-called Moscow Trials. Several of them were personally known to the author. This book is dedicated to their memory.[8]

Darkness at Noon focused in on the "flexible" morals of the Soviets, the end justifying the means. It actually told the truth about communism, which explained its rejection by Hollywood.

In 1946 Victor A. Kravchenko wrote a typically hefty, Russian-style book, the kind you need a forklift to get home and you brag to your friends that it only took you half an hour to read. The literary piece was called *I Chose Freedom,*[9] and it detailed the intense suffering of those who were caught in the clutches of a lunatic leader. On its Web site, The Learning Channel references Kravchenko's work and describes the Ukrainian starvation in this way:

> More than seven million Ukrainian peasants died as a result of a man-made famine during the winter of 1932 in the richest agricultural region of the Soviet Union. The Kremlin used the famine as a means of breaking the resistance of the independent Ukrainian farmers to Stalin's collectivization of agriculture, and as a political weapon to destroy Ukrainian aspirations for independence. The Soviets were confiscating and exporting the Ukrainians' grain while doing nothing to save them from starvation. Cannibalism broke out, and the peasantry, the core of the Ukrainian state, was crushed. The famine has assumed mythic proportions for the Ukrainians. It has come to symbolize the horror of Russian domination and the necessity of Ukrainian liberation.[10]

Les Lettres Francaises, a French weekly controlled by the communists, called Kravchenko a liar and a spy. So he decided to try out a handy little tool that's used with exuberance in the West. It's the good old lawsuit.

Guess what? Kravchenko won. The trial was an embarrassment for the Soviet slugs. Witnesses told of being snatched from their homes. They told of being stripped of belongings.

They told of kids being tossed out into the snow. And they told about the death trains, where people were hauled away to labor camps in cattle cars.

The Soviet embassy in Paris tried to help out with the defense. The embassy brought over witnesses from the Soviet Union to testify in the Paris court. At one point the communists alleged that Kravchenko was not really a big-shot metallurgical engineer at all. But Kravchenko had dug up a copy of *Pravda* that contained an item on a well-known metallurgical engineer, who would oversee a new factory in Vladivostock. The engineer was Kravchenko himself.

Kravchenko was really stunned by the Stalinist grip on American intellectuals. He explained that the positive image of Soviet socialism had been imposed on the American mind "by the best propaganda machine in all history." He found that slave labor, police-state tactics, purges, the meager standard of living, and the great famine of the early 1930s had virtually been ignored. And he may or may not have known that in Hollywood, Stalinist censors were working hard to make sure that the subject matter he was writing about would never make it to the big screen.

On the other hand, films that portray communists in a good light seem to have no problem making their way into the theaters.

Take a Hayek

In the winter of 2002, Salma Hayek created a lot of flack with a little flick called *Frida*. Mexican critics were generous with their grousing. Some said the movie sensationalized the lives of Frida Kahlo and her husband, muralist Diego Rivera. Others were dissatisfied because the film was in English.

Both camps missed the mark. What was really wrong with the film was that it celebrated a couple of U.S.-hating Soviet-style communists.

Apparently, Hayek served as one of the film's producers. She described the movie as a story of unconditional love. But Kahlo and Rivera's politics weren't some sort of quaint artistic eccentricity, like Nick Nolte's driving.

Just what is the real scoop on Frida Kahlo and Diego Rivera? Well, in 1936 Rivera petitioned the Mexican government to give asylum to one of the founding fathers of communism, Leon Trotsky, when he and his wife were forced out of Norway. The Trotskys ended up staying in Kahlo's family home. Kahlo then seduced the older man, kind of like Monica Lewinsky without the pizza. One of Kahlo's self-portraits is actually dedicated to Trotsky himself.

When the wild-eyed revolutionary was assassinated, Kahlo did an about-face and acted like a member of the politburo. She claimed that Trotsky was a coward and had stolen from her when he stayed at her house.

Kahlo attacked Trotsky because she had become a dedicated Stalinist. And she continued singing Stalin's praises even after finding out about his culpability in the death of millions. In fact, one of Kahlo's last paintings is called *Stalin and I.* Her diary is filled with references to Stalin and her yearning to meet with the tyrant. Kahlo's art also reveals her deep hatred of the United States, and of people with any measure of space between their eyebrows.

Knowing all of this, who would ever have thought that Americans, left or right, would applaud the movie. Or that the Academy would give it a couple of Oscars. Or that—and this is no joke—the U.S. Postal Service would put Kahlo's unhappy face on a stamp.

Plagued by Apparitions

It's strange how modern-day Tinseltown folks like to invoke the "ghost of blacklist past." They do it whenever they want to attack someone, and they need a little dramatic flair in their deliverance.

In February 2003, Sean Penn seemed to be living out the lines of a B-movie script. The Iraq News Agency had played him for a fool, by putting words in his mouth, after his much-publicized anti-war journey to Iraq.

Later Penn claimed that his public position on the war in Iraq was the reason that he didn't get a juicy movie role. The actor alleged that when producer Steve Bing didn't cast him in the film *Why Men Shouldn't Marry,* Bing was "borrowing a page from the dark era of Hollywood blacklisting."

There it is—the reference to the "dark era." Bing's been a huge contributor to liberal causes and candidates, so he must've been shocked to be publicly characterized as a blacklister.

In another use of the handy-dandy blacklist label, the Screen Actors Guild released a piece of creative writing that was supposed to protect some of its members. The guild was coming to the rescue of a group of vocal celebrities who were claiming to be against war but were actually busy making major fools of themselves. So how did SAG come to the aid of the throaty thespians? It pulled out the blacklist card. And here's what it looked like:

March 3, 2003

Screen Actors Guild Releases Statement

Regarding Free Speech

Los Angeles–Screen Actors Guild released the following statement today:

As our country again considers the possibility of war, it is the fundamental right of citizens to express their support or their fears and concerns. While passionate disagreement is to be expected in such a debate, a disturbing trend has arisen in the dialogue. Some have recently suggested that well-known individuals who express "unacceptable" views should be punished by losing their right to work. This shocking development suggests that the lessons of history have, for some, fallen on deaf ears.

Over 50 years ago, this nation was faced with a monumental challenge: whether the world's greatest democracy was strong enough to truly allow its citizens the exercise of their rights of free speech and assembly during a time of international tension known as the "Cold War." Most of America failed that test, averting its eyes as the House Committee on Un-American Activities persecuted citizens, destroyed careers, ruined lives and gave rise to the notorious "blacklist." During this shameful period, our own industry prostrated itself before smear campaigns and witch hunters rather than standing on the principles articulated in the nation's fundamental documents.

Today, having come to grips with its past, having repudiated the insult of loyalty oaths and examined its own failings, our industry, perhaps more than any other, understands the necessity of guarding and cherishing those rights for which Americans have fought and died.

In that spirit, the Screen Actors Guild Board of Directors, appreciating the value of full and open debate and devoted to the belief that the free flow of information, opinions and ideas contributes to the health of our nation, supports the right of all citizens, celebrated and unknown, to speak their minds freely, on any side of any issue, as is their Constitutional right. In the same vein—and with a painfully clear appreciation of history—we deplore the idea that those in the public eye should suffer professionally for having the courage to give voice to their views. Even a hint of the blacklist must never again be tolerated in this nation.

SAG says that during the Cold War era, America was guilty of "averting its eyes as the House Committee on Un-American Activities persecuted citizens, destroyed careers, ruined lives and gave rise to the notorious 'blacklist'." The idea that folks in Hollywood would be "persecuted" for left-leaning rhetoric is so absurd it sends most people into a laughing fit. In reality, those who fail to jump on the Bolshevik bandwagon are the ones who need serious protection. That's the real blacklist that exists today. Do you suppose that SAG will ever intervene on behalf of those with genuine politically incorrect views? Don't bet the bank on it.

But this is the kind of thing that happens when the truth gets twisted up. The revised history of the blacklist era hangs over Tinseltown like 70 pounds of smog. There's no doubt that it's one of the heftier reasons for Hollywood's leftward tilt. Maybe someday the townies will have the sense to just get over it.

CHAPTER TWO

Decade of Change

Sometimes it appears as though even the Hollywood sign slants left. We get a glimpse of why the celebrity crowd is so comfy leaning in this direction when we look at the 1960s. That decade was, after all, the dawn of Hollywood liberalism.

It may sound strange, but the Hollywood version of the blacklist fable is something that energizes many of the lefties in Tinseltown to this very day. Part of the reason for this is fear. After all, the freedom to make second-rate films that make a ton of money is extremely important to these folks. Any threat, real or imagined, to the "Do anything I want" pursuit really scares them.

Let's take a peek at history to get some insight into the left-ist Hollywood mind.

Blacklist phobia was something that kept Hollywood liberals pretty much bottled up through the 1950s. You have to admit, the fifties were simpler times. Families had single breadwinners, taxes were actually payable, and married couples slept in separate beds, at least in TV land.

There was, however, some indication in the 1950s of what was to come. Things were starting to loosen up. Rock 'n' roll ruled the airwaves, Elvis perfected the sneer, and teens danced their skorts off on TV. All the while, Hollywood was taking careful notes.

Leftist sensibilities began to stir, and the seeds of upcoming scorn for the establishment started to be sown. Hollywood pumped out movies like *The Wild One* (1954) and *Rebel Without a Cause* (1955). Films like these usually showed a moody young guy from the wrong side of the tracks being rejected by the community. He's welcomed with open arms, though, by a kind-hearted girl who's able to see through his crude exterior. Buried in the plots of these films was a mutiny against the whole freakin' adult world. And this was way before smart-aleck kids started bossing their dopey dads around on TV.

Still, changes seen in the fifties were zilch compared to the massive overhaul that took place in the sixties. The transition to a new decade brought peace marches, love-ins, and the unmistakable smell of pot. Creative products coming out of Hollywood were revolutionized. This included music, television, and film. The hibernating lefties of the West were gearing up.

The movies of the sixties tell a lot about the attitudes that were taking shape in Hollywood. In 1960 *Inherit the Wind* went to great lengths to make people of faith look like blessed buffoons. The film also gave a boost to the theory that everyone except Hollywood celebrities came from monkeys. Most of the film takes place in a southern courtroom with lots of people sweating, especially the southern white guys.

New themes that had not been explored much on film before started to show up. *To Kill a Mockingbird* (1962) was another chance for the public to see southern white guys sweat. In the film, Atticus Finch is a 1930s defense lawyer in a pre-Rainbow Coalition Alabama town. He takes on the job of defending a young black man who is charged with raping a white woman.

Now a black man raping a white woman in the 1930s South was not your run-of-the-mill crime. The people of the town were not happy with Atticus's decision to defend this kid. They try to "persuade" Atticus not to take on the job. But Atticus is the epitome of the liberal view of nobility, a real social-justice superhero. Not even an angry mob of locals is going to stop this fella.

> Buried in the plots of these films was a mutiny against the whole freakin' adult world. And this was way before smart-aleck kids started bossing their dopey dads around on TV.

Atticus was the ideal role model for the Hollywood Left—a courageous crusader. But the film included some clear, definite moral lines. That little "oversight" would be corrected in the future.

The honorable side of social justice was still on display in a series of 1960s films. The films featured a black actor who would go on to transform the racial attitudes of a nation. Sidney Poitier showed that talent and ability could not only succeed in America, it could also get people to accept a black guy with a French name.

From *Lilies of the Field* (1963) to *A Patch of Blue* (1965) to *To Sir with Love* (1967) to *In the Heat of the Night* (1967), Poitier's films broke new ground. But the film that hit the race issue the hardest was *Guess Who's Coming to Dinner* (1967).

The movie plot involved a common parental nightmare of the times, one that was not confined to the South but included the northern suburbs as well. A successful, affluent couple is feeling very cheerful about news that their daughter's boyfriend, who just happens to be a wealthy doctor, has proposed to her.

Cheerful, that is, until they actually meet the husband-to-be. The idea of a black son-in-law illustrated how northern suburbanites could sweat just as much as southerners. It also exposed some of the real racial tensions that existed in society.

During the sixties there was a lot of worry about what was called the atomic bomb. Schools had regular air raid drills, where those who wanted to live or avoid deformity would "duck and cover."

Three films from 1964 made marks on the left lanes of Hollywood that remain to this day. There was an underlying tone of distrust for the government, for the military, and for anyone who wore a sheet. The films exposed suspicions about, and dislike for, people who were unemotional, insensitive, mean-spirited, callous, reckless, and abusive—in short, people who were conservative. And they gave the impression that stripping arms from the military was the only way to avoid a series of bad war movies and doomsday.

Failsafe was a 1964 film that was actually written by Walter Bernstein, one of the former blacklisted writers. In the film, a U.S. airplane equipped with nuclear bombs finds itself on its way to Moscow, thanks to a glitch in technology. An unthinkable diplomatic solution is eventually reached by the president, played by Jane Fonda's dad. (You knew the Fondas had to be involved.) In order to avoid a nuclear holocaust, the United States has to drop a few bombs on its own people, but hey, at least the planet is saved.

Another film, *Seven Days in May* (1964), showed the terrible threat to America that supposedly lurked in its own military. In watching the movie, you get the feeling that the top brass are probably all conservative, anti-communist, Republican types, especially since they allow Burt Lancaster to lead them. The audience is left with the impression that grave danger could come from the Right at any moment.

In the 1960s the only thing that scared budding baby boomers more than Spam was the atomic bomb. That dread of world nuclear annihilation became a somber spoof in a bizarre Stanley Kubrick satire called *Dr. Strangelove or: How I Learned to Stop Worrying and Love the Bomb* (1964).

Using dark comedy and a whole lot of weird music, the film tells the tale of a U.S. Air Force general named Jack D. Ripper, who has lost his mind. Unfortunately, the crazed general has the power to order a nuclear attack on the Soviets.

General Ripper believes that the communists in the Soviet Union are conspiring to pollute the precious bodily fluids of the American people. The Soviet ambassador informs the president of the United States that if the Soviet Union is hit with a nuclear weapon, an apparatus will automatically be activated that will wipe out all life on Earth, except for a few monks in Tibet and maybe Mike Wallace.

A plan is implemented by the U.S. and the Soviets to shoot down American jets. One of the planes manages to survive. It ultimately drops its payload on the designated target, finishing the film with the end of the world.

The lead character, Dr. Strangelove, who is played by Peter Sellers, is a caricature of a fascist. He's a man with a knockwurst-sized German accent and a twitch in the form of a Nazi salute. He accidentally refers to the president of the United States as "fuehrer." And he gives the prez the skinny on how the government can continue to exist after nuclear doomsday occurs. Clearly, the film presents the military in the most unattractive way possible. Let's just say it would never have made it as an Air Force recruiting film.

End-of-the-world flicks reverberated outside of movie houses, too. In fact, they had an impact on the White House itself. Remember the campaign ad of the same year, 1964, when Lyndon B. Johnson ran against Barry Goldwater? The scene shows a lovely, peaceful day in rural America. A little girl is slowly counting as she plucks daisy petals in the warm sunshine. In the background, an announcer's voice also counts down—10, 9, 8, 7, . . . Suddenly, there's the sound of an explosion. The camera pans into the little girl's eyes just in time to capture the reflection of a mushroom cloud. Although he's never mentioned by name, the implication is clear: Barry Goldwater is really Dr. Strangelove.

Another bizarre spectacle that mottled the landscape of the 1960s was the student protest. The first protests sprang from a bitterness that had been brewing about the draft, the Vietnam War, and actually having to work for food. But it didn't take too much time for long-haired, bell-bottom wearing, Sonny and Cher look-alikes to start protesting lots of other things.

Bras, draft cards, flags, and Robert Goulet records were unceremoniously burned. Protests against school schedules and grading policies were next on the picket circuit. It got to the point where protests became an event. Nobody much cared what was being protested. It was just hip to walk and balk.

In the latter part of the decade, the real far-left themes began to emerge. Films got downright belligerent when it came to dealing with good and evil. In 1967 two films came out that redefined the sport of rule breaking. Traditional ideas of right and wrong were turned inside out in *Bonnie and Clyde* and *The Graduate*.

Teens fell in love with the idea of making heroes out of a couple of depression-era bank robbers. Who wouldn't, when the characters in *Bonnie and Clyde* (1967) were played by two of the most glamorous stars of the time, Faye Dunaway and Warren Beatty. Young movie-goers were enticed into theaters with the cute little slogan "They're young, they're in love, they kill people." It was pretty obvious that virtue wasn't going to be the strong suit for the movie's lead thugs, even if they did look good.

Bonnie was a kind of forerunner for twisted feminist characters that were to come. In the 1920s women were supposed to be at home raising the kids and cleaning the house, not robbing banks and murdering men.

The movie has a scene that shows a romanticized view of events through leftist lenses. When the wanted criminals, Bonnie and Clyde, arrive at a migrant camp, they're treated like rock stars. And the residents of the camp are portrayed as gangster groupies. It's enough to bring tears to the eyes of Trotsky followers and Susan Sarandon fans.

Young movie-goers were enticed into theaters with the cute little slogan "They're young, they're in love, they kill people." It was pretty obvious that virtue wasn't going to be the strong suit for the movie's lead thugs, even if they did look good.

As if youthful defiance in the form of robbery and murder weren't entertaining enough, another film introduced promiscuity, incest, and serial adultery. In *The Graduate* (1967), the main character, Benjamin, played by a young Dustin Hoffman, has just finished college. Benjamin is like most college grads. He doesn't have the slightest idea what he's going to do after graduation.

Lots of adults give him advice. Ben questions the wisdom of his elders but is still willing to listen. He's especially attentive when a guy named Robinson tells the young man that he should take advantage of every situation presented. After all, Ben would only be young once and should grab for all the gusto he can get. Today is the first day of the rest of your life, blah, blah, blah.

Ben takes it to heart. Robinson's wife (Anne Bancroft) seduces Benjamin with a little stripping and a lot of alcohol. Since she's old enough to be his mother, Ben soon finds the age difference thing depressing. So in order to relieve his pain, Ben hits on Mrs. Robinson's daughter, Elaine (Katherine Ross). This infuriates Mrs. Robinson, and thus, a twisted love triangle is born.

The year 1968 was a turning point in the decade. That year Martin Luther King Jr. and Robert Kennedy were both assassinated. A demonstration in Chicago turned into an intense clash between young protesters and police outside the Democratic National Convention. "The whole world's watching" was the chant heard around the globe. But just in case anyone missed it, the group Chicago engraved the phrase onto one of its albums.

The same year yielded a couple of celluloid creations, which carried 1960s' themes farther left than they'd been taken before. Teens usually have a way of convincing themselves that they're smarter than adults. This phenomenon often occurs when adolescents are at the pinnacle of their ignorance. But during the sixties, high schools actually started to teach students how to be thoroughly stupid. For those who remained just a little bit smart, drugs were readily accessible to take care of any errant brain cells.

The youth of the sixties really believed that the world would be better off if adults no longer ran things. And Hollywood tapped into this sentiment with Marxist glee. In a twisted, kid-oriented flight of imagination, Hollywood served up a movie where youngsters took over America and sent adults packing—to concentration camps, that is. *Wild in the Streets* (1968) was the heart-warming little flick that had the elder sets' knees knocking all over the place.

College students, too, started getting creative. They invented a new kind of road trip. They'd travel around in packs through towns in middle America, fighting convention, challenging authority, and essentially acting snotty.

Three actors who ended up perfecting the art of snottiness were introduced to the public in 1969. Peter Fonda, Dennis Hopper, and Jack Nicholson rumbled onto the big screen in *Easy Rider* (1969). Their characters were ignorant young dudes who acted immature and used a bunch of drugs.

The movie plot involves a search for something. But the characters in the film aren't really sure what they're searching for, if you exclude the notion of a good time. The country is projected through the main characters' eyes as being hopelessly corrupt. An "Easy Rider" America is populated with mindless numbskulls who always do the "acceptable" thing. Actors, directors, and enlightened bikers are, of course, the exception.

Although it was made in the same year as the Woodstock bash, the movie didn't share Woodstock's aura of optimism. Instead, it was dreary and depressing. The two bikers manage to snake across the nation on their Harleys. Their names are Wyatt and Billy, conjuring up images of cowboy outlaws.

In a yuppie-like display of defiance, Wyatt tosses away his watch. He and his pal hit the road as credits roll along to the Steppenwolf tune, "Born to Be Wild." The song romanticizes the idea of taking a trip and having no destination. The two rogues of the road "head out on the highway, lookin' for adventure" and whatever comes their way.

So what happened in Hollywood in the 1960s when a low-budget film defied convention and featured sex, drugs, and violence? It got showered with awards, of course.

It's not long before the main characters of the film need to make some money. What better way for free-spirited individuals to pick up a few bucks than by selling drugs? The men buy some cocaine in Mexico and smuggle it into California.

So what happened in Hollywood in the 1960s when a low-budget film defied convention and featured sex, drugs, and violence? It got showered with awards, of course. *Easy Rider* won Best Film by a New Director at Cannes. And it received two Academy Award nominations.

Easy Rider opened the doors for new directors to break more norms. Warped heroes, unresolved moral tensions, and free-wheeling misbehavior suddenly became cool. Hollywood's new generation of the Left now had the perfect role models for society to emulate. And Left Coast activists would hold fast to their counterculture dreams for many years to come.

Rock Your Worldview

Cinematic anti-heroes weren't the only rebels that surfaced during the 1960s. Campus radicals, the organized Left, and Students for a Democratic Society joined in on the radical revelry. But there was a louder group that screamed out a theme of revolt against the "establishment." It was rock musicians, and their music laid out quite a soundtrack for the decade of transformation.

The music itself sparked an anti-government, anti-parent, anti-tradition, and anti-bathtub crusade. It helped fashion one of the most self-absorbed and deluded generations in all of American history—the baby boomers. The boomers would eventually grow up, physically at least, and spread the virus of liberalism throughout Hollywood.

Right before the sixties started, vanilla-flavored music acts took over. Performers who wore matching outfits were all the rage. Artists like Pat Boone, Frankie Avalon, and Fabian had the parent seal of approval pressed into their foreheads.

Still, sixties' audiences longed for a return to the more edgy stuff that had been present in the early 1950s. And a lot of rock performers in the mid-to-late sixties had actually cut their teeth on Chuck Berry, early Elvis, Jerry Lee Lewis, Little Richard, and Buddy Holly. They loved the driving force of the music, but they needed to make it their own. So they created lyrics to make themselves look politically, socially, and culturally defiant. Some of the music that drained into the brains of baby boomers poured out of the likes of Bob Dylan, Neil Young, and the Grateful Dead.

They say music soothes the savage beast, but the sounds of the sixties stirred up a cultural monster. It wasn't just any old music. It was momentous, so momentous that dancing wasn't allowed. The music was to be absorbed while sitting on the floor in the lotus position, uttering phrases like "Wow," "Heavy," and "Please pass the bong, man."

It was a kind of rock that was otherworldly. As one former editor of the *Rolling Stone* put it, it "was tied to a counterculture professing to be so firmly against commercial and social conventions that the notion of a 'rock and roll business' seemed an oxymoron."[1]

Despite the counterculture's so-called rejection of all things conventional, the business of rock would turn out to generate moolah—tons of it. Rock stars became bandana-headed warriors, battling rules with electric guitars that they pointed like futuristic weapons at the old guard. For some hard-line lefties, the phrase "Social force for change" meant "Let's have a double shot of revolution in our beer." Young radicals complained about capitalism, but they still participated in the system by shelling out lots of cash for records and concert tickets.

Organizations on the far left, on the other hand, looked at the sixties as key to their efforts to bring down the establishment. A song recorded by the Rolling Stones illustrates how 1960s' music was thought of as a vehicle for political rebellion.

The 1968 tune "Street Fighting Man" embodied the themes of the radical Left. The song declared that the time was "right for fighting in the street." In another stanza of the same song, the Stones spoke of "a palace revolution."

How it must flip out leftists from the sixties to see the "street fighting" Rolling Stones of today trying to camouflage their age spots and grabbing for the tube of Ben Gay.

Even though the music of the 1960s inspired the Left, a lot of the musicians and bands of the era differed dramatically in their values, beliefs, and bank accounts. The more politically provocative rockers deserve a closer look.

Deliberately Dylan

In July 1965 a young singer was scheduled to perform at the Newport Folk Festival. The festival was put on by Pete Seeger and Theodore Bikel, two solid pillars of the Left. The singer performed a traditional acoustic rendition of folk songs. All of a sudden, musicians holding electric instruments sort of magically appeared onstage with the singer. The bunch pounded out a song, and bedlam followed. The song was called "Maggie's Farm." The folksinger was Bob Dylan.

This was the first concert Dylan, backed by the Paul Butterfield Blues Band, did with "support." The performance was roundly booed. Dylan's manager allegedly engaged in a fistfight with one of the promoters.

Later that year, Dylan and company toured the United States, Australia, Scandinavia, the United Kingdom, and France. The boos continued.

Although Bob Dylan is often viewed as the poet who raised the music of the 1960s to the level of art, the artist himself was a fabrication. He was a calculated creation, a product of a well-executed self-marketing campaign.

The guy known as Bob Dylan was actually born in 1941 as Robert Zimmerman of Hibbing, Minnesota. He was the son of a middle-class furniture store owner. In his youth, he listened to early rock and played piano in various bands.

After finishing high school, Zimmerman went to the University of Minnesota. He spent time with folk musicians in the coffeehouses of—this is no joke—Dinkytown. He hadn't changed his name or his voice yet. That would come at a future date.

Zimmerman was following the dictates of today's Dr. Phil, who tells his viewers to "build a whole new you." The singer would later refer to this process as "building a character."[2] Building a character meant finding a new identity, personality, style, and look. He chose Woody Guthrie as his model. Guthrie was a musical vagabond in the book, and subsequent film, *Bound for Glory*. Zimmerman was already familiar with Guthrie and knew a lot of his repertoire.

With his "new package" concept, Zimmerman decided to build a folk style that was deliberately unpolished. He took on an Okie accent and cultivated a James Dean image. He met a blues musician named Jesse Fuller, who had developed a style of playing the harmonica (with the help of a harp holder) and strumming the guitar at the same time. Zimmerman taught himself the technique. He was ready. He changed his name to Bob Dylan. And like Neil Sedaka with a head cold, he set out to conquer the pop rock world.

> Zimmerman decided to build a folk style that was deliberately unpolished. He changed his name to Bob Dylan. And like Neil Sedaka with a head cold, he set out to conquer the pop rock world.

Zimmerman had done a first-class job. Bob Dylan took the Greenwich Village folk scene by storm. His early reviewers often praised him for his loose, spontaneous authenticity. You have to admit, the whole thing is kind of ironic.

Still, in 1962 one of the most famous political songs ever written flowed from Dylan's pen—"Blowin' in the Wind." And it moved through the studios, mansions, and limousines of Hollywood like incense to a leftist god.

During the same year, another influential folksinger hooked up with Dylan, musically and personally. Joan Baez recorded Dylan's songs and sang his praises. They ended up being romantically involved.[3]

Both the new Left and the civil rights movements were motivated by the music of Dylan. But he himself had no intention of getting involved. Strangely enough, he was pretty much apolitical.

Commenting on politics, Dylan said, ". . . I've found out some things. The groups promoting these things, the movement, would try to get me involved with them, be their singing spokesman—and inside these groups, with all their president–vice president–secretary stuff, it's politics. Inside their own pettiness they are as bad as the hate groups. I won't even have a fan club because it would have to have a president, it would be a group. They think the more people you have behind something the more influence it has. Maybe so, but the more it gets watered down too. I am not a believer in doing things by number. I believe the best things get done by individuals."[4]

Then There Was Woodstock

The Woodstock Festival was a musical event that defined the flower-power generation. Eventually, it spread political pollen all over the hills of Hollywood. It was a large outdoor rock affair that lasted an entire weekend. The best of the sixties' counterculture songwriters, musicians, and bands took part in it.

It was more than just a single concert where long-haired inebriated adolescents and post-adolescents spent a few hours losing their hearing and lapsing into unconsciousness. It was a long, drawn-out series of concerts where long-haired inebriated adolescents and post-adolescents spent a few *days* losing their hearing and lapsing into unconsciousness.

Organizers of the event had something big in mind. They wanted a name that would capture the mood of the times. In 1969 the former Robert Zimmerman was living in Woodstock, New York. Festival organizers decided to name their landmark event after the hometown of Bob Dylan, the singer-songwriter who epitomized the tone they wanted to convey.

True to sixties' form, the festival was not held anywhere near the actual town of Woodstock. Instead, it was held on Max Yasgur's farm in Bethel, New York, located about 100 miles outside of New York City. Stephen Stills would make sure no one would forget that bit of trivia. He carved Yasgur's name into the annals of rock history with the song "Woodstock." As for Dylan, he'd be a no-show.

Organizers wanted the world to take notice. Woodstock was going to be huge. It would be the biggest party ever, with girls, rock 'n' roll music, drugs, and, oh yeah, peace on Earth.

Before the epic event took place, the largest rock concert had had an audience of about 20,000. Organizers figured about 200,000 might come to Woodstock, but they said they only expected about 100,000 so as not to alarm anybody. Promoters sort of snickered to each other, "We'll fool the press. The event will be twice as large as they're thinking." When the final tally was in, it was more than four times as large as the number they'd initially thrown out.

It was billed as the Woodstock Music and Art Fair: Three Days of Peace and Music. It turned out, though, that in addition to peace and music, hippy-dippy listeners were subjected to traffic jams, pouring rain, mudslides, and equipment failures.

More than 450,000 young rock fans came to the upstate New York farm like pilgrims to Mecca. Roads leading to Bethel couldn't handle the traffic. Even the New York State Thruway was jammed. Millions were trying their best to attend.

Organizers had only set up three ticket booths. They were so utterly overwhelmed by the crowd they were forced to change the event into a gateless, free festival. Some attendees parked miles away and trudged to the concert site. They arrived to see a picnic, which changed into a crowd, which became a small town, which grew further still.

Overnight an unplanned city sprang into being—the third most populated city in the state of New York. Services normally connected with a city had to be improvised. It was a miracle that no serious crisis occurred during the weekend, except when they needed more toilet paper.

Musicians arrived and left via helicopter and astral projection. Neil Young was there, performing with Crosby, Stills and Nash. The Grateful Dead showed up live as well. Other sixties' luminaries included Jimi Hendrix, Arlo Guthrie, Janis Joplin, and Jefferson Airplane.

The nature worship that we see in full bloom today was just beginning to bud. Scads of hippies were trying to get in touch with the elements. Those who attended Woodstock ended up linking with a part of nature that some found disagreeable—nonstop driving rain. It poured from Friday night on, but diehard fans seemed unfazed.

The ground turned into a muddy mess. Even the stage became a musical mudslide. The water, the mud, the music, and the massive crowd melded together in harmony. And Woodstock was transformed into a banner fable of the Left.

Eventually, Woodstock ripened into a full-blown mythical account of legendary proportion. It was the place where liberal dreams had become a reality. Almost 500,000 people gathered together. They lived by their own anti-establishment rules. And they sought pleasure together.

"See," said the Left. "This is what we can build for all of society."

The fairy tale continues to live on in the hearts and minds of the Hollywood Left, many of whom witnessed Woodstock in person or experienced it vicariously in film and song. There's never really been anything like it. Despite attempts, organizers were never quite able to duplicate it.

Day of the Grateful Dead

One Woodstock band, though, would make a lasting impression and end up taking a leftward lead. They were a group of folk and bluegrass musicians. They got together in 1963, calling themselves the Mother McCree's Uptown Jug Champions. In 1965 they renamed the band The Warlocks. And they made some changes that would forever alter the American pop scene.

They added electric instruments, along with some elements of rock 'n' roll. A pop genre was in the offing. Jerry Garcia, the dominant member of the group, claimed in 1965 that while he was stoned on a hallucinogen, he opened up a dictionary. The first thing that he saw, when his eyes could focus, were three words: "The Grateful Dead."[5] The words became the group's name, and fans became known as Deadheads. Fans and band alike became linked to the one thing that would taint many of the ideals that came out of the sixties—mind-altering drugs.

The drugs used were experimental. Almost everyone involved now admits it was wrong. Suicides, homicides, induced psychoses, and ravaged lives prove it. The band itself was allied with psychedelic gurus Ken Kesey and Timothy Leary, who encouraged young people to screw up their minds and their bodies.

The Dead debuted in San Francisco, home of the acid rock scene. It was a drug user's Disneyland, where so-called Ken Kesey Acid Tests took place. The band and buddies consumed manufactured LSD and recorded music while on the stuff.[6] Concerts became longer than a Mahler symphony or an Al Gore speech. Who would sit patiently on the floor while improvised acid rock went on for hours on end? Deadheads would.

> Concerts became longer than a Mahler symphony or an Al Gore speech. Who would sit patiently on the floor while improvised acid rock went on for hours on end? Deadheads would.

Deadheads knew that the heart and soul of the band they adored was founder and lead guitarist Jerry Garcia. "Captain Trips" was his nickname. He earned the title as a result of the journeys he took on LSD and other psychedelic drugs.

When Garcia died in August 1995, he'd been in the process of trying to overcome a drug addiction. He was only 53 years of age. The way in which his death was covered showed how much the lefty boomers had infiltrated the press. The leader of the free world at the time, Bill Clinton, showered Garcia with praise. He called him a genius. In San Francisco, flags were flown at half-mast. The whole thing was reminiscent of the loss of JFK and Martin Luther King Jr.

Garcia was viewed as the king of counter-culture. His music was a backdrop for those who claimed to loathe the establishment. Now he was being treated like a member of the very same establishment. He must have been trippin' in his grave.

The Youngster

There was also a guy in the sixties who sang in high falsetto voice. No, it's not who you think. These were pre-solo Michael Jackson times. This high-pitched troubadour was Neil Young.

Young was born in Toronto, Canada, in 1945. He came from creative parents, a TV celebrity mom and a sportswriter dad. In his early music days, Young drove around in a hearse and kept his guitars inside a coffin tray.

Like so many other boomers, Young was seduced by rock in the 1950s. His first bands had a series of fanciful names like The Shocking Pinks, Gone with the Wind Orchestra, and Young and Restless. Those crazy Canadians. Why couldn't he come up with a sensible American name like Hootie and the Blowfish?

When the sixties began, Young was influenced by Bob Dylan and became a folky. After drifting back to rock in the middle of the decade, he drove his hearse to Los Angeles and met up with Stephen Stills. Young and Stills put together a new group, but they didn't have a name. Some steamrollers that were fixing the streets inadvertently supplied one. The steamrollers had nameplates with two words that would eventually level the minds of a generation—Buffalo Springfield.

Hollywood embraced the "fun at all costs" lifestyle that sixties' rockers were supposed to have invented. Unlike many of his contemporaries, though, Young questioned the direction that the hippy movement was taking. In the latter part of the decade, Young took a second look at the rock 'n' roll message. After years of forbidden substances, groupies, senseless behavior, and shoes that gave you nosebleeds, he started commenting in his songs on sixties' musicians and their fans.

In 1969 Young went on his own with a new back-up band called Crazy Horse. The following year brought Young into Crosby, Stills and Nash, probably because Steve Stills of Buffalo Springfield was a driving force in the band. Crosby, Stills, Nash and Young made their entrance at the Woodstock Festival. Young's gig with the band only lasted about a year. He returned to a solo career. Rumor has it that part of the reason he left was because of his growing disdain for drugs.

Young has always been a unique political figure in the Hollywood music scene. He wrote a song in 1970 that was a rock 'n' roll smack at then President Richard Nixon, after four students at Kent State were killed during an anti-Vietnam War confrontation. But in the 1980s, Young endorsed Ronald Reagan for president. Then he flipped over in the late eighties and supported the far-left presidential candidacy of Jesse Jackson.

In December 2001, Young had many in the Hollywood establishment gagging on their hors d'oeuvres. He showed up at a Beverly Hills banquet to receive an award. The honor was a Spirit of Liberty lifetime achievement award, which was being given by the inaptly named People for the American Way. Some of the Hollywood lefties couldn't believe their ears as Young used the occasion to strongly support President George W. Bush and his policies in fighting the war on terror.

Young even talked of the need for sacrifice during a time of war: "To protect our freedoms, it seems we're going to have to relinquish some of our freedoms for a short period of time."

He'd always been a politically outspoken musician. After all, his song "Ohio" was released days after the Kent State University students were shot and killed. And the late eighties tunes "This Note's for You" and "Keep on Rocking in the Free World" became theme songs for activists of all stripes.

But in 2001, Young wrote a song to memorialize the travelers who took over the legendary Flight 93. United Airlines

Flight 93 crashed in Pennsylvania after it was commandeered by hijackers on September 11. Young's song is based on the telephone call from passenger Todd Beamer, who told an operator about a plan he and other passengers had to take on the terrorists. The last words Beamer was heard saying were "Let's roll." The words became the title of Young's song.

> We've got to get inside there
> Before they kill some more
> Time is running out
> Let's roll.

CHAPTER THREE

The Manna from Havana

The Hollywood community often acts like Mr. Magoo. Remember the cartoon character that lived in a world of illusion? His vision was frightfully bad, but he didn't want to admit that his eyesight was failing. Instead, he just sort of bumbled his way through life, oblivious to the numerous near misses he encountered every hour of every day.

Like Magoo, a lot of leftist celebrities pretend to walk around as if they're stone-blind. But their condition differs from our animated friend in a couple of ways.

First, Magoo didn't have control over what he couldn't see. And his lack of vision was non-specific. In other words, he saw all things with equally poor clarity. In contrast, the situation with left leaners in Tinseltown is self-imposed. They have what's called selective blindness. This may be a purposely acquired trait, kind of like air kissing. In any event, those afflicted refuse to see the cruelties, atrocities, misdeeds, and mayhem committed by official commie tormentors the world over.

The second way in which Hollywood leftyweights differ from Magoo has to do with their bumbling. It's not funny at all.

Why would anyone ever want to confer star status on human scum? It remains one of those unsolved Left Coast mysteries. It's hard to swallow, but the usual gang of entertainment elite—the directors, actors, filmmakers, TV producers, et al.—like to ignore "inconvenient" facts. Things like statistics, human rights records, and eyewitness accounts don't matter much in their historically edited world. They're always finding new oppressors to shower affection on. Their current favorite is a guy who's turned his country into a tropical prison camp. He's the finger-pokin', cigar-smokin', gun-totin' Fidel Castro.

Whenever Fidel drops in on a capitalist country, libs flock to the site just to swoon left. A number of Hollywood luminaries have actually traveled to Cuba to spend some non-proletariat time with him. The list includes Danny Glover, Harry Belafonte, Ed Asner, Spike Lee, Sydney Pollack, Oliver Stone, Robert Redford, Leonardo DiCaprio, Kevin Costner, Chevy Chase, Naomi Campbell, Kate Moss, Jack Nicholson, and Steven Spielberg.

Some of the more inane celebrity statements reveal their paper-thin understanding of the Cuban dictator. For instance, in 1998 Jack Nicholson took some time away from basketball viewing to go meet with Fidel. *Daily Variety* reported that Nicholson described Castro as "a genius." The actor said that during his three-hour meeting, the two "spoke about everything." Wonder which one played the joker in that little melodrama.

In the late 1990s, supermodel Naomi Campbell went to Cuba along with the undernourished Kate Moss. The *Toronto Star* reported that Campbell was "nervous and flustered" over meeting with the infamous dictator. Maybe it was his camouflage pants. At any rate, Campbell remembered Castro said that "seeing us in person was very spiritual." For anyone who hasn't already heard, Castro is renowned for his record-breaking womanizing. So meeting with the two top supermodels was a spiritual experience? Yeah, right. It was one of those holy Charlie's Angels encounters.

On Earth Day 2000, Chevy Chase informed the public that "socialism works" and "Cuba might prove that." In an effort to

> Whenever Fidel drops in on a capitalist country, libs flock to the site just to swoon left.

give his statements that air of artistic legitimacy, Chase added, "I think it's conclusive that there have been areas where socialism has helped to keep people at least stabilized at a certain level." What do you suppose the ideal level to be stabilized at in Cuba is? Abject poverty? Wholesale indigence? Third-world destitution? Chase must have been using those SNL rules of logic again.

The *New York Post* reported that the head of MTV, along with the president of CBS television, visited Cuba in 2001. One of the media execs described Cuba as "the most romantic, soulful and sexy country I've ever been to in my life." Nothing like staged bliss to get a Hollywood mogul's motor running.

Also in 2001, Kevin Costner jetted over to Cuba. Seems *Thirteen Days,* Costner's film about the Cuban missile crisis, was in need of a little publicity. So the actor went to show the flick to Fidel. In his typically flat manner, Costner said, "It was an experience of a lifetime to sit only a few feet away from him and watch him re-live an experience he lived as a very young man." Think Costner may have lingered a little too long in Waterworld?

Turns out that two of Hollywood's top bananas in the field of directing, Steven Spielberg and Oliver Stone, have both visited Cuba and met with Castro.

Spielberg traipsed off to the mock enchanted setting in November 2002. *E.T.*'s prime mover was opening a festival of his work on the island. His spokesperson, Marvin Levy, told Reuters, "Steven has always said that film is a universal creative medium that can reach out to people across national boundaries and cultures." Hey, it worked for Jerry Lewis, didn't it?

While in Cuba, Spielberg wanted to meet with the country's "filmmakers," talk to students at an international film school, and visit whatever's left of the Cuban Jewish community since it dwindled from 15,000 members before Castro's revolution down to 1,500.

According to official delegates, Spielberg spent eight hours in conversation with Fidel. For most people, that would be about as interesting as being subjected to 56,000 hours of NPR. Maybe not for Spielberg. He purportedly rated the time spent with the Cuban dictator as "the eight most important hours of my life."[1] The pair supposedly discussed cultural exchanges, history, the environment, and the U.S. trade embargo. Chances are they never got around to talking about private property, free speech, due process, civil rights, or how to get those stubborn bloodstains out of your carpet.

The bespectacled director summed up his sentiments this way: "I feel so much at home here. I hope to come back many times in the future." For a truly authentic experience, Spielberg ought to try making the trip across the sea via inner tube.

Oliver Stone is apparently a Castro fan, too. Ever notice how his films tend to be on the paranoid side when it comes to U.S. activities and institutions? Well, he doesn't seem to be at all paranoid when it comes to a certain communist government.

Stone actually met Castro back in 1987 at the screening of the film *Salvador*. The tyrant obviously made a deep impression on Stone because in February 2002, Stone decided to go on his own excursion to Cuba. He supposedly went there to do some research for a film project.

"I am here to interview Fidel for Spanish television," Stone told Reuters at a convention center where he had heard Castro speak.

In order to make a movie that features the communist country and its self-appointed president, Stone worked with Fidel friend and former head of Cuba's state cinema institute Alfredo Guevara. He's said to have met with Castro's older brother, Ramon, too. And he's had a couple of sessions with el presidente himself.

Conspiracy buff Stone says that in making a documentary about Fidel Castro, he didn't let the despot's supposed charm affect his objectivity. Stone let loose with this statement on the Cuban oppressor-in-chief: "We should look to him as one of the Earth's wisest people, one of the people we should consult." Yeah, if we ever want to know the most efficient way to torture mass numbers of people and subjugate a nation.

As is typical of left-leaning nincompoops, Stone was eager to tell the press about the glorious triumphs of the Castro regime. You know, things such as the extraordinary educational system and other services it has developed. He forgot to mention the innovative way of getting prisoners to talk using the lit end of the finest Cuban cigars.

> Stone said that he wanted to show Fidel's "human side." Attempting to portray the human side of Castro is like trying to show the softer side of Jeffrey Dahmer.

Stone's HBO documentary premiered at the 2003 Sundance Film Festival. In speaking of the flick, Stone said that he wanted to show Fidel's "human side." Attempting to portray the human side of Castro is like trying to show the softer side of Jeffrey Dahmer.

The film publication *Variety* said Stone's documentary was being produced by Spanish film companies. It was supposed to include extensive interviews with the 75-year-old plátano-puss. The movie's original title was *Looking for Fidel*. It should have been renamed to fit its conscience-challenged namesake. Maybe something like *Looking for Mr. Crowbar*. But instead decision makers went with Fidel's nickname, *Comandante*.

Comandante was supposed to air on cable in Spring 2003, but the folks at HBO actually made a decent decision. No, it wasn't the one about putting *Sex in the City* out of its misery. It was the one about dumping Stone's Castro oblation. HBO dropped from its lineup the one-sided piece of pro-Castro propaganda because of some of the things that Fidel had done in Cuba earlier in the year.

It seems that Castro had taken advantage of the media focus on the war in Iraq and engaged in some trademark crackdowns on dissidents. Four men were given life sentences, four alleged hijackers were sentenced to prison terms, and three alleged ferry hijackers were executed by firing squad.

Word has it that Stone wants to go back to Cuba and interview Castro about the executions. The so-called documentary may return with additional footage attached. Havana forbid.

God Bless the Child

Many of the same folks who claim to abhor violence and detest firearms somehow managed to twist things around in a big way back in 2000. They nodded in approval when armed paramilitary officers helped to deliver a defenseless six-year-old child back into the arms of Fidel Castro.

You see, Elian Gonzalez was the little boy who survived the journey across the Florida Straits to escape his homeland of persecution. He survived the tragic loss of his mother, who died in the ordeal. He survived being stranded alone at sea for two days in shark-infested waters. He survived the media onslaught, which followed his rescue on Thanksgiving Day by a fisherman who spotted him adrift in the water. He survived for months living under the piercing lenses of about a million cameras, while government officials, lawyers, and talking heads debated his status. But he couldn't survive the sick political chess game that eventually determined his fate.

The knee-high refugee was snatched in the dead of night by armed federal agents, after folks standing vigil outside were gassed. Torn from the grip of the same fisherman who had saved him, the boy's heavy sobbing couldn't be muffled by the blanket flung hastily over his head. He was whisked away, his sacred sanctuary, precious playthings, and innocent trust kicked aside. It was the eve of Easter.

The Pulitzer Prize–winning photo of little Elian, paralyzed with fear at the sight of an automatic weapon lodged a few inches away from his head, says it all. It's one more supernatural fingerprint on the record for us to ponder—that someone was there at just the right moment and captured the truth.

Unbelievable as it was, the trauma done to Elian didn't seem to faze the usual Left Coast gun grabbers, or the pistol poachers on the East Coast either, for that matter. Why not? Well, part of the reason is because these are some of the same folks who want to open up the nation's borders and bring anyone and everyone into the country, as long as they'll vote the liberal party line. The Cuban community was not exactly a stronghold for the Democrats at the time of this fiasco. But even if it were, Elian was a bit too young to qualify to vote, even in Florida.

Michael Moore, left-wing demagogue extraordinaire, ended up giving voice to the Hollywood thinking on Elian. If you're not familiar with Moore, he's the guy who never misses an opportunity to slam President Bush. And he's forever expressing his disdain for the United States.

The generously proportioned joker wrote that the only thing Elian Gonzalez had to fear in returning to Cuba was "receiving free health care" and "an excellent education." He added that Elian had a better chance of his "baby brother being born and making it to his first birthday than if he had been born in Washington, DC."

Moore was only reflecting the same sentiments as his allies on the other coast. On NBC's *Today* show, morning cornflake Katie Couric used one of her favorite techniques for implying objectivity. She used the routine where she begins with the phrase "Some suggested." A lot of people in the mainstream press like to begin their questioning and so-called reporting with cute little mind-massage words like "Some say," "Some feel," or "Some recommend." They know just how to finesse the language, so to speak.

Anyway, regarding the Cuban community in Florida known as Little Havana, Couric said, "Some suggested over the weekend that it's wrong to expect Elian Gonzalez to live in a place that tolerates no dissent or freedom of political expression. They were talking about Miami. All eyes on south Florida and its image this morning. Another writer this weekend called it 'an out-of-control banana republic within America.'"

Most people listening probably thought Katie had suddenly been hit with a bout of journalistic dyslexia. "Didn't she mean to say Havana instead of Miami?" trucker Bob asks waitress Betty over at the Sioux City, Iowa Truck Stop.

No, folks. Katie gets paid megabucks for her unparalleled skill at reading prepared scripts. Unfortunately, she meant exactly what she said.

Actually, coddling commie regimes seems to be a hobby for all of the alphabet soup broadcast networks. For instance, CBS had its blurry eye on the Elian saga. On the morning the little guy was forcibly abducted from his relatives, Dan Rather spit out the following: "While Fidel Castro, and certainly justified on his record, is widely criticized for a lot of things, there is no question that Castro feels a very deep and abiding connection to those Cubans who are still in Cuba. And, I recognize this might be controversial, but there's little doubt in my mind that Fidel Castro was sincere when he said, 'listen, we really want this child back here.'"

Rather had little doubt in his mind that Castro was sincere? Based on what? The creamer in his coffee? Hey, Dan, no Pulitzer for you!

Brook Larmer and John Leland of *Newsweek* described the wonderful life the young boy would face in the communist haven this way: "Elian might expect a nurturing life in Cuba, sheltered from the crime and social breakdown that would be part of his upbringing in Miami . . . Cuba now even has ATMs that dispense dollars from foreign banks. The education and health-care systems, both built since the revolution, are among the best in the Americas, despite chronic shortages of supplies. . . ."

> Once in a while it would be nice if Americans could pick up a magazine and "oscillate to the contrary rhythms" of the truth about Cuba.

How do these guys come up with this garbage? Last time anyone bothered to look, there weren't a whole lot of waiting lists to get into Cuban hospitals or schools.

Larmer and Leland continue, "The boy will nestle again in a more peaceable society that treasures its children. But his life will oscillate to the contrary rhythms of this central Cuban paradox. As a shining symbol of the Communist state, he will have access to the corrupting fruits of the new economy. He'll enjoy the best Cuba has to offer, the things only dollars can buy."

Once in a while it would be nice if Americans could pick up a magazine and "oscillate to the contrary rhythms" of the truth about Cuba.

Tender Tyrant

There have been a number of movies where Hollywood's taken the opportunity to demonstrate its love for Fidel.

In 1990 Sydney Pollack came out with a flick called *Havana*. The movie looked at the relationship between a drifting loaner-gambler and a valiant female communist who was dedicated to the Castro revolution.

The film was slow moving and boring. Of course, movies that try to shove a political agenda down the throats of an audience usually are. This one essentially portrayed communists as cardboard cutouts of nobility. Commi-babe Lena Olin fawned over her hero, Castro. Like some sort of sensual snake charmer, she lured others into the leftist realm.

In the fall of 2002, a documentary called *Fidel* was brought to the screen. It was billed as an objective biography of the Cuban leader. The film followed the life of Fidel from his teenage years, to his revolution against the Batista regime, to the modern-day non-statesman that he is. *Fidel* was the creation of Estela Bravo. Bravo attempted to acquaint viewers with Castro through interviews with the man himself and a variety of his leftist admirers. Alice Walker, Harry Belafonte, and Sydney Pollack gave their perspectives on Castro's personality. Current and former U.S. government figures, including Arthur Schlesinger, Ramsey Clark, and Congressman Charles Rangel, offered their political and historical musings on Castro and Cuba.

The audience was treated to scenes of the paranoid dictator swimming with bodyguards, visiting his childhood home and school, joking with Nelson Mandela, Ted Turner, and Muhammad Ali, and meeting Elian Gonzalez. Thankfully, viewers were spared the sight of Fidel being given a bubble bath.

Even the usual politically sympathetic film critics couldn't help but notice the giant load of half-truths that came down the pike in the distorted documentary. Ken Fox of *TV Guide* acknowledged bias, although he said that the film was "no more biased than most right-leaning treatments of Castro's career, . . . the lack of opposing viewpoints soon grows tiresome—the film feels more like a series of toasts at a testimonial dinner than a documentary."

The Hollywood Reporter's Frank Scheck said that *Fidel* took the form "of an unabashed love letter." Dusting the film with faint praise, Scheck wrote that it "sacrifices the value of its wealth of archival footage with its less than objective stance."

> Even the usual politically sympathetic film critics couldn't help but notice the giant load of half-truths that came down the pike in the distorted documentary.

A review called "Documentary Gets Cozy with Commie," written by V. A. Musetto of the *New York Post*, asked, "Looking for an objective portrait of Fidel Castro? Then this documentary by Estela Bravo isn't for you." Musetto noted, "Bravo's love fest has only nice things to say about Cuba's bearded leader, as it chronicles his life from childhood to the present."

But A. O. Scott of the *New York Times* had possibly the most biting quote. Scott sniped, "This is an exercise not in biography but in hero worship." Scott also pointed out that the harshest criticism of Castro in the film was made by American novelist Alice Walker, who was surprised that Castro can't sing or dance. "It's a good thing he's got all of those other good qualities," she said. Yeah, like his expertise in backstabbing.

Scott summed things up by saying, "This is bad cinema and bad history."

Castro worshipers must have spent most of their lives OD'ing on bad cinema and bad history. That's about the only way to account for their strange affection toward this guy.

In December 2002, Harry Belafonte, one of the star interviewees in *Fidel*, teamed up with Danny Glover to knock the Bush administration around a bit. Both were in Havana attending a film festival. Reportedly, the pair accused the administration of pressuring Hollywood into making war movies and violent films. The duo's comments were graciously reported by Radio Havana.

The actors theorized that there was an ongoing effort by Bush and Co. to promote the administration's war machine. They said that because Hollywood is controlled by large corporations, war movies and violent films are shaped by the "interests of the Pentagon and the White House."

In another lapse of patriotic memory, Belafonte, who apparently thinks Fidel Castro is fantastico, told the press that September 11 gave President Bush an excuse to implement plans "to control the world militarily, economically and culturally."

Bad history can sure hide the facts. Four decades of totalitarian communism have left Cuba in a state of anything but paradise. Thousands of people each year risk life, limb, and property to escape the tropical slave plantation.

Human rights organizations cite Castro's as one of the world's most repressive regimes. Block spies, members of a group that's officially known as Committees for the Defense of the Revolution, spy on neighbors and report back to the regime. And news from the block spies travels faster than a gossip columnist after a double espresso.

Even speaking to a foreigner can result in your being questioned about your loyalty to the Castro dictatorship. Gulags are loaded with political prisoners, and many of those incarcerated have done nothing more than speak out against the crimes of Castro or try to exit the country.

Most people are aware that one of the primo causes of the Hollywood crowd is the AIDS epidemic. Folks are also attuned to the fact that most libs in Tinseltown cringe at the mention of the "Christian Right." They see conservative Christians as runaway extras from *The Exorcist* set, whose pupils change into crosses whenever their eyelids are shut. Such religious monsters are assumed to be gay haters. Of course, they're not. Demon runaways, eyeball wizards, monster zealots, or gay haters, that is. But Castro may be. He's displayed a loathing of the pink community in Cuba that makes Jerry Falwell look like a Teletubby.

Fidel has had a long tradition of placing homosexuals and transsexuals in prison, based on mere suspicion or rumor. When the various stars are pledging their devotion to Castro, do they have any idea what Castro's response to AIDS has been?

Turns out AIDS is not only hazardous to your health in Cuba, it's fatal to your freedom. Testing is mandatory nationwide. Anyone who tests positive for HIV is incarcerated. No contesting. No due process. No reasoning with officials. Bet you've never heard Fidel branded with the homophobic label, though. Not by the adoring celebrity set anyway.

In letters smuggled out of Cuba, it was discovered that some of those imprisoned for their HIV-positive status were intentionally starved to death. The reason? They had the audacity to ask for better food.

Yes, life in Cuba really does stink. How desperate do you have to be to purposely shoot yourself up with HIV-infected blood? It's been reported that some young people have done exactly that. They'd apparently rather be sent to a prison than have to endure the humiliation and torment of forced labor.

We can't be too tough on the celebrities, though. They're so accustomed to Hollywood sets they can't see through one that's been erected just to fool them. They and other influential visitors to Cuba are shown Potemkin villages, phony little cities like the ones put up in the former Soviet Union, designed to disguise the truth. Somehow they buy into the ruse. To keep the facade going, Cuban citizens are actually denied access to certain beaches and restaurants. There's even a nickname for the whole thing. It's called "tourist apartheid."

Health care is another thing that's touted as one of Castro's wonderful accomplishments. But statistics scream otherwise. In 1959 Cuba had 337 hospitals. In 1989 the number had decreased to 264. Disease in Cuba has steadily risen since Castro took over. Suicides have doubled. And that's without the benefits of Hillary-care.

One thing Castro likes to brag about to celebrities is a cinema school. It was founded by a guy named Gabriel García Márquez. In *World Net Daily,* Joseph Farrah wrote about a friend, Merle Linda Wolin, who visited the Cuban cinema school for *Premier Magazine.* Wolin, an acknowledged liberal, was shocked to find out that all of the student work at the school is subject to censorship, Cuban intelligence agents are involved in every aspect of the school and watch over everything, and the idea that it's some sort of a place of freedom and creativity is a lie. The school was set up as bait for Hollywood. And it managed to hook in a number of star fish.

Hollywood needs to educate itself about what life is like for Cuban artists, too. All over Cuba, writers and artists know that if they want to continue in their careers, they have to embrace the idea, and spread the message, of the Cuban regime as benefactor.

In Cuba literature and art are sponsored by the government. The government will only provide support if a writer or artist serves the political agenda against capitalism and against the United States of America. Artists live under a system where all of their work must reflect what is called "socialist realism." Painters, sculptors, authors, actors, choreographers, dancers, directors, and playwrights are in constant danger of a purge, where they face exile from normal social standing. And that doesn't mean being seated at the table nearest the kitchen at Spago's.

It's a shame that some of these same Hollywood celebrities can't visit with the folks who are locked up in Castro's gulags.

It's a shame that some of these same Hollywood celebrities can't visit with the folks who are locked up in Castro's gulags. But even though they can't, they should at least look at the facts. Here's a guy who has imprisoned and tortured dissidents. He's kept fugitives from U.S. justice. He's maintained total control through use of intimidation and kangaroo courts. He's been a ruthless dictator for decades. He's denied his people freedom of speech, freedom of press, and freedom of association. Most celebs wouldn't last a nanosecond without limousine service, never mind having to survive in a place like Cuba.

Still, they carry on their long-distance love affair with the Latin Joe Stalin. Like filmmaker Saul Landau. He produced four documentaries on Cuba for PBS and CBS. He won an Emmy Award for an anti-nuclear piece, and he directed a CBS documentary with Dan Rather in 1974 called *Castro, Cuba and the U.S.*

Landau told CNSNews.com that Cuba is a better place than the United States of America, when it comes to "the right to food, the right to shelter, the right to a job, the right to a retirement." He claims not to have seen any evidence that Castro is a sadistic monster or a brutal dictator. Landau chalks up the suppression of a free press, free elections, and free association to revolutionary necessity. The filmmaker says in a revolution, "they broke a lot of eggs" to achieve their aims.

Thank God we don't make those kinds of omelettes in the U.S. of A.

How a Political Issue Becomes a Hollywood One

Ever wonder how liberal political issues always seem to end up in the celebrity spotlight? Here's how it works.

The process begins with a memo. The memo is written by a staffer at the Democratic National Committee, a liberal-leaning think tank, a leftist advocacy group, or an assistant to Fidel Castro.

After the memo is approved by Queen Hillary, it's forwarded to the Committee of Lefty Dinosaurs (COLD). This is an ad-hoc group made up of Ed Asner, Ted Danson, Jane Fonda, Barbra Streisand, Robert Redford, Mike Farrell, Martin Sheen, and Susan Sarandon.

COLD sends the memo to get feedback from the secretary-general of the United Nations, Eleanor Clift of *Time* magazine, and Ted Turner, wherever he happens to be vacationing. It then assigns the task of promoting the issue to one of the many non-profit organizations in Hollywood, depending on the type of issue that's at stake.

If the issue concerns the African-American community, it's necessary to have Jesse Jackson, Al Sharpton, and Maxine Waters place their imprimatur on the memo before any action is taken. If finances are tight, a request will be made that Jesse Jackson conduct one of his shakedowns to generate cash flow.

Next, leftist lobbying organizations get the creative types in Tinseltown to sneak related ideas into the content of television, film, music, and video games. At the same time, a delegation of stars, usually young women, go to Washington, D.C., to hold a march or testify in front of Congress.

Full-page ads are purchased in major newspapers and publications to promote the issue and demonize anyone who might oppose it. Rich people in Malibu, Pacific Palisades, Brentwood, and Beverly Hills are hit up for moolah by making them feel even more guilty than they usually do. If extra cash is still needed, benefit concerts, performances, and events are held to raise additional funds.

Sometimes a press conference is conducted, where a gaggle of celebrities shows up to spout off. Photos of the stars pontificating are published in newspapers around the world.

Celebrity spokespeople then hit the TV talk-show circuit. With furrowed brows, they appear on cue to speak out. Some of the braver ones even try to get in the last word with Bill O'Reilly.

The goal is to make the issue look cool. Young successful stars of stage, screen, television, and music jump on the bandwagon. Soon everyone is wearing a ribbon, pin, T-shirt, or tattoo.

Success is measured in a number of ways. Congressional committees may have stars out to the Hill to testify further, *60 Minutes* may do a stealth promo piece, or politicians, especially during a presidential election cycle, will debate the issue.

Then, in the end, conservative talk-show hosts make fun of it.

How a Political Issue Becomes a Hollywood One

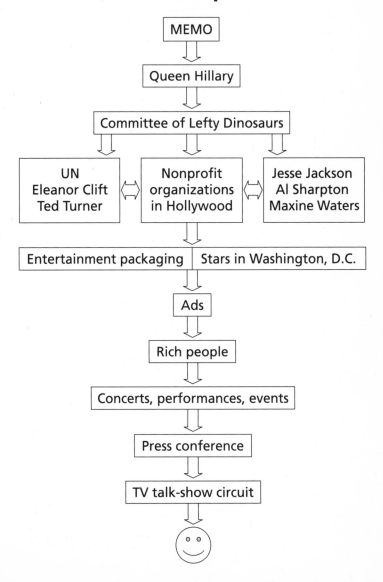

MEMO

Queen Hillary

Committee of Lefty Dinosaurs

| UN
Eleanor Clift
Ted Turner | Nonprofit
organizations
in Hollywood | Jesse Jackson
Al Sharpton
Maxine Waters |

Entertainment packaging | Stars in Washington, D.C.

Ads

Rich people

Concerts, performances, events

Press conference

TV talk-show circuit

CHAPTER FOUR

The Celebrity Booster Club

Ever heard of the Creative Coalition? Billy Baldwin's president of the group. And Robin Bronk is the executive director. The group's not just known for its creativity. It's known for its activism as well.

Founded in 1989 by Ron Silver, Christopher Reeve, Susan Sarandon, Stephen Collins, and others, the Creative Coalition is dedicated to the art of activism. Its Web site speaks of wanting "to stimulate constructive dialogue about vital public issues and to encourage informed advocacy within the entertainment industry." Translation: Celebrities in the group want to be noticed for something other than their latest program, flick, or tune.

Bronk gave a statement to CNSNews.com on December 17, 2002. It illustrated what all first-rate stars must have on their bio in this day and age. The executive director said, "We live in a society here in the U.S. where celebrities are put out there as opinion leaders. Just as many have their agent and their manager and their publicist, they are expected to have their issue."

Interesting word Bronk used—*issue*. For stars and wanna-be's, that's the thing that's getting to be as much of an essential in Hollywood as a mansion in the hills or a friendly doctor who dispenses pills. It's the absolutely vital, must-have, gotta be known for—cause.

These days, actors aren't just phoning up agents to ask about gigs or to get the skinny on a new script. They want a good charity or a good cause to be associated with. Besides being good for their image, it can help them get a leg up on the competition. And it can come in handy when their criminal record starts to get too bulky, or on those hectic days when they're caught with their pants down on PCH.

The cause is generally picked less for how it may help society or the country and more for how it might help a career. There are cases where the cause doesn't involve politics, but that's rare. Most of the time, it's politically charged and reveals the liberal mind-set that saturates Tinseltown. If you close your eyes, it's easy to imagine the inevitable call from star to agent, seeking the perfect organization to attach name and likeness to.

STAR: Can you get me a good disease?

AGENT: Hmmm. What'd ya have in mind?

STAR: I'd like something that people really care about. What about AIDS?

AGENT: You gotta be kidding. AIDS is what everybody wants in Hollywood. Anyway, Liz Taylor has that one sewn up. And even if she did give it up, or couldn't handle it anymore, there's a waiting list a mile long.

STAR: Okay, okay. How about one of those kids' diseases?

AGENT: All taken. Let's see. Are you interested in herpes, pinworms, or psoriasis?

STAR: Isn't there anything other than a disease?

AGENT: Well, there's the UN. It always needs celebrities to promote it. But you'll have to travel, and the characters you'll be hanging with are pretty boring.

STAR: Oh, heck. Just give me psoriasis. I've got an audition in three days. But let me know if a spot opens up for a cancer or a mental illness.

AGENT: Will do. Hey, break a leg on the tryout.

STAR: Ooh, that reminds me. Are broken bones available?

Yes, getting a good cause can really be a tough job. As you can see, not all causes are alike. Some are highly desirable and enlarge your status. Others aren't as fashionable or as career boosting. In fact, a number of causes are avoided by Hollywood celebs altogether because, for whatever reason, they've fallen out of favor, they border on political incorrectness, or in the worst case, they're just too stinkin' normal.

Because of the left-of-center peer pressure that covers every inch of the entertainment capital, getting involved with certain causes can be bad for one's livelihood. These are the kinds that should come with a written disclaimer:

WARNING—The Mayor of Hollywood has determined that being associated with the following causes can be injurious to your employment potential, occupational path, and social activity for the duration of what is bound to be your miserable life.

Some of the causes to steer clear of, if you ever want to walk the streets of Hollywood without unopened cans of near beer being flung at you, include the following:

Gun Shy

Tom Selleck was skewered by Rosie O'Donnell. Charlton Heston was ambushed by Michael Moore. This is the way Hollywood treats those who dare to stand up for the right to bear arms. Second Amendment champs get thrust into the same category as land mine manufacturers and WorldCom execs.

It's because guns are dark, ugly things that can never be warm or fuzzy, even when they're carried in grandma's knitting bag. Despite what the facts might be, in Hollywood's leftist mind, guns are for celluloid satisfaction only. No matter how handy firearms are for defending your life and protecting your family, or how beneficial they are for giving thugs something to think about before targeting your community, such reasons will never be enough to counter the Hollywood anti-gun hysteria.

Star libs wouldn't be caught dead hanging out with anyone who's in favor of individual gun ownership, unless, of course, the person, or behemoth-sized crew, happens to be their personal bodyguard brigade.

Risky Business

You won't see many Hollywood stars coming to the aid of hardworking individuals who venture to take risks and start businesses. Illicit rackets of the Heidi Fleiss or drug-oriented kind don't count.

Let's face it, burdensome regulations and sky-high taxes aren't sexy issues. And even though job growth and prosperity result when small businesses flourish, how do you match a slogan like "Save the Whales" with a string of accounting terms? Besides, the whole thing takes way too much rational thought.

Residents of Tinseltown wouldn't recognize basic economics if it bit them in their lipo-sucked bottoms. More and more often, actors, directors, producers, and other industry types are making trips out of the country to places like Vancouver to produce films and TV shows. This is happening because of the lower taxes, cheaper labor, and more welcoming business climate found in just about every place other than California. In fact, some people are speculating that if California gets unfriendly enough to commerce, Hollywood itself may be moved out of the state, or maybe even out of the country. You can bet if relocation takes place, it won't be transported to Cuba, North Korea, or China. It will be to a place that allows businesses to make a—dare we say—profit.

GI Jitters

Although lately Hollywood's a bit more divided on this one, the military is generally looked at with scorn. After all, the Left has a tradition of distrust to live up to. And the Tinseltown mentor, the president that Hollywood adored, the one who put the "X" in ex-president, once wrote that he loathed the military.

Unfortunately, the military is involved right now in the rather unpleasant task of fighting a war on terror. Hollywood libs think war is bad—that is, unless one of their own guys happens to be leading the charge. Lately we've seen a resurgence of involvement in USO activities, though, and some celebrities have even gone to visit the troops. Most are careful to distinguish between supporting the troops and supporting the actual war.

> The problem is that it takes some extra thought to understand that the world contains quite a few nasty people who don't think peace is a positive thing.

The problem is that it takes some extra thought to understand that the world contains quite a few nasty people who don't think peace is a positive thing. These folks aren't very nice at all. And when Gandhi-like tactics are used on them, the response, after their belly laughs subside, is to methodically grind their opponents into meatballs.

Still, Hollywood sentiment leans toward the unilateral embracing of peace. The residents forget about the hostile things that have occurred in the world, like the flattening of students by tanks in Tiananmen Square or the mowing down of Christians via machete in the Sudan. "Peace" as a cause is just so darn emotionally fulfilling, it can make the brightest of lefties lose their heads.

School's Out

Loads of Hollywood celebs have kids of their own. In the normal course of Left Coast events, the tykes are nurtured by nannies, pre-taught by tutors, and formally educated at the finest private schools around. Sound familiar? Yes, they're just like our politicians.

But providing vouchers or tax credits so that ordinary Americans can have the same privileges as they do isn't a hip enough cause for a star to get involved with. Oh, it would help the children, but the liberal teachers' unions might get a tad testy. Anyway, can you imagine how a "Hollywood Gala for School Choice" would go over? It just doesn't have the same ribbon-wearing potential that other causes do.

This Land Ain't Your Land

As the green noose of environmental regulation sweeps across our municipalities, counties, states, and federal government, individual property owners are suffering terribly. But you're not likely to hear much talk about compassion for the victims or urgency to protect this fundamental liberty coming out of the Hollywood ranks. No one's ever received an Academy Award and said, "I'd like to dedicate this award to the victims of environmental abuse and to the preservation of property rights in the United States of America." If someone had, you would have heard scores of chin implants drop to the ground in unison.

When celebs themselves, though, are the target of overzealous environmentalists, they start whistling a completely different tune. But then again, they usually have a little more clout when it comes to fighting the system because, goodness knows, the world can always use one more 342-room cabin on 7,000 acres of privately owned forest.

The stars shy away from more causes than those just mentioned. But the ones they embrace, the ones they lust after, the ones they'd give their veneered teeth to be connected with are a lot more revealing. Let's take a look at them.

The Top Seven Hollywood Causes

Cause #7
Anti-Smoking

This is one of the newer causes, and a lot of celebrities have taken it up—the cause, that is. Hollywood gave it the full-flick treatment in the tobacco executive hit piece *The Insider*.

A group of entertainment bigwigs are now officers on the smoking police patrol. They're busy classifying stars according to tobacco habits, meaning those who smoke are more dangerous than those who don't. Smoking scenes are frantically being edited out of films, too. Writers, producers, and directors are under pressure to keep cigs off the screen. However, sneaking out to the bathroom to satisfy personal addictions is still allowed.

Although this cause is not as glamorous as some of the others, or as commercially appealing, there's an added joy for Hollywood folks devoted to this particular brand of activism. They get to fight the evil enemy, Big Tobacco. And they don't even have to give up their weed.

Cause #6
Gun Control

This cause is for the slightly more aggressive libs in Hollywood. The lefties who choose it get to make fun of a whole host of targets—white males from the South, militia members, hunters, and the like. But they have to be careful when they adopt this issue. There's actually the possibility of getting a few swings flung back in their own direction. Not to worry. Sarah Brady and her "gun violence" envoys are more than happy to appear on stage at a moment's notice to put an end to coherent discussion. The emotional photo-ops gained are worth the occasional friction. Celebs just have to remember to shout, "Stop the violence!" Then promote the passage of more laws as the solution. They come out smelling like anti-gunpowder heroes.

Cause #5
Feminism

This is a favorite cause of quite a few Left Coast women, and a number of faux-sensitive men. You know, wimpy males who claim to be getting in touch with their feminine side. Those who sign up for this activist craze get to walk around and sanctimoniously condemn the objectification and exploitation of the female sex. They usually do this while displaying their surgically enhanced silhouettes, or those of their significant others. The great thing about the whole situation is that stars of both genders get to live out the clichéd experience of wanting and having it all, and neither side complains a bit.

Cause #4
The Environment

A lot of the stars who live in houses 200 times the size of most Americans' love to express their compassion for Mother Earth. And many who get driven around in stretch Mercedes limousines take great pleasure in preaching about the need to conserve energy. To supposedly prevent various calamities—like global warming, global cooling, and global just right—they gather together on days like Earth Day and condemn evil corporate types for wanting to construct buildings, manufacture products, and find new supplies of fuel. They seek to preserve the Earth in all of its wilderness glory, as long as it's outside of their own bulldozed sanctuaries. And psychics to the stars have assured them that those plants and animals in environmentally sensitive areas that bite the dust during movie-making would voluntarily give up their lives for the sake of the "art."

Cause #3
Peace

Celebs love to carry the banner for peace. Peace on Earth, peace in the nation, peace in our cities, peace on the playground, peace at the office, peace in the cop car, peace at the nail salon, peace in the bank lines, peace at the auto mechanic, peace at the 50%-off designer wedding gown sale. Pick your peace. It's anywhere, except on the big and little screen.

Those who embrace peace as their cause are in for a treat because nothing they do has to make any sense. They just have to spout things like "tranquility," "positive vibes," and "the need for understanding." Then end every rally, march, speech, or appearance with a big old group hug.

Cause #2
Animal Rights

Defending animals is so-o-o popular in Hollywood. What could be warmer or fuzzier than protecting little puppies, kittens, and other Bambi-like creatures? Female stars who take up this issue get to pose in provocative outfits and sometimes even go nude. And no one thinks badly of them for doing it because they know it's for Whiskers, or Fluffy, or Willy—the whale, not the former commander in chief. This, of course, encourages adolescent males to become some of the staunchest defenders of animals on the face of the Earth. And the activist streak lasts until they're old enough to buy mature magazines.

And the #1 Cause Is ... (Drum Roll, Please) DISEASE!

Yes, disease is the most popular cause of the liberal Hollywood set. Breast cancer, emphysema, cystic fibrosis, diabetes, bony-knees syndrome . . . Any one of them can earn celebs the coveted "humanitarian" label. And that can take you a long, long way in Tinseltown.

Charity Begins at Hollywood

Sometimes the pages of fiction contain chunks of fact. This was the case with *Cause Celeb,* a novel written by British journalist Helen Fielding. The book took a peek at the curious relationship that seems to have developed between celebrities and charities. Even though the work was published in 1994, the public only really caught wind of it after Fielding's second and third novels, *Bridget Jones's Diary* and *Bridget Jones: The Edge of Reason,* became famous.

Cause Celeb is set in the mid-1980s. In the story, the main character of the book, Rosie Richardson, leaves the comforts of England to go off and work in a refugee camp in Africa. Unfortunately, famine hits the population of Africa so hard, there's danger that far more people will be in need of help than the workers can handle. After struggling to find a solution, Rosie decides to go back home and address the situation by putting together a celebrity fund-raiser. That's when the games begin.

The book pokes some fun at star involvement, and at the idea that a cause like famine could somehow become fashionable. After hearing a bit of the book's plot, some of you may be reminded of an event that took place in the mid-1980s for real.

Only this one would forever change the way the famous looked at themselves and their involvement with causes.

Live Aid

It was the tail end of 1984. Bob Geldof sat stroking his chin. His band, the Boomtown Rats, was in the latter part of its career and about to release a final album. After seeing pictures of hungry African children on television, Geldof was so moved he decided to donate all of the proceeds from the next Boomtown Rats' record to an African relief agency.

He did something else as well. He created another record, with a group of English musicians who called themselves Band Aid. On November 25, 1984, almost 40 pop stars arrived at a studio in West London to record a song. Sting, Phil Collins, George Michael, Duran Duran, Culture Club, Spandau Ballet, Bananarama, and Bono were present. At the time, all were chart toppers.

The song they performed was released on December 7, 1984. The record was called "Do They Know It's Christmas?" It was the fastest-selling single up to that time. And it ended up raising $24 million for the hungry in Sudan and Ethiopia.

After personally visiting Africa in 1985, Geldof got together with pre-baby-dangling Michael Jackson and singer Lionel Ritchie for another project. With an all-star lineup of musical celebrities, the tune "We Are the World" was laid down. If its purpose hadn't been so darn praiseworthy, the single might possibly have been remembered as one of the most aggravating tunes ever written. It's rumored that some people listening to the song for the 9,014th time donated bucks just to make it go away.

Taking part in the recording of "We Are the World" gave Geldof the idea of putting together a concert to raise money for the starving people of Africa. He ultimately called the event Live Aid.

Live Aid took place in 1985 as a joint London-Philadelphia rock concert. It included topflight musical artists from overseas, like U2, Paul McCartney, the Who, Led Zeppelin, and David Bowie, and from the U. S., the Hooters, Paul Young, Simple Minds, and the Thompson Twins.

With the stadium settings of Wembley in England and JFK in Phillie, it was like a giant, dual-country, rock 'n' roll telethon. And it was broadcast to most of the world. No doubt Dick Clark was hit with a bad case of TV-production envy.

Singer-songwriter Phil Collins ended up performing on both sides of the Atlantic. First, he appeared in London. Then he jumped on a Concorde and jetted to New York, where a helicopter brought him to Philadelphia and he appeared again. That had to have future Clonaid doctors really intrigued.

The extravaganza reached an estimated audience of 2 billion people. It generated more than $100 million. That's the kind of bread that gets everybody's attention. Almost half of the money was spent on food aid. The remainder went into long-term development. Sadly, even with all of the celebrity pull, 1.2 million people still starved to death.

But what about the rocker who was in the twilight of his career when he organized the whole thing? You can call him Sir Robert Geldof now. He was knighted. And he was nominated for a Nobel Peace Prize, too, for putting the whopping charity event together.

Of course, the accolades didn't go unnoticed by the celebrity crowd. Geldof's acclaim opened up a new chapter in the Hollywood cause competition.

It's sort of fitting that Live Aid happened during the image-loving 1980s. It was during this decade that the pop culture reached new heights of artificiality, particularly in the music business. After all, a new tool was available to help construct any kind of persona one could imagine. It was the music video. And it would be used to the hilt by stars to manipulate the media and catapult celebrities with the hankering right into the spotlight.

Of course, the accolades didn't go unnoticed by the celebrity crowd. Geldof's acclaim opened up a new chapter in the Hollywood cause competition.

The Live Aid concert inspired Neil Young, John "Cougar" Mellencamp, and Willie Nelson to organize a similar fund-raiser for American farmers who were hurting. It was dubbed Farm Aid. A series of the happenings were held, but no one was knighted, nominated for a Nobel Prize, or even given a golden cowpie. Still, the events were a hit, especially with the agricultural crowd.

Folks continue to try and duplicate the Live Aid format. Several Tibet Freedom Concerts have been held. And when Paul McCartney put together a concert for the victims of 9/11, he dubbed it Live Aid II. There was also NetAid, which had the aim of raising money and awareness to combat poverty. The organization used three overlapping concerts in London, Geneva, and the New York area for its 1999 event. Among the performers who participated were Bono, Sting, Pete Townshend, Puff Daddy, David Bowie, George Michael, and Bryan Ferry.

The three concerts were broadcast and webcast live around the world. The NetAid audience was huge, approximately 1 billion people. But unfortunately, after all was digitally said and done, the fund-raiser only managed to net about a million dollars. Guess a lot of people still like to donate the old-fashioned way.

Live Aid was a turning point for celebrities, in terms of advocacy and activism. The link between stars and causes was cast in stone. Now we have Leonardo DiCaprio serving as chairman of the Earth Day festivities, the Beastie Boys organizing concerts for Tibet, and Sting rushing off to save the rain forests.

But Geldof's success in the charity arena would end up having one of the most enduring effects on the life of a particular friend of his, Paul Hewson. We all know him simply as Bono.

Bono

Who would have thought back in 1984 that the Live Aid concert would end up producing a celebrity activist who would eventually jet around the globe influencing the most powerful people in the world?

As it would happen, one of the groups that performed at Live Aid was the Irish rock group U2. Its lead singer would emerge as a man dedicated to a series of activist causes. And that man would just happen to be the intriguing charmer with the often mispronounced single name of Bono.

In the fall of 2002, the U2 front man was named the most powerful guy in music, according to a poll of top music industry execs. Was it because of his soaring Irish rock voice? His trademark wraparound shades? His swaggering stage presence? Nope. According to the British music magazine Q, which publishes the list, Bono was named because of his involvement in high-profile political issues, ranging from Third World debt to enlargement of the European Union.

The singer found a way to use his rock 'n' roll clout to get face-to-face contact with international political leaders. He even met with the Pope.

Time magazine dedicated a 2002 cover to the crooner, with the accompanying headline "Can Bono Save the World?"[1] Who knows, but the Nobel committee thinks he may be prize-winning material.

Whenever he's not lobbying politicians, Bono's singing lead for one of the most enduring successes in the music industry. U2 remains a force 25 years after the group first began pumping out music.

Can you imagine a rock star trotting over to Washington, D.C., to demand more U.S. foreign aid? Well, Bono did it. The fact that the United States is the largest provider of foreign aid the world's ever seen didn't deter him either. In 1986 Bono lent his name to an Amnesty International Tour. As a result of the rocker's involvement, Amnesty International's membership surged.

Bono has embraced his activist identity. He's lent his celebrity power to organizations like Greenpeace, Artists Against AIDS Worldwide, and a children's charity called War Child.

But his number one cause by far has been trying to get the debt of Third World countries forgiven. He's basically asked the West to "fahgetaboutit." The debt, that is. He's been able to lobby Congress to try and convince members to approve hundreds of millions of dollars in debt relief for dozens of countries.

In May 2002, before Treasury Secretary Paul O'Neill stepped down from office, he and Bono went on a fact-finding tour of Africa. The Bono & O'Neill road show included stops in Ghana, South Africa, Uganda, and Ethiopia.

Bono always seems to make friends with people you wouldn't expect a rock star to give the time of day to. Folks in D.C. say the reason he's capable of finding common ground with those on the Right is because U2's main man is a devout Christian. One case in point serves as an example of perhaps the oddest coupling ever seen in the nation's capital. Following a meeting with a well-known conservative senator, Bono developed a close relationship with the powerful former legislator. The senator was Jesse Helms. At Bono's urging, Helms went to his first rock concert ever, so he could hear Bono and U2 perform. One of Helms's senior staffers, Lester Munson, told the *Guardian,* "The senator is very much a fan of Bono."

The fact that he's a multimillionaire who's speaking for the oppressed and the poor of the world is something Bono doesn't mind talking about. "I'm uncomfortable being a rich rock star doing this. I'm unhappy with that juxtaposition. I would love not to be doing this—for somebody else to do it who is not as compromised as me. That guilt has driven me to be a policy wonk. It makes me queasy to turn up just for the photo opportunity, so I turn up for the briefing as well. I go to bed with World Bank reports. These issues are bigger than whether it makes me comfortable or not. So the band might cringe, I might wince, but I went to Washington to get a check, and I'm going back to get a bigger one."

> Bono says he wants a bigger check from the taxpayers? Maybe he should stick with the leading-by-example stuff and give away his own money— not ours.

Bono says he wants a bigger check from the taxpayers? Maybe he should stick with the leading-by-example stuff and give away his own money—not ours.

Bono told *People* magazine in 2002 the following tale: "There's an old story about an American and an Irishman looking up at a mansion. The American looks at it and says, 'One day I'm going to live in that place.' The Irishman looks at it and says, 'One day I'm going to get the bastard who lives in that place.'"[2]

Well, it's pretty clear. In a Bono-fied world, the mansion is America, with all of her riches, and we the people are the "b" words. Bono doesn't seem to pay attention to the fact that a lot of governments, which receive foreign aid, pocket the lion's share for themselves and dole out very little to the people who need it.

It turns out that in Europe, plenty of people in the music business claim legal residence in Ireland because of the country's favorable tax laws. Bono's birthplace has no income tax on the money earned from record royalties. There's something a wee bit hypocritical about a dude who wants to raise our taxes but lives in a musician's tax haven himself.

When Bono's standing up for the Third World, the starving, and the hungry, it's a pretty strange sight anyway. He always seems to be donning designer sunglasses, which if auctioned off on eBay would probably fetch enough to pay off three-quarters of the entire Third World tab.

More and more these days, Bono's strategy is to behave less like a fund-raiser and more like an international lobbyist. We all know how persistent lobbyists can be. The folks in the White House even have a nickname for him. They call him "The Pest," which gives you a hint about his determination.

The Pest has gotten some good results. Along with Bob Geldof, he's been able to get meetings with Secretary of State Colin Powell, National Security Advisor Condoleezza Rice, former Treasury Secretary Paul O'Neill, and even Senior White House Advisor Karl Rove.

And it's really something when you can garner the attention of the president of the United States himself. On the Bono effect, President Bush told the press that "Dick Cheney walked into the Oval Office and said, 'Jesse Helms wants us to listen to Bono's idea.'"[3] Wonder if anyone considered whether or not it was appropriate to laugh.

Celebrities and the UN

The UN has a long history of recruiting Hollywood stars to assist in promoting its image. The organization even has a bunch of fancy titles for its celebrity helpers—advocates, spokespersons, messengers of peace, goodwill ambassadors, yada, yada, yada. Using the attractive designations and noble causes as bait, the UN reels in people from music, film, art, sports, and literature to lend a hand.

In June 2002 dozens of celebrities came together for a star-studded UN meeting in New York City. Luminaries included Roger Moore, Danny Glover, Harry Belafonte, Angelina Jolie, Peter Ustinov, and Vanessa Redgrave. The celebs were dazzled. It was all about one of their favorite causes—peace.

According to a UN News Service press release of June 12, 2002, Gillian M. Sorensen, Assistant Secretary-General for External Relations, stated, "The purpose of the meeting is to deepen their understanding of the UN and its many roles, to strengthen their connection to the whole UN system, and to reinforce their roles as advocates and spokesman who inform, who inspire and raise awareness and raise funds, who travel to the frontlines and help us carry our message to a larger public."

Sorensen added, "We think this is a very special gathering—we know that [celebrities] reach audiences and younger people and that our own speakers sometimes do not. . . ."

The UN usually sounds good, but the problem is that it's primarily made up of VITs—Very Important Thugs. The official officials of the body like to treat international agreements as if they were used hankies. And they like to ignore the human rights violations of China, Cuba, Vietnam, and a host of other countries, and jump on the U.S. for trumped-up wrongs while they're at it.

The inaptly named UN Commission on Human Rights is a virtual rogue's gallery of nations, with members that have, to their discredit, some of the worst human rights records imaginable. Celebs usually do the "see no evil, hear no evil" act, when acquiring the "facts" about these countries.

In September 2000 the UN sponsored the largest gathering of world leaders in history. It was called the UN Millennium

Summit. Now no gathering of world leaders would be complete without a corresponding meeting of celebrities. So right after the big summit, the UN hosted a kind of jamboree for the rich and famous. The guest list included Michael Douglas, Danny Glover, Susan Sarandon, Mia Farrow, Peter Ustinov, former Spice Girl Geri Halliwell, and, of course, Harry Belafonte, proving once again that razzle-dazzle globalism sells a whole lot better than the typical Kofi Annan pitch.

The UN first fell in love with the idea of celebrity ambassadors in the 1950s. It all started with Danny Kaye, who was used to promote children's rights. In 1954 the comedic actor was made UNICEF's first ambassador at large. His task was to make the needs of children known throughout the world.

Audrey Hepburn became a goodwill ambassador for UNICEF in 1988. She held the position for five years. Other celebrities took notice as she journeyed to Ethiopia, Guatemala, Somalia, Sudan, Thailand, and other countries to advocate children's rights.

> Most of the big names are personally recruited by the UN secretary-general himself. Can you imagine the bedlam when an agent in Hollywood gets a call from Kofi Annan? At first, the agent probably thinks it's a foreign producer. Then again, it kinda is.

Hepburn also testified before several U.S. congressional committees about world hunger. A lot of stars probably fantasized about the kinds of meetings Hepburn got to attend. Just think—presidents, prime ministers, queens, and kings. It's enough to make Eliza Doolittle quit selling flowers for good.

Some celebs are brought into the organization through its various agencies. But most of the big names are personally recruited by the UN secretary-general himself. Can you imagine the bedlam when an agent in Hollywood gets a call from Kofi

Annan? At first, the agent probably thinks it's a foreign producer. Then again, it kinda is.

Sometimes celebs get involved with one of the many international summits, conventions, symposia, or other kinds of phony meetings of the organization. For instance, the ultra-busy Leonardo DiCaprio helped to promote the UN-sponsored Earth Summit, and he took the opportunity to bash the U.S. in the process.

In August 2002 the actor called the United States the world's biggest polluter and urged President Bush to make a statement in favor of the environment by coming to the Earth Summit in South Africa. DiCaprio said, "Mr. Bush, we are asking for your support, to be the President that looks towards the future."[4]

Later in the month, DiCaprio's commitment was called into question in a report by the BBC. In an August 28 article called "Stars Steer Clear of Summit," the BBC reported that although DiCaprio had asked President Bush to attend the summit, he himself was a no-show. Leo's lame excuse was that "he had contractual obligations" in the United States. Guess he was just a little too busy raking in the bucks.

Susan Sarandon and *Star Trek* actor Patrick Stewart also called on Bush to go to the summit. Funny thing was, they didn't show up either. Other absentees, who had been at the 1992 Earth Summit in Rio but failed to make this one, included Sting, the Beach Boys, Jane Fonda, and Shirley MacLaine.

In August 2001 Angelina Jolie was named a UN goodwill ambassador. This was timed to correspond with her box-office hit *Tomb Raider*. The UN apparently liked the idea of an attractive, computer-generated fighting archaeologist becoming an ambassador of goodwill. Chris Janowski, spokesperson for the UN High Commissioner for Refugees, indicated that Jolie's popularity was what the UN was tapping, saying that she "can naturally bring in our message to youth, people who are not usually interested in the UNHCR or the United Nations."

The U.S. Fund for UNICEF has its own roster of titles. Celebs get to be crowned with labels like "national ambassador" or "special representative." Stars who have served as national ambassadors include Maya Angelou, Katie Couric, Jane Curtin, Laurence Fishburne, and Edward James Olmos. Sarah Jessica Parker was granted the title of special representative for the performing arts. And Paul and Heather Mills McCartney were named goodwill ambassadors for the UN's 2002 Adopt-A-Minefield campaign.

The UN wants its celebs out front, proudly wearing titles, pins, and slogan-soaked clothing. So do a lot of other causes that look to the stars to carry their messages.

Star Stumping

Stars choose to stump for lots of different causes. Sometimes they get involved with a charity because they or their families have been personally affected. Sometimes their careers, and/or their rears, are beginning to sag and they're in need of a boost. Whatever the reasons, the whole scene makes for some interesting magazine covers and press conferences.

Ed Harris on Manhood

In the middle of the war on terror, some Hollywood celebs took a breather from spouting anti-war nonsense long enough to gather in D.C. and attack President Bush for being pro-life.

At a Planned Parenthood gala, Camryn Manheim told the *New York Daily News,* "We are in dire jeopardy of losing the right to choose." And Cybill Shepherd lamented that "they are clearly capable of dooming Roe v. Wade."

But Ed Harris took a different tack. He focused on the president's manhood. Harris told a group at a NARAL Pro-Choice America gala, "Being a man, I have got to say that we got this guy in the White House who thinks he is a man, who projects himself as a man because he has a certain masculinity."

Harris babbled on, saying, "He's a good old boy, he used to drink, and he knows how to shoot a gun and how to drive a pickup truck. That is not the definition of a man."

The slur brought out a roar of approval from a crowd that included Kathleen Turner, Tipper and Karenna Gore, Ossie Davis, and Madeleine Albright.

Here's a definition of a man for Harris—one that's been around forever, is morally sound, and speaks to the best part of ourselves. Real men protect the innocent.

Ed Asner Battles Age Bias

Hollywood has always favored younger actors for its glamour-oriented roles. Apparently, things aren't that much different now. But hope springs eternal for Ed Asner. He's trying to re-verse the trend.

The elder actor appeared in Los Angeles to announce the formation of a new group that is supposedly going to help older actors and writers get more work. The group is called the Industry Coalition for Age Equity in Media. It includes repre-sentatives and support from the Writers Guild, the Screen Actors Guild, AARP, Women in Film, and the California Com-mission on Aging.

Asner, along with some fellow liberal activists, is pre-dictably turning to government to provide "teeth" for the organization via legislation. California State Senator John Vasconcellos has authored a bill that, if passed, would require the state to "work with the entertainment industry to change cultural attitudes toward older adults and make the work force more responsive."

Can you smell an affirmative action plan for underemployed seniors in the works? Just think—if a quota system is implemented, we may just see scantily clad seniors shaking their booties on MTV.

Julia Roberts Heads for the Hill

Julia Roberts wouldn't appear nude in the movie *Full Frontal*. But she did appear in front of Congress in the flesh.

In an attempt to focus some attention on Rett syndrome, a neurological disorder that mainly targets young girls, Roberts gave testimony on Capitol Hill. The Oscar-winning actress spoke to members of the House Appropriations Subcommittee for Public Health Funding about the disease, which affects about 200,000 girls and women around the world, rendering them unable to communicate or control bodily functions. Sporting glasses and dressed in a suit, Roberts broke down in tears as she described the death of Abigail Brodsky, a 10-year-old Brooklyn girl with the disease. Before dying, the young girl was able to film a documentary with the actress.

Roberts asked the subcommittee to set aside, in its 2003 budget, $15.5 million for research. But then the star got in trouble with those who would normally be in her camp. It seems that some animal rights groups were upset that Roberts urged Congress to support animal therapeutic studies.

It's hard to believe that there are people in this country who will rush to save the lives of lab animals that serve to assist science, but they'll turn their backs on human animals in distress.

Richard Gere Suffers from Bubba Backlash

According to *New York* magazine, after Hillary left an American Foundation for AIDS Research event, Richard Gere lobbed the following remark out in his speech: "Senator Clinton, I'm sorry, your husband did nothing for AIDS for eight years."

Did we hear that right? A Hollywood star saying something tangentially critical of St. Hillary?

Apparently so. The *Washington Post* reported that there were gasps from the crowd. Sharon Stone, Ralph Lauren, Natasha Richardson, and Lorne Michaels were in the audience and were probably some of the stunned ones there.

Senator Christopher Dodd took on Gere with one of his typically vacuous remarks. "He's such a jerk," Dodd said, minus any of the grace that you'd expect of an elder statesman.

The senator added, "That was just rude. I would love to get him and Hillary in a room alone together. Let's see what would happen then."

Can't you just see it now? Gere and Clinton locked in a room alone together. . . . In this corner, tap-dancing his way to the Tibet meditation marathon . . . and in this corner, fast dancing her way into the Senate and onto the Armed Services Committee . . .

Rosanna Arquette Fights Elder Starlet Abuse

Rosanna Arquette has made a unique film. Inspired by a fellow actress's decision to leave Hollywood a number of years ago, Arquette conducted interviews with 30 actresses, including Meg Ryan, Sharon Stone, Vanessa Redgrave, Gwyneth Paltrow, Daryl Hannah, Frances McDormand, Melanie Griffith, and Jane Fonda. Then she turned the project into a documentary called *Searching for Debra Winger*.

The film made its debut at the Cannes Film Festival, and apparently it's packed with emotion. But the feelings expressed by the actresses involved are chiefly those of anger. It seems that the women are mad at the male studio bosses for treating them as sex objects. They also resent being pressured into having to have surgery to enhance their looks.

Arquette describes what she thinks is driving the surgery mania. She says that Hollywood is a place "where youth is revered and physical perfection is achieved through body-altering surgery."

Frances McDormand of *Fargo* fame begs her fellow thespians not to "succumb to the tyranny of plastic surgery" within the profession.

It all kind of makes you long for the days when people talked about natural beauty radiating from within, and they really believed what they said.

Janet Reno and the Rocket Man

What's a candidate for governor to do to exceed the support already shown from Rosie O'Donnell, Alec Baldwin, Martin Sheen, and a disco-dance fund-raiser? Look to the world of aging rockers.

When she was running in the gubernatorial Florida primary, Janet Reno, champion of the little guys and gals, hosted a private $500-per-ticket event at a suburban Fort Lauderdale hotel. Senior pop star Elton John even signed up to sing for dollars at the 2002 September fund-raiser.

At the time, Reno spokesperson Nicole Harburger told the Associated Press that Elton would "do anything to support her campaign."

It's not certain whether Elton John participated in the new Democrat tradition of kissing, but if he did he most likely needed a heck of a long time to recover.

John Kerry Courts Hollywood Cash

John Forbes Kerry took the first step toward a 2004 presidential bid. The U.S. senator filed the necessary papers to establish an exploratory campaign committee. He also cozied up with some heavy hitters in Hollywood.

As far back as March 2001, NewsMax.com reported that Kerry had already informed the all-important Tinseltown brigade that he would run for prez. Kerry whispered the announcement at a pre-Oscar gathering at a posh estate in Beverly Hills. Included among left-leaning party pals were Kate Hudson, Russell Crowe, Julian Schnabel, and Miramax chief Harvey Weinstein. Weinstein's apparently a perennial favorite of Dems. In the past, he supported Bill, Hill, and Al.

According to Seth Gitell of the *Boston Phoenix*, Kerry went to the Bel Air home of Lawrence Bender. Bender is the producer of such feel-good films as *Pulp Fiction* and *Good Will Hunting*. Despite his professed devotion to campaign finance reform, Kerry was apparently sniffing out some campaign cash.

Let's face it. There's no amount of groveling at Hollywood's feet that's going to turn this JFK into another JFK. Brother Ted, maybe, but JFK—no way.

Stealth Endorsement

Another kind of star marketing is going on, but this one's taking place in a much more clandestine manner.

People who tuned into ABC's *Good Morning America* on February 19, 2002, were treated to a heartrending story from actress Kathleen Turner. Diane Sawyer conducted the interview with her trademark furrowed brow, which is meant to convey compassion but sometimes looks more like the expression of a person who's experiencing irregularity. Turner lamented the on-going battle she's had with the disease rheumatoid arthritis.

At a key moment in the program, Sawyer asked Turner whether or not she was still in pain. Turner responded with the address of a Web site, where the viewers could go to get help. Was the actress doling out this valuable information in order to help fellow sufferers? She may have been. But what the public didn't know, she was also aiding her own bank account.

It turns out that Kathleen Turner was being paid for her revelation by two different drug companies, as reported by Lawrence Goodman in Salon.com and by CBSNews.com.[5] Yes, that's right. She was being compensated for talking about her illness on the tube. Turner never had to mention the names of any drugs, but the Web site info she dispensed, with the help of Diane Sawyer, was actually sponsored by two different companies.

The two firms work together to sell an arthritis drug. A spokesperson for one of the companies confirmed to CBS that Turner was compensated by both firms for lending her star power to what he called an "unbranded campaign to educate people who are stricken with this disease."[6]

This type of celebrity-enhanced campaign is a strange breed. It looks like your average, ordinary interview with a star, but it functions like an advertisement. As a matter of fact, when a sympathetic celebrity is relaying his or her story, and you reach for the nearest tissue in which to catch your tears, you're probably thinking that the star is doing a public service. He or she is, but with a catch. When the audience gets sucked into the drama of the celebrity's personal struggle, or that of a family member or friend, the last thing viewers think of is that the star may be doing it for the bucks.

The dollars we're talking about here can be tremendous. Former *West Wing* actor Rob Lowe reportedly obtained a very lucrative arrangement for his involvement with a drug company campaign. The company manufactures a product used to lessen the side effects of cancer treatment.

NBC ended up canceling a scheduled appearance by Lowe to speak about the drug, because of the financial arrangements.[7]

"This has become a hugely gray area as to where the star's charitableness begins and where the financial interests begin." So says Barry Greenberg of the Celebrity Connection, which enlists stars for the companies.

Drug advertising has become more prevalent because the government has loosened up regulations. We saw Joan Lunden pitching the allergy drug Claritin in 1998, and Bob Dole told us all about his little blue pill, Viagra, in 1999.

The ads weren't at all subtle. Anyone watching them knew the stars had a connection with the products. But some backlash occurred as a result, and some stars started to feel as though their highly prized reputations were in danger of being sullied. So a more subdued approach was developed.

In addition to the assault of TV advertising, pharmaceutical companies came up with a new way to capitalize on celebrity influence and help to increase business at the same time. The idea was pretty clever. Celebrities could receive bucket-loads of cash to do free-flowing interviews. They could speak about a particular illness that they themselves suffer from, or one that a friend or relative has, and vent their frustration on camera. They wouldn't even have to mention the name of the product. All they would have to do is recommend that people go to see their doctors or go to visit a Web site.

From a star's point of view, it's a win-win deal. Celebrities get to appear noble, like they're performing a crucial public service that will help make folks aware of serious conditions and corresponding treatments. And they can make megabucks doing it.

Lauren Bacall was featured on NBC's *Today* show in March 2002. She talked with the dutifully dour Matt Lauer about macular degeneration, a serious eye disease. During the conversation she brought up the drug used to treat the condition. Once again the viewers had no idea that she was being compensated by the manufacturer of the drug for airing her views.[8]

> Celebrities get to appear noble, like they're performing a crucial public service. And they can make megabucks doing it.

On May 23, 2000, viewers of the Fox News Channel saw an interview with Olympia Dukakis. The actress talked about a disease called post-herpetic neuralgia, which is caused by another malady that's been around for a while called shingles. Dukakis described her mother's pain. "She couldn't even touch her hair. That's how painful it can get." She also described new treatments that were available and mentioned the names of a couple of drugs. Dukakis was paid by a drug manufacturer to do the interview. This tidbit of info was confirmed by a gal who was hired by the drug company that put together the campaign.

Here's the way zippy Paula Zahn, Fox News Channel anchor at the time, introduced Dukakis. "The tireless actress is constantly on the move, but now she set her sights on helping to ease the pain of more than a million Americans." Guess with the money she was getting, Dukakis was also easing the pain of her business managers, accountants, agents, and creditors.

Remember the two sisters who fronted a rock band called Heart back in the 1970s? The lead voice of the group was and still is Ann Wilson. She now supplements her record royalties with some moolah that she gets for talking publicly about Lap-Band surgery. Wilson guested on CBS's *Early Show* in July 2002 to promote the Lap-Band surgery rather than her rock band. She got her money from a PR firm retained and paid by the company that makes the Lap-Band.

You've probably heard about another pop singer with the same last name as the Heart singer Ann. It's Carnie Wilson. She used to weigh close to 300 pounds, and since having a stomach reduction procedure called gastric bypass, she's lost somewhere in the area of 150 pounds. Wilson's been front and center for years, talking about the surgery and the benefits of it. She's been interviewed on both ABC's *Good Morning America* and *20/20* numerous times.

Here again we have a celebrity who says she's just trying to help people. And she is. But the singer is also helping Carnie Wilson. She gets paid to do appearances whenever she talks about her surgery. A company that runs hospitals that perform gastric bypasses and another company that makes the equipment used to do the surgery provide Wilson with her compensation.

Wilson apparently doesn't think the money connection is unsavory in any way. She says, "I don't need the money. That's not why I do it. But every day of my life, I'm committed to people in helping them get healthy."

There's a problem here for the networks, though, because they don't exactly know whether a celebrity guest is getting paid or not. If they knew for sure, they would be obliged to tell the public. But if a celebrity keeps it to him or herself, there's not much the networks can do. In fact, many executives say that if a celebrity has a story to tell, the media are going to have to tell it.[9]

Maybe the best description of this kind of celebrity involvement was given by Esai Morales, an actor who plays Lieutenant Tony Rodriguez on the TV series *NYPD Blue*. When talking about his link to the Center for Disease Control's anti-smoking campaign, Morales said that he allows himself "to be used to draw attention," and he describes himself as "a cause slut."[10]

Sounds like Morales has hit the nail right on the head.

When Celebrity Endorsements Backfire

Organizations that use celebrities as spokespeople can sometimes end up with more than they bargained for.

There's the story of the female star who was flown in to be the guest of honor at a party. She was put up at a hotel, where she proceeded to make a number of long-distance calls and empty out the minibar. Her adventures ended up costing the organization a bundle.

And then there's the story of the singer who offered to sing for free, but the backup singers, dancers, lighting engineers, and everyone else involved in the production cost the charity hundreds of thousands of dollars.

Getting a celebrity to front a cause or charity can sometimes be a double-edged sword. It can get the cause a lot of publicity, but it can also mess with the message.

In the late 1960s, Jim Morrison of the Doors was recruited for a health advisory radio campaign. The spots were never aired because Morrison had sabotaged the recording with the following statement: "Hey, kids, stop doing amphetamines. Do acid instead."

Shannen Doherty was involved in an anti-smoking campaign for the government. Just a few months later, a photographer snapped her picture in a nightclub. She was caught red-handed with a nicotine stick.

Supermodel Naomi Campbell provides an example of a celebrity endorsement gone wrong. She had been one of the celebrity spokes-posers in the People for the Ethical Treatment of Animals' anti-fur campaign. The campaign featured Campbell in some provocative posters that were adorned with the slogan "I'd Rather Go Naked Than Wear Fur." To what certainly must have been PETA's horror, Campbell appeared at a fashion show in 1997 wearing—you guessed it—fur.

More recently, after Britney Spears was paid a huge amount of money to be a Pepsi promoter—oops!—the pop singer was spotted drinking Coke instead.

Julie Nathanson, a publicist at Rogers and Cowan, said, "The way to get to the media is by having celebrities, which is not necessarily a good thing. It is just the way of the world at this particular point."[11]

Nathanson tells a story she heard about a young actress who had her limousine driver take her over to a giant charity event, where she was asked the question "What brings you here tonight?"

As Nathanson recounts it, the young actress said, "Well, you know, I have a new series and everybody is paying attention to me, and I decided it's time for a charity."[12]

Guess in Hollywood, charity is all about "me."

CHAPTER FIVE

Hollywood's Fuzzy Thinking

If you exclude disease, the cause that stars love to champion the most is the protection of those furry little critters. Anyone who spends time in Hollywood knows how easy it is to get to the point where you'd rather be with animals than with people. But that's another story.

The interesting thing in Tinseltown is that most of those who call themselves animal rights supporters don't really mean *all* animals of the world. They mean critters of the cuddly variety. You know the Big Bird, Winnie the Pooh, and Teddy Kennedy types. So far, there haven't been a whole lot of celebs who have stepped forward to trumpet the cause of protecting termites, rats, parasites, or lice from the cruelty that's inflicted by exterminators, medical practitioners, or cosmetologists.

Bunnies, puppies, and kittens have managed to pull at the heartstrings of stars and starlets, so much so that many of them have decided to reject real fur and leather, as well as sloppy joes and fish tacos.

Now if you've ever tried to walk around for more than 15 minutes in state-of-the-art vinyl shoes, or if you've attempted to stick with a diet of tofu, rice crackers, and lima beans, you know that such personal sacrifice is difficult to maintain. Well, stars are no different than the rest of us in that regard.

The vegan diet is an especially tough one. The vegan purist eats no dairy, no eggs, no fish, and no chicken. However, wilted leaves, wet straw, multicolored seeds, and small pebbles are eaten in ample amounts.

> The interesting thing in Tinseltown is that most of those who call themselves animal rights supporters don't really mean *all* animals of the world. They mean critters of the cuddly variety.

The hardship surrounding the whole PC menu has given birth to an easier form of vegetarianism in Hollywood. It's called "beady-eyed vegetarianism." No kidding. This approach to protecting animals involves a certain amount of compassion, but not too much. You only eat foods that come from animals without big round eyes, the kind of peepers that can come back to haunt you after you've overeaten and passed out on the sheepskin rug. So you can't eat cow, lamb, rabbit, deer, and the like. But creatures with ball bearings for eyes, like fish, lobster, and crayfish, you can scarf down with abandon.

This brings to mind one aboveboard member of the entertainment community who's an avid hunter. It's Ted Nugent, and he's labeled animal rights activists with the nickname "fantasy-based hippies." Wouldn't it be great if Nugent, who has already written a cookbook, could come up with his own answer to beady-eyed vegetarianism? Maybe he could call it the bull's-eye diet planner—any animal that comes within bull's-eye range qualifies as chow.

There's another animal that seems to be kicked aside by most of the animal rights crowd, when it comes to protection. It's called a human being. Over and over again, these extreme activists find themselves at odds with the rights, needs, desires, and sometimes even the very existence of humans. This, unfortunately, puts them in conflict with various causes across the liberal spectrum.

A number of organizations claim that their goal is to protect animals. The biggest group is People for the Ethical Treatment of Animals, or PETA, as it's more commonly known today. This bunch seems to be everywhere—working with kids in schools, recruiting big-name stars, plastering posters around town, sponsoring events, doing TV and radio interviews, issuing press releases, advertising, etcetera, etcetera, etcetera. Part of the reason for this is because the group raises a ton of money. By the end of its fiscal year 2000, it had brought in more than $17 million.

Now anybody who wants to change the world through activism is going to experience a misstep now and then. Chance statements get made and controversial things get endorsed. But PETA has managed to offend its own members, big time, as well as a lot of the folks on the Left.

A little background is in order here. Conservatives believe in good and evil. But conservatives also believe that there are ways to tell when one thing is more evil than another.

Now some people like to say that certain things are equal when they aren't. Sort of like when we were kids and we were told that we had to share the Snickers bar (the one we'd carefully stashed away in our sock drawer) with our little brother. We'd keep the whole candy bar to ourselves and hand an old jawbreaker to our screaming sibling, telling him that the two were totally identical.

That's kind of what Ingrid Newkirk, a co-founder of PETA and a national director of the organization, tried to do when she said this: "Six million Jews died in concentration camps, but six billion broiler chickens will die this year in slaughter-houses."[1]

What the heck is she talking about? They're *CHICKENS!* She craftily put a big fat equal sign where it doesn't belong. Let's see . . . in this hand there's the untold suffering, maximum depravity, and wholesale evil of the Holocaust. And in this hand, there's a mom at a drive-through window picking up a bucket of the Colonel's secret recipe to feed her kids for dinner. What kind of yahoo could think of equating these two? Somebody needs to find the lady a conscience that works.

Isn't it strange that folks who call themselves animal rights activists tend to have an atheistic view of the world? They love Chuckie Darwin and buy into the idea that "it"—meaning life—"happens," kind of like that slogan we see on the back of grunge T-shirts.

When we look at nature, we see the principle of survival of the fittest on display, all right. What we don't see is the gazelle family suing the pack of hyenas for eating one of its cousins. Not yet, anyway. The only "right" that seems to be in full operation is the right to be eaten by another animal.

So if we humans are a part of nature, or at least that's what we've been told, shouldn't we be able to eat just like the rest of the animal kingdom?

Many lefties also believe that it's just an accident that human beings are smarter than other animals. It's just a fluke that we actually learned to create, use tools, hunt, ranch, and raise our own food.

Of course, the truth is that we really are smarter than pigeons and rats. And yes, God is the one who designed these fantastic noggins for us. Now if we could just get liberals to use them.

Animal rights activists like to gloss over the normal behavior of wild animals. If an activist stumbled upon some lions and tigers and bears in the forest, would he or she try to convince the creatures about the virtues of joining Animals for the Ethical Treatment of People? That speech would be over in a single bite.

And what about the use of the term *rights?* It's ludicrous, but that hasn't stopped some law professors from pushing to allow chimpanzees to have their day in court. Not to say that there isn't a lot of monkeying around with the law that goes on in courthouses each day.

If animals have rights, they must have equal protection. That would include, for example, tapeworms. Just because these animals happen to reside *inside* of humans doesn't mean that we have the right to kill them and remove them. After all, the aforementioned Ms. Newkirk of PETA spoke these astonishing words, too: "A rat is a pig is a dog is a boy." This was reported in the September 1989 issue of *Vogue.* So why not "a rat is a pig is a tapeworm is a man"?

> Most people in this country love animals. And every decent person abhors the idea of treating animals in a cruel fashion. But most people also value Aunt Edna over Rover.

Most people in this country love animals. And every decent person abhors the idea of treating animals in a cruel fashion. But most people also value Aunt Edna over Rover.

Animal rights activists talk a lot about ethics. *HEL-LO!* Animals are incapable of ethics. The Golden Rule is still one of the best moral principles in the world. Animals can't comprehend such a concept. But animal rights activists continue to say that some creatures should be treated the same as, or better than, humans.

Clash of Causes

The errors surrounding this Hollywood cause are so great they could make your mind explode. But oddly enough, a rift has developed between Hollywood's #1 and #2 causes.

Now we know that Hollywood stars love the disease cause. And one of the most sought-after diseases to represent in Tinseltown is AIDS. Everyone remembers seeing star after star wearing the mandatory AIDS ribbon on each of the awards shows, despite the fact that it's gotten extremely difficult to find a spot on the body that's got enough clothing to pin the darn thing to.

Hollywood's gotten in the habit of holding AIDS banquets, AIDS quilt displays, AIDS runs, AIDS walks, AIDS parades, AIDS concerts, and AIDS tractor pulls, all to accomplish what has been dubbed "AIDS awareness." There's a problem, though. Apparently, the animal rights activists aren't in sync with the AIDS cause.

One of the most evil beings in the world, according to animal rights activists, is the scientist who still uses animals to do research. Some of the more rabid Hollywood celebs do the swearing off of the meat eating and fur wearing thing. But they also go to events where there are signs that say things like "Stop Animal Research" or "Scientists from Hell." These extremists basically like to broadcast their hatred for animal experimentation.

Former Hollywood actor Chris DeRose is now director of an organization called Last Chance for Animals. DeRose was a regular on the TV magazine series *Hard Copy.* In early 1999 he produced a pilot called *Hollywood Animal Crusaders*. Guest stars included John Travolta, Cher, and Don Johnson.

As reported in the *Los Angeles Times*, April 12, 1990, DeRose said this: "If the death of one rat cured all diseases, it wouldn't make any difference to me." One gets the feeling that DeRose might have a somewhat different opinion if he or his kid were the one with the disease.

The host of ABC's former late-night TV show *Politically Incorrect* was the "satirized for your protection" Bill Maher. The comedian now has a similarly biting show called *Real Time* on HBO. Here's an example that captures Maher's feelings about scientific experimentation: "To those people who say, 'my father is alive because of animal experimentation,' I say, 'Yeah, well, good for you. This dog died so your father could live.' Sorry, but I am just not behind that kind of trade off." Maher made this very politically correct statement on his ABC program of October 22, 1997.

In 1992 Michael J. Fox, former advisor to the Humane Society of the United States, wrote a book published by St. Martin's Press called *Inhumane Society: The American Way of Exploiting Animals*. In it, Fox penned the sentence "The life of an ant and that of my child should be granted equal consideration." Wonder if his children appreciated their dad's sentiment when they heard that.

A lot of prominent animal rights activists reject the idea of placing meat in their mouths but don't seem to be bothered by the regular insertion of "foot." There's an encyclopedia's worth of celebrity hooey that's been hurled around in the name of animal rights. Some of the more high-stupidity highlights deserve a closer look.

As cited in the *New York Times*, January 14, 1989, one of the co-founders of PETA, Alex Pacheco, said, "We feel animals have the same rights as a retarded human child."

This is a man who also said, as reported by the Associated Press on January 3, 1989, "Arson, property destruction, burglary and theft are 'acceptable crimes' when used for the animal cause." Guess it's okay to do the crime, as long as you get the right amount of Hollywood face time.

A lot of prominent animal rights activists reject the idea of placing meat in their mouths but don't seem to be bothered by the regular insertion of "foot."

We talked about Ingrid Newkirk earlier. Remember, she's the one who said that a human child and a rat should be treated the same. Newkirk echoes the feelings of a lot of the goofballs in the celebrity ranks.

According to the PETA Web site, actor Harry Hamlin apparently graced the world with this questionable piece of profundity at a PETA gala: "It's really important that we understand that animals deserve to be here as much as we do and that we must treat them with the same respect that we would treat our fellow man." Sure hope Hamlin doesn't mean the kind of respect where we all line up to be spayed and neutered.

Recording artist Pink expressed similar feelings to those of Hamlin. She's quoted on the PETA Web site as saying, "I've always felt that animals are the purest spirits in the world. They don't fake or hide their feelings, and they are the most loyal creatures on Earth. And somehow we humans think we're smarter—what a joke." Now aren't you ashamed of yourself for believing all this time that you were smarter than a snail darter?

If someone said Linda Blair of *The Exorcist* fame had written a book, what type would spring to mind? A book on head-twisting aerobics or perhaps on pea soup recipes?

Well, Blair has written a book called *Going Vegan*. It seems that she, like so many other celebrities, is dedicated to animal rights. Bill McCuddy of Fox News points out that, in a particular passage of her book, Blair is horrified that Mike Tyson keeps a tiger as a pet. Blair called Tyson's choice of pet "morally horrible." With all that Tyson's been involved in, it seems a bit unusual that an exotic pet is what earned him such a low ranking in Blair's eyes.

Some might question Blair's own choice of animal companion. Her stable of pets includes one hefty-looking bulldog type. Blair's fervor for protecting animals spills over into animal fashion as well. Apparently, it's a self-mage thing—the animal's, that is.

In an interview with Bankrate.com's Tamar Alexia Fleishman, when asked if she bought fancy outfits for her pets, Blair replied, "God, no. In the animal rights movement, we don't decorate our dogs; it lowers their self-esteem."

Back in 1997 Blair kicked off a PETA campaign by urging people to donate only to charities that don't fund animal experiments. She appeared in an ad with the slogan "Animal experiments make my head spin."

Now there's nothing inherently wrong with going vegan, but it's important to remember that when it comes to actually sticking with the diet, the devil is in the details.

Cameron Diaz has a unique reason for giving up the "other white meat." The PETA Web site indicates that the actress gave up eating pork because she was told pigs share the same mental capacity as three-year-old children. Babe was undoubtedly happy to hear that one.

One of the basic premises of the whole animal rights movement is that animals are very, very nice. And the more cuddly ones are actually nicer than humans. So if we follow through with this kind of reasoning, animals should be treated just like people, right? It all sounds good except when we begin asking, Which animals are they talking about? And what about when we're faced with the choice between saving an animal or saving a person?

When we're trying to determine which creatures rate higher than others, a passage from the techno-rocker Moby reflects the general sort of feeling in Hollywood. This Moby moment arrives courtesy of the PETA Web site: "Certainly I'd love to live in a world where everyone was a vegetarian and animals didn't have to suffer for human purposes. A goal of mine is to one day live on a big spread of land with tons of animals—a big menagerie of dogs and cats and chickens and pigs. But until that time comes, I just choose to live the way I do. Hopefully, other people will see that it's ethical and healthy, and some of them just might choose to live that way themselves."

So Moby dreams of a big animal menagerie. And his animal utopia is made up of "dogs and cats and chickens and pigs." What about lizards, scorpions, snakes, and killer bees? How come they're left out? Must be that sage Orwellian axiom—some animals are more equal than others.

Speaking of equality, when an equal sign is placed between animals and human beings, animal research suddenly becomes one huge Hollywood dilemma. If you look at the big medical breakthroughs that have occurred in this century and the last, you realize that animal research has played a major part in the discoveries.

The U.S. Department of Health and Human Services determined that the life expectancy of human beings has increased by almost 21 years, thanks to the scientific research that's been conducted on animals. Reputable science, health, and government organizations all point to the need for continuing the practice.

Take the issue of breast cancer. It's one that's important to most feminist groups. And the matter of heart disease is of concern to a whole slew of organizations. Animal studies are helping researchers discover information that could lead to cures for these and hundreds of other diseases.

Funny how it is when someone you love dies of a disease. All of a sudden you develop less of a concern about the hamster that "helped out" in the lab and more about the urgency of finding a cure for the illness in question. Does that mean as a society, or as individuals, we stop caring altogether about whether an animal is mistreated or has to suffer? Of course not, but we understand that when it comes to priorities, placing people over pets is the moral, ethical, and compassionate way to go.

Nothing has collided quite as forcefully in Hollywood as the anti-animal research campaign and the subject of AIDS. We know that experimentation on animals saves lives, finds cures, and eases people's suffering. And we know that this premise applies to *all* illness. That means it applies to the one that's been the most politicized and PC sanitized—the affliction of AIDS.

Here's where the dilemma comes in. AIDS affects homosexuals in disproportionate numbers. And Hollywood wholeheartedly supports gays and the gay rights movement. So what's an activist to do?

The truth is that without animal research we're not ever going to get a cure for AIDS. As reported in the September 1989 issue of *Vogue*, PETA priestess Newkirk stated that humans were less important than animals. She's even indicated that if animal research was to produce a cure for AIDS, the organization still wouldn't be supportive. "We'd be against it," she said.

Some animal rights activists have really stooped low to further their goals. One of the most infamous bully squads is the Animal Liberation Front (ALF). The FBI has actually gone as far as to classify ALF as a domestic terror group.[2]

In 1989 ALF broke into a laboratory at the University of Arizona and liberated some mice. Although the little rodents were undoubtedly reveling in their newfound status, some of the humans weren't as chipper about it. You see, these weren't your average run-of-the-mill Mickeys and Minnies. They were part of a research project to develop a treatment for cryptosporidium, a potentially life-threatening condition for anyone infected with HIV.

As it turns out, the scientists lost valuable time in their research. And as fate would have it, in 1993 cryptosporidium hit the city of Milwaukee hard. More than 300,000 people were affected, and the lives of more than 100, many of whom were AIDS sufferers, were lost.[3] Here's where we're apparently supposed to say that at least the mice were okay.

In 1997 when animal rights activists traveled to Washington, D.C., on their annual trip to demonize animal testing, they were surprised to find AIDS activists waiting for them. A group called Americans for Medical Progress had brought an AIDS victim named Jeff Getty to speak at a press conference. It seems that Getty had received baboon bone marrow in order to treat his AIDS condition. He said that since treatment began, animal rights activists, including members of PETA, had called him a "victim of mad science" and sent him "obnoxious messages."

Getty went straight for the bottom line when he said, "Stop research and you stop life. My life and the lives of millions of people with HIV or AIDS depend on scientists working with animals to develop new therapies."[4] AIDS activists went on to speak publicly about the importance of the use of lab animals to find cures for various diseases.

When you're dealing with the liberal Hollywood community, facts never seem to stand in the way of a fashionable cause. Animal rights activists have filed lots of lawsuits against the government to try and slow down scientific research. And their lobbyist friends push to pass laws that would oppose laboratory animal research. Thanks to generous donations from wealthy Hollywood types, these people-pooh poohers have been able to propagandize kids and adults, with their one-sided tale of the pain and suffering that lab animals have to endure. The human face of the one who might be saved in the process is conveniently left out of the discussion.

The same celebs who wear AIDS ribbons and champion the need for a cure can't go out and support animal rights, can they? Or the feminists who say they want to eradicate breast cancer can't really jump on the PETA bandwagon, can they? Apparently, a lot of them can and do. Let's look at a few.

A Zoological Catch-22

Alec Baldwin is a perennial PETA person. He's been a celebrity host for PETA's Animals Ball and Humanitarian Awards Gala. Baldwin told a Los Angeles TV station that there are "a lot of human subjects . . . who would be more than willing to become live experiments."[5] It seems that Baldwin is suggesting that we think about using people instead of animals in our research experimentation. Wonder if there's a lab cage with Baldwin's name on it, waiting for the actor to do his part.

Appearing on the TV program *Extra* on December 16, 1996, Baldwin said, "A lot of medical experimentation, perhaps all of it, is a sham. . . . I know that it's kind of ludicrous to continue the charade, this kind of lazy, outdated science as an answer."

Baldwin is on record as being firmly opposed to scientific experiments using furry creatures. But like the rest of Hollywood, he seems to want to continue his support for AIDS organizations. The *Sunday Times* (London) of January 19, 1997, spoke of his backing of animal rights. It also told of how the actor had "drawn support for AIDS causes." Doesn't anyone in La La Land see a contradiction here?

Baldwin also strongly supports breast cancer research, partly because his mother was diagnosed with breast cancer. The *People* magazine issue of December 8, 1997, reported that Alec helped raise more than $500,000 for the Carol M. Baldwin Breast Cancer Research Fund, Inc. In a press release from the fund dated May 29, 1987, the actor endorsed the facility. He said, "We are making this pledge so that our wives and daughters—along with your wives, daughters, sisters, and mothers—will some day be able to live secure in the knowledge that breast cancer has been eradicated."

It seems that Baldwin is suggesting that we think about using people instead of animals in our research experimentation. Wonder if there's a lab cage with Baldwin's name on it, waiting for the actor to do his part.

Here's that nasty little problem again. Breast cancer, just like the other major maladies, can't be wiped out without the assistance of animal testing. And yes, if it wants to make progress on the cure front, the institution that Baldwin pledged money to has to engage in the "detested" animal research.

Baldwin's ex-wife, Kim Basinger, is another one of PETA's favorites. She also seems to be standing on the precipice of a conflict with herself. According to an Associated Press report of September 17, 1997, Basinger tried to persuade a New Jersey laboratory to stop its research. The lab was attempting to acquire new data on osteoporosis. With PETA's help, the actress was hoping to stop some proposed experiments on dogs.

Now these pooches were not your everyday Fido types. The canines had been specially bred for research. The study was being conducted to test a new medicine that would help treat the potentially crippling bone disease. While Basinger's star status did help to improve the conditions for the animals, it didn't halt their use. The research continued anyway.

Basinger has been an active Hollywood PETA player for years. On November 20, 1996, Paramount Pictures issued a press release that indicated she would be the co-host of PETA's 1996 Animals Ball and Humanitarian Awards Gala.

On the December 16, 1996, TV show *Extra,* Basinger made this statement about animal research: "It's outdated and it's our ethical responsibility to really catch up with new technology, and there is technology out there."

And in the April 25, 1997, *Washington Post,* Basinger talked about animal research in this way: "I don't believe in any kind of experimentation on animals . . . it's all about money, that's all it is."

Most everyone except the left-wingers knows that animal research is about saving human lives and preventing human suffering. Then again, years of crass materialism can really do a number on your objectivity and reason.

While Basinger basks in the approval of PETA, she also seems to want to be identified as someone who cares about cures for AIDS and breast cancer. She was involved with the Carol Baldwin fund-raiser for breast cancer, too. And she and then-husband Alec Baldwin actively supported the AIDS cause while they were campaigning against animal research at the same time. Another glaring example of inconsistency in motion.

Then there's the Hollywood happy puss that loosed Ed Asner on America. Also a PETA spokesperson, she tried to urge women to quit taking a drug because it contained horse urine. The smiley face is Mary Tyler Moore. The drug is a hormone replacement treatment that helps prevent osteoporosis, the same bone-weakening condition mentioned earlier that makes life miserable for those unfortunate enough to develop it.

In June 1999, Mary Tyler Moore went to Washington, D.C., to lobby for another cause. The actress coordinated an event where she arranged to have 100 young people gather together on Capitol Hill. The purpose was to seek funds to help cure juvenile diabetes. Moore was the chairwoman of the Juvenile

Diabetes Foundation. She said that she wanted the money for the "more than 16 million people who, like me, have diabetes."

Once again there's a strange irony at work. Any money that would go to studying juvenile diabetes would most likely involve animal research. But to a Hollywood liberal, political correctness seems to be able to iron out all the wrinkles in a lumpy rationale.

Comedienne Sandra Bernhard is a PETA award winner, too. She's been involved with ads sponsored by PETA. But Bernhard went to a Playboy AIDS benefit and a fund-raiser for the American Foundation of AIDS Research as well. In 1994 Bernhard attended a tribute that raised half a million dollars for the AIDS Project Los Angeles. And in April 1997 she performed at an event to raise money for a group called Gilda's Club, a cancer support center.

Like other celebs before her, she's basically opposing herself, because, quite frankly, there is no cure without the fur.

Some celebrities appear to be in disharmony with PETA and AIDS organizations on the animal issue. Melissa Etheridge has actually withdrawn her public support of PETA. But Etheridge is a pure political liberal, so why would she suddenly turn away from the group? It seems that the singer came to the realization that advances in curing AIDS have been made precisely because of animal research. Etheridge learned the truth the hard way. The rocker said this to a reporter: "My father died of cancer and I've lost too many friends to AIDS, so I do believe in animals losing their lives to eradicate cancer and AIDS from our lives."[6]

Most of the folks in the entertainment industry, though, don't yet see the incredible contradiction in supporting animal rights and, at the same time, wanting desperately to cure AIDS, cancer, diabetes, and other diseases. But if they took the time to think it out, they'd find that you can't wear the animal rights banner and the AIDS ribbon at the same time. Etheridge came to know the truth and was bold enough to admit it in Hollywood. Maybe there's hope for the rest of them.

PETA in Tinseltown

No one does Hollywood quite like PETA does. It's aggressive in its approach, but in a hip and trendy kind of way. And it's been able to create a peer pressure among the famous that's stronger than the Hulk on steroids.

PETA has actually put together two animal rights recordings. One's entitled *Animal Liberation* and the other is called *Tame Yourself*. The albums feature big musical names like Chrissie Hynde, the Indigo Girls, Michael Stipe, and Belinda Carlisle.

Chrissie Hynde's contribution to the PETA Web site shows her appreciation for the group's in-your-face approach. "I like the fact that PETA gets up people's noses and they make people think and that they're confrontational. [Some] people don't like their methods, but I'll tell you something, we don't like [animal abusers'] methods. People think PETA is confrontational. Well, we're never as confrontational as to trap something or put a gun to its head." Makes you wonder what gets up Chrissie's nose.

PETA also staged some rock concerts. One was called Rock Against Fur, and another was Fur Is a Drag. Artists who participated included the B-52's and k.d. lang. PETA was even given permission to set up tables and distribute literature on former-Beatle Paul McCartney's world tour.

Animal rights groups in general and PETA in particular have really hit pay dirt in Hollywood with the issue of fur. They've been able to reach some powerful players in the entertainment capital with their message.

Martin Scorsese and Oliver Stone have pledged to PETA that they'll keep fur off of their movie sets. Brad Pitt implied that his line of clothing will conform to political PETA correctness, saying, in *Details* magazine, "Maybe I'll design a line of clothes like Puff Daddy, but all in synthetic fur. . . ." And Ashley Judd, when commenting on her Catwoman costume for one of the *Batman* movies, let everyone know in advance, "It won't be leather. I love animals, so it will probably be pleather or some other animal-friendly material."

If these folks could get their way, they'd probably insist that U.S. Marine Corp members now be called "pleathernecks." Makes you wonder how long it'll take environmentalists to get the stumped look off their faces when they find out that pleather isn't biodegradable.

Kristen Johnston, the statuesque blonde from the former TV sitcom *Third Rock from the Sun,* bowed to PETA pressure. She told *Glamour* magazine, "In some roles I have to wear fur, and I always make sure it's fake, like in *Austin Powers: The Spy Who Shagged Me.* Faux fur is great because it shows people that faux can look fabulous." Isn't "faux can look fabulous" the official motto of Tinseltown?

> Makes you wonder how long it'll take environmentalists to get the stumped look off their faces when they find out that pleather isn't biodegradable.

In 2001 PETA had a 20th birthday bash. It was held on both coasts, in two of the most elite private nightclubs—the Viper Room in Hollywood and the Spa Nightclub in New York. Celebrity PETA princess Chrissie Hynde was the West Coast host; she and the Pretenders performed on the Sunset Strip. In an attempt to up the hipness factor, Jenna Elfman and Thomas Gibson of the departed sitcom *Dharma and Greg,* Pamela Anderson, Toby Maguire, Bill Maher, and Alicia Silverstone were invited. It's not known whether non-human animal representatives like Kermit also made the guest list.

Tinseltown even has its own version of animal rights awards. It's called the Genesis Awards, and it honors members of the entertainment industry who help PETA and its buddies. Like every other self-indulgent event on the Left Coast, the awards are presented annually at a star-studded ceremony. Celebrity presenters are, of course, mandatory. Stars who have played the presenter role in the past include James Cromwell, Pierce Brosnan, Martin Sheen, Kelsey Grammer, Charlotte Ross, Alicia Silverstone, Bill Maher, Wendie Malick, David Hyde Pierce, Dennis Franz, Sidney Poitier, and Doris Roberts.

The Genesis Awards television special actually airs nationwide. The show is in its 17th year and is chaired by Hollywood actress Gretchen Wyler. Wyler is executive producer for the program. And it just so happens that Wyler is also the founder of the Ark Trust, now known as the HSUS Hollywood Office. This is a media lobbying center, one of the many in Hollywood.

Hollywood efforts to influence the media are as common as stretch limos on Rodeo Drive. In addition to the sway that the Genesis Awards has on the content of films, music, and television, the Humane Society of the United States Hollywood Office acts like a watchdog on the entertainment and information media. It puts out a bimonthly publication called the *Media Monitor* and a yearly *Foe-Paw Report,* which point the finger at anti-animal messages in the media.

HSUS also sends out an electronic news bulletin called *Animal Issues Now!* It's distributed throughout the entertainment media in hopes of indoctrinating them with current animal rights themes. Like other media lobbyists, the HSUS Hollywood Office recommends story lines to producers, directors, writers, and other creative minds in the industry to help shape the substance of TV and film projects.

PETA regularly works the industry over with campaigns, events, awards ceremonies, and its media center. In many cases, the animal rights message suggests lifestyle changes for the pampered human pups of Tinseltown.

One of the PETA commandments is "Thou shall not consume meat." To get people to adopt the mandate as their own, the organization sponsors a "Live and Let Live" vegetarian campaign. Actress Jennie Garth, tennis star Martina Navratilova, and supermodel Tatjana Patiz have all participated.

Even Oprah Winfrey has accepted the PETA pedagogy. The TV diva is quoted on its Web site as embracing the beefless way of life. "I've stopped. I'll never eat another burger," Oprah told the *Newark Star-Ledger*.

And Rue McClanahan of the now-syndicated *Golden Girls* sure thinks a vegetarian diet is the answer to making life meaningful. "If you carry the power of compassion to the marketplace and the dinner table, you can make your life really count," the actress sermonized to the *Newark Star-Ledger*.

Some stars come up with surprising commentary about their veggie diets. Country singer crossover Shania Twain told *TV Guide*, "I love to cook. Very healthy eating . . . Nothing that had to die." Apparently, when it comes to the plant kingdom, words can be parsed with no problem. Guess Shania doesn't worry about her greens unless she hears some screams.

Cameron Diaz explained to *Esquire* magazine, "My niece was 3 at the time, which is a magical age. I thought, Oh, my god, it's like eating my niece!" Looks like Cameron skipped the course "Persuasion and Reason" in college. Either that or she's been listening to too many of those Deepak Chopra tapes.

But seriously, the peer pressure to go along with this stuff is enormous. And PETA

If you're in the cause biz, you can learn a lot from the manner in which the folks at PETA operate. They've infiltrated the celebrity world in a big way, and it's paid off.

knows just how to make people in Hollywood walk the PC line—appeal to their vanity.

In May 2002, in an effort organized by PETA, 100,000 voters took part in an online poll to choose the world's sexiest vegetarians. The winners were Toby Maguire and Natalie Portman. The previous year's winner was the aforementioned linguistic whiz, Shania Twain.

If you're in the cause biz, you can learn a lot from the manner in which the folks at PETA operate. They've infiltrated the celebrity world in a big way, and it's paid off. A U.K. magazine, *Time Out,* called animal rights the number one "hip cause," due to the high-profile campaigns of "super trendy PETA."[7]

But even the hippest of organizations can't please all of the liberal powers in Hollywood all of the time.

PETA Has Feminists Fuming

PETA knows what everyone else in the marketing world knows. Sex sells. So the organization goes out of its way to find the most attractive, slinky, sexy female celebrity supporters it can to carry its message forward.

PETA even has its own pinup calendar. It has featured *Baywatch* beauties Pamela Anderson and Traci Bingham, *Lolita* star Dominique Swain, *NYPD Blue* actress Charlotte Ross, Playboy Playmate Kimberly Hefner, supermodel Carré Otis, and *Clueless* actress Alicia Silverstone. PETA's Web site explains, "Their revealing photos are meant to turn you on—to a more caring, respectful attitude toward animals." Yeah, the only problem is the same revealing photos might turn some of the gazers into animals themselves.

The group's best-known campaign is "I'd Rather Go Naked Than Wear Fur." Over the years, it has featured a string of sexy celebs, including Tyra Banks and Christy Turlington. This activity got the feminists all fired up. They're incensed with PETA's use of foldout imagery.

Pamela Anderson of *Baywatch*, *V.I.P.*, and Kid Rock fame lent her image to a PETA anti-fur billboard, which was erected in Times Square. Here's Pam's PETA quote: "It amazes me that some designers still turn animals into fashion victims. I've written to them all to say, 'Foxes and chinchillas are anally electrocuted, beavers are drowned in underwater traps, and minks are injected with weed killer or have their necks broken, all for a tacky coat that makes women look like Bigfoot! Why?' C'mon, ladies, it's time to remove that unsightly hair from your back—in other words, your fur coat!" Now that's some powerful stuff from Pamela.

Some of the PETA pinups of the past were sensual stunners from a top modeling agency. Boss Models had eight of their eyefuls pose in the buff with their backsides displayed in their au naturel state. A caption on one of the ads read, "Turning your back on fur." They may have gotten a couple of their body parts mixed up here.

Continuing on the rear theme, the PETA Web site says this about Charlotte Ross: "Sure, both David Caruso and Dennis Franz bared their butts on *NYPD Blue*, but fans went gaga for the 'derriere extraordinaire' of their costar Charlotte Ross, who donned a white bunny—and nothing else—for PETA's poster reading, 'I'd rather show my buns than wear fur.'" Charlotte Ross's bun show paid off when she received the Celebrity Animal Advocate of the Year Award.

Alicia Silverstone posed for PETA in the phony leather substance called pleather. To make it more appealing and authentic looking, pleather in the shade of black was chosen. Silverstone wore a low-cut biker vest and a studded cap, both of which were 100 percent synthetic. The caption on the ad read, "Pleather yourself." A little too punny, don't you think?

Patricia Monterola did something bold for PETA. She let her naked body be painted with stripes. Then the Mexican pop singer appeared in a Spanish and English ad that launched in Miami. It was all part of an attempt to reach Spanish-speaking audiences with a message that people should boycott circuses. PETA's Web site stated, "Patricia's provocative pose proves that she is willing to 'show her true colors' about animal rights." Boycott? It would seem as though the circuses would be jammed with guys looking for pop singers in cages.

Supermodel Carré Otis went topless for PETA. For her poster, Otis dressed up as an underwater mermaid and preached this message: "Try to relate to who's on your plate." Do you get the sense that PETA is targeting one gender in particular—the one that's least likely to give up the beef?

Otis apparently thought long and hard about cuisine. She had some unique insight on "wrongful discrimination" at one eatery. "I was in a sushi bar over a year ago, and it was just one of those moments that it dawned on me—it hit me over the head—how could I just discriminate between a cow [and] a fish? Both had a consciousness, and what right did I have to discriminate between the two?" Supermodels just need celery sticks to stay alive anyway, don't they?

Actress Kathy Najimy, who was in *Hocus Pocus* and *Sister Act,* jumped in bed with a guy for PETA. In the resulting picture, Najimy winked as she said, "If you need fur to keep warm, you've got problems." Seems men in particular spend the majority of their lives trying to deal with that shaggy issue.

Kimberly Hefner, one of the former spouses of Hugh Hefner and past Playboy Playmate, donned a low-cut, cleavage-exposing Uncle Sam outfit for PETA. The attached message on a parody of the World War II recruiting poster read, "I want you—to go vegetarian." Bet if nothing else, it made a lot of guys stand up and salute.

Sometimes PETA's approach basically borders on soft porn. Bonnie Jill Laflin, who is both a former *Baywatch* gal and Dallas Cowboy cheerleader, posed nude on a pile of hay, holding only a cowboy hat. To match the seductive look on Laflin's face, the caption read, "Nobody likes an eight-second ride."

Apparently, Laflin used to be a rodeo fan, but now she's concerned about the insensitivity that's being shown to bulls. She says, "If rodeo riders took a few jolts from a 9,000-volt hot-shot and had straps cinched around their groins, they'd be singing a different tune—mostly high notes." No guy wants to hear himself making that sound.

Sheryl Lee, the actress who played Laura Palmer on the television series *Twin Peaks,* did a naked corpse scene for PETA in what appears to be an autopsy room. The caption for her picture said, "I wouldn't be caught dead in fur." Lee's approach seems a bit rigid.

Another sand-brained *Baywatch* star, Traci Bingham, did the nude PETA poster thing. In her poster, Bingham is shown with her back to the camera and her body marked like a side of beef. Areas of her torso were marked with labels, like she was destined to be cut up and cooked. The subtitle read, "All animals have the same parts." Now Bingham won't be able to tell her dates not to treat her like a piece of meat.

In June 2002, hip-hop star Pink did her part for PETA. She promoted a fur-free door policy at nightclubs around the United States. A PETA poster showed Pink in a "fur-free zone" at a chichi New York club called Central Fly. Like some other women who are known by a single name only, Pink thinks a lot of herself and her opinions. The pop artist summed up her feelings on fur wearers this way: "I hope they someday get bitten in the ass by the same kind of animal they wear on their back."

Christina Applegate, who played Kelly Bundy on the TV show *Married . . . with Children,* handled the 2002 Christmas campaign for PETA. In keeping with the pinup girl motif, Applegate wore little more than a diamond cross, gloves, and a sensuous smile.

In December 2001, Britney Spears was asked to go nude for the animal cause. But her representatives were furious over a report in the *New York Post* that gave the impression she was willing to participate in an anti-fur, in-the-buff photo shoot. Spokespersons for Britney suggested that, when it came to their client, People for the Ethical Treatment of Animals could've used a lesson in ethics. Apparently, Spears was going to supply PETA zealots with a photograph of her clothed self, but after reports of nude expectations, she canceled any involvement with the project.

"Notwithstanding the meaningful work that PETA does, we cannot be involved with an organization that would distort the truth," Spears's publicist told Reuters.

Britney recognized that PETA distorts the truth? Guess she's not that innocent after all.

The organization actually acknowledged that it's come very close to porn promotions. PETA spokesperson Dan Mathews told the *Calgary Herald* in January 2002, "We are soft-hearted, it doesn't mean we can't be soft-core." Guess it's okay to be soft on decency, too.

When Mathews made this statement, he was holding a news conference to publicize actress Dominique Swain's poster. The PETA picture of Swain capitalized on the actress's role in the 1996 film version of *Lolita*. It showed Swain in her birthday suit, standing in a schoolroom at the chalkboard. The message, "I'd rather go naked than wear fur," was written on the board a number of times, presumably as a punishment for wearing an animal by-product. If this is any indication, punishment in school sure has been altered in a major way since we were kids.

A spokesperson from Media Watch, the Toronto-based group that speaks out against exploitation of female images in the media, said, "I wasn't really clear what naked women have to do with the animal cruelty."

You've got to admit, Media Watch has a point. And a lot of the people on the Left are ticked off about the approach PETA's using. Many are self-proclaimed feminists, and they get madder than usual when they see organizations like Playboy and Frederick's of Hollywood sponsoring animal rights events. What they're angry about is the sexist imagery and objectification of women. Hey, isn't that what Hollywood's famous for?

PETA Tweaking

In 2001, according to a PETA release, Drew Barrymore said, "I love animals, so I can't eat them." The actress explained that she wanted to "save all the little lobsters in restaurants and throw them back into the ocean." PETA rewarded Barrymore by praising her for turning down a cover on *Vogue* magazine because of her anti-fur beliefs.

Maybe the organization celebrated her too soon. In August 2002, Barrymore, the apparently not so die-hard vegan, announced that she was forgoing the meatless path for a typical sort of celebrity reason—it just wasn't exciting enough. She told IMDb.com that she doesn't eat a ton of meat. And she added, "I don't wear a ton of leather, but I don't put strict limitations on myself anymore." Ah, yes, those strict limitations can really be a drag when you're trying to party hardy.

Animal rights activists had a banner year in 2002. For some reason, fashion designers got the urge to use lots of fur in their clothing. About 10 times as many designers featured fur in their collections as compared to the previous season.

To PETA's horror, some of the glamour pinups of the animal rights movement started showing up in public wearing—fur! Celebrities like Jennifer Lopez, Halle Berry, P. Diddy, and Posh Spice wore it with panache. And some who were previously anti-fur, like Cindy Crawford, Kate Moss, and Madonna, were actually enjoying being politically incorrect. Guess it had to happen. A lot of the stars initially got involved with the animal rights cause for superficial reasons.

But when you think about it, fur wearing has been a long-standing tradition in Hollywood, like gaudy jewelry and permanent tans. Fur has always been the most noticeable sign of glamour and the ultimate indicator of success. All-time classic stars like Marlene Dietrich, Marilyn Monroe, and Liz Taylor wore full-length minks to keep their personas in high gear.

When PETA launched its "I'd Rather Go Naked Than Wear Fur" campaign in 1994, it showcased five supermodels—Naomi Campbell, Christy Turlington, Claudia Schiffer, Cindy Crawford, and Elle Macpherson. Of the original models, only Turlington and Macpherson retained their anti-fur position.

Cindy Crawford had a falling-out with PETA in 2002. The model appeared on the catwalk of designer Roberto Cavelli's fashion show wearing a chocolate mink fur coat. This was in stark contrast to an earlier PETA ad that had her wearing nothing but a fake fur hat. Crawford's publicist, Annett Wolf, responded by saying Crawford was only being nice to PETA and hadn't really agreed to the anti-fur message in 1994. "[PETA] is not her cause. She has been really nice about the PETA ad, but it's just not her thing."

In January 2002 activists were all over the Walt Disney Company over a Cuba Gooding Jr. movie called *Snow Dogs*. The movie featured Gooding as a dentist who went to Alaska to get his inheritance. Only the inheritance included a pack of sled dogs, and Gooding had to learn to mush. Animal rights activists were up in arms over what they thought was cruelty to huskies.

Forget about insider trading, stock dumping, and corporate impropriety. Those offenses are nothing compared to animal rights violations. It seems that animal rights activists got angry over some remarks Martha Stewart made on her TV program a few years ago. At that time, the domestic diva alluded to the Iditarod dogsled race in Alaska as a wonderful example of dogs and people working together.

Unfortunately for Martha, the episode aired a second time, and it stirred up a sleigh full of anger in a group called the Sled Dog Action Coalition. The group decided to pressure animal rights advocates to snarl and bark at Stewart and at Viacom CEO, Richard Bressler.

Maybe Martha ought to get busy doing canine penance and knit those Iditarod doggies some leg warmers and booties.

Gisele Bündchen committed a cardinal sin, at least according to PETA. Not only did the supermodel cut a deal to appear in Blackglama fur ads. She showed up on the runway in a custom-made mink wrap. She even said that "fur is the hottest material to work with right now."

So it was not a complete surprise when, at a TV taping of the *Victoria's Secret Fashion Show*, Bündchen came down the runway in a beaded bra and panties and was greeted by some gals who had a beef with her. The four females carried signs that read, "Gisele: Fur Scum." They screamed epithets at the model as she calmly strutted her stuff.

The PETA-philes were unceremoniously dragged offstage, and the Gisele segment was retaped. As Bündchen came down the catwalk in the second shoot, the audience broke into spontaneous applause.

Maybe someday we'll hear more applause in Hollywood for folks who resist the furry state of mind.

The Left Coast's Greatest Hits

"Shop Around"   Winona Ryder

"You Talk Too Much"   Alec Baldwin

"Still Crazy After All These Years"   Ed Asner

"Good Vibrations"   Richard Gere

"Love the One You're With"   Jennifer Lopez

"Both Sides Now"   Ann Heche

"He Ain't Heavy,
   He's My Brother"   Roger Clinton

"Show and Tell"   Christina Aguilera

"The Day I Found Myself"   Pee-Wee Herman

"The Great Pretender"   Martin Sheen

"'Knights' in White Satin"   Robert Byrd

"Money"	Michael Moore
"The Hustle"	Jesse Jackson
"Runaround Sue"	Susan Sarandon
"What a Fool Believes"	Sean Penn
"Oops! . . . I Did It Again"	Jane Fonda
"It's My Party"	Barbra Streisand
"Don't Know Much"	Sheryl Crow
"Wild Thing"	Joe Lieberman
"Saturday Night's Alright for Fighting"	Russell Crowe
"Runaway"	Roman Polanski
"I Fought the Law"	Robert Blake
"Kind of a Drag"	RuPaul

CHAPTER SIX

Reverse Blacklisting

Liberals in Hollywood love to talk about tolerance. They claim to be accepting of everyone on the face of the Earth and totally open to all of the ideas out there. They really want people to buy into the notion that they're pleasant folks, who walk around with arms wide open, always ready to join in singing a round of "Kumbaya." Their actions, though, with respect to one particular group in society, communicate something very, very different.

There's a kind of caste system that's in place in Hollywood. It's similar to the type that we've seen over the course of history, where people are divided into classes based on wealth or religion or heredity, that sort of thing. In a system like this, somebody's going to be stuck at the bottom rung of the social ladder. And the unfortunate souls in this position have traditionally been called, among other things, the "untouchables."

In the Hollywood version of the caste system, the untouchables are those individuals who hold ideas that are alien to the

Left. Such type of independent thinking is considered to be impure, or even filthy, in Tinseltown.

Now you would expect that the accepting liberals we spoke about earlier would gladly put up with someone who happens to have a different belief system than they do. Not so, in Hollywood. Those who reject the approved roster of thinking are treated like pariahs, as if they have some sort of contagious disease.

> In the Hollywood version of the caste system, the untouchables are those individuals who hold ideas that are alien to the Left.

Of course, being labeled in this manner can be very hazardous to a music, TV, or film career. It's the mark of the political beast, which means the person is a *REPUBLICAN!* (Note: The labels of "conservative" and "Christian" in Hollywood are equally despicable ones and can be used interchangeably with Republican.)

When Hollywood stars talk about Republicans, they get that look on their face like they've just taken a swig of cod-liver oil to wash down the third helping of Aunt Gladys's headcheese casserole. It's an expression of unmitigated, full-blown nausea. Their quotes say it all.

Out of the Mouths of Knaves

During the 2000 presidential campaign, the Republican nominee—who went on, by the way, to become president of the United States—was the topic of conversation in Tinseltown. Speaking about George W. Bush, Julia Roberts said, "The man's embarrassing. He's not my President and he never will be either."

In a dead giveaway that she's a rock-solid Democrat, Roberts's rehearsed quip went like this: "Republican comes in the dictionary just after reptile and just above repugnant."

Actor Alec Baldwin has a number of numbskull quotes to his credit. Can we ever forget his call to violence against key Clinton impeachment player Congressman Henry Hyde, along with his family, on *Late Night with Conan O'Brien* in December 1998?

Baldwin said, "I am thinking to myself, if we were in other countries, we would all right now, all of us together . . . would go down to Washington and we would stone Henry Hyde to death. We would stone him to death. Wait! . . . Shut up! No, shut up! I'm not finished. We would stone Henry Hyde to death and we would go to their homes and we'd kill their wives and their children. We would kill their families."

Now granted, Conan's program is no *Meet the Press*. But even if Baldwin was only kidding, it was way over the top, if not illegal, to suggest that one of our national leaders, along with his family, be killed.

Even after the impeachment was over, Baldwin wasn't done with his tirade. In an interview in *The Nation* magazine in April 1999, Peter Biskind recorded this little Baldwin gem: "They were on their knees praying to God at night for some kind of situation that would create an ethical parity between their two parties that would enable them finally to put Nixon to rest, where they could say, 'we are not the only party of rich white guys who keep women down.'"

Apparently, stars like Alec believe Republicans are basically people haters who have the worst possible interests of the poor, minorities, and women at heart. In the same *Nation* interview, the actor declared, "The extremist Republican leadership are destroyers, they're not builders. How can you come in and say that a welfare system, with as many warts as there were on that system, wasn't a valid attempt by a very intelligent and well-meaning group of people several decades ago to address a serious moral problem. . . . The extremist Republicans would rather shut it down and have nothing, rather than repair it. And if we consign a generation of people to abject poverty and ignorance and poor health and illiteracy and so forth, then that's just too bad."

When the would-be incoming Majority Leader Trent Lott was facing media scrutiny after making a racist at worst, stupid at best, remark during Senator Strom Thurmond's 100th birthday festivities, the media elites tried a gazillion different ways to equate Republican ideas with racism.

One of the members of the Black Caucus, Congressman Benny G. Thompson from Mississippi, suggested that if Trent Lott wanted to redeem himself and his racist soul, all he had to do was embrace an agenda that included more money for affordable housing, a higher minimum wage, national health care, and prescription drug benefits. In other words, he should sacrifice himself on the DNC altar.

Well, Hollywood folks play by the same set of rules as Democrat politicos. And rule #1 goes something like this: "The only good Republican is the one who turns into a Democrat."

Bashing Republicans

If we take a peek back at history, we can see that batting Republicans around has been a pastime in Hollywood for quite a while. There are lots of reasons to explain the phenomenon.

La La locals consider those on the Right to be racist, sexist, homophobic, and xenophobic, whatever that Scrabble jewel means. Even though many Hollywood industry people are incredibly wealthy themselves, it seems they're always nagging Republicans to try and get them to spend other people's money, namely ours. In their minds, it's the Republicans' fault that homelessness, poverty, AIDS, and failing schools exist.

The lefty celebs also believe that Republicans have a ton of dough at their disposal, but they're just plain stingy. They think that Republican politicians hoard dollars so that they can give them to their corporate buddies. And this supposedly makes it impossible for Democrats to go out and save the world. The idea that the money really belongs to the taxpayers or that if star libs wanted to cure all of the ills of the world they could do so by reaching into their own pockets never occurs to them.

> The truth is that here on the Left Coast, members of the entertainment community have billions of dollars in combined net worth. Why don't the whiners in the bunch use their own bucks to alleviate the suffering that plagues their consciences?

The truth is that here on the Left Coast, members of the entertainment community have billions of dollars in combined net worth. Why don't the whiners in the bunch use their own bucks to alleviate the suffering that plagues their consciences?

Don't mention tax cuts to them either. They don't want tax cuts because they want *bigger* government. They wouldn't know limited government if it bit them in their Versace flood pants. And free market? They think that's where the underprivileged go to pick up their package of government cheese.

If they'd only *think* for a moment instead of emoting, they'd realize that there are conservative ideas that are grounded in compassion, like enterprise zones, empowerment zones, school choice, and privatized plans for social security. And if these ideas were given half a chance, they'd actually work.

Hard-core libs really get into the knee-jerk emotional response to Republicans. Sometimes when Republican administrations are in power, the Left and its causes get more attention from Hollywood than they otherwise would.

In the liberal-leaning magazine *The Nation,* an article by
Mark Cooper called "Under the Cloud of Clintonism" featured
a host of liberal producers, directors, and actors waxing nostal-
gic about when Ronald Reagan was president.[1] Not that they
liked Reagan, mind you. It's just that Reagan was a lightning
rod that energized and unified the Left.

It seems the far left in Hollywood really misses the hate that
Reagan generated. That's because the anger served a very important purpose. It motivated the Trotsky troops to bring in the
bucks.

You see, the emotion dropped dramatically during the Clinton years. They had their boy in office, and life was oh so good.
But when Republicans got back in the driver's seat, the Hollywood Left started ratcheting up the energy again.

The origin of the hatred
for the Bush administration
needs to be explored a bit further. The roots are actually
found back in the presidency
of Ronald Reagan.

> It's strange that Reagan,
> who'd been a Hollywood
> actor, would be so disparaged
> by his compadres in the cine-
> matic community.

It's strange that Reagan,
who'd been a Hollywood actor,
would be so disparaged by his compadres in the cinematic community. The antagonism directed toward him began as soon as
he was elected governor of California. But what really sent the
Hollywood community reeling was his ascent to the White
House in 1980. And the electoral slaughter of Jimmy Carter
made matters all the more worse because that meant he had a
clear mandate.

The same kind of hate speech we hear hurled at George W.
Bush was spewed by celebs against Reagan as well. Although
enemies in Hollywood and other places never acknowledged
Reagan's intellect, they did credit him for being an accom-

plished actor. In fact, the tale told in Tinseltown was that Reagan used his cunning acting ability to bewilder the public and propel himself into office.

Current activist and pre-eminent lefty Mike Farrell had this to say about Reagan's victory: "What we were seeing was Frankenstein's monster in a sense; we were seeing this media product . . . and we knew! We knew who this guy really was!"[2]

The idea that this fellow in the White House was once a Hollywood actor actually emboldened entertainment professionals to hike up their activist activity. "If he's an actor," they'd say, "that means I can get involved in politics, too!"

When Jane Fonda was asked by an interviewer whether the use of celebrity for political activism was appropriate, she responded, "At a time when we have a former actor as President of United States, I don't see how anyone can ask that question."[3]

But the Reagan era had other powerful influences on the Hollywood community. During Reagan's tenure, Hollywood libs latched onto a host of causes that pushed them even further left. These pinko-hearted activists hopped around from supporting a nuclear freeze, to advocating environmental and arms control initiatives, to backing the Sandinista government in Nicaragua, to propping up Walter Mondale in 1984.

In 1982 a liberal who was said to be part of the "Malibu Mafia" backed a ballot referendum to create a State of California endorsement of a nuclear freeze. The nuclear freeze movement in Hollywood took off. The frosty front man for the cause was Paul Newman. Sally Field was also involved as a fund-raising hostette. This led to a television debate on a late-night ABC program called *The Last Word*. Charlton Heston and Paul Newman debated the issues of nuclear weapons, national defense, and a nuclear freeze. The idea of having serious policy debated by Ben-Hur and Cool Hand Luke was a little hard to take, and credibility took a bit of a wallop.[4]

There were also stars like Mike Farrell, Robert Foxworth, Mandy Patinkin, and Richard Gere who came forward to support the Sandinista government in Nicaragua. Hollywood created its own pro-Sandinista group called the Committee of Concern for Central America, which lobbied in Washington, D.C. The group even brought Daniel Ortega, the Nicaraguan communist, to speak to Hollywood celebrities at town meetings.

In 1984 the hatred for Reagan motivated Hollywood to back Walter Mondale with a vengeance. Celebrities were recruited to raise cash for the Democratic National Committee. Even Jane Fonda and then-husband Tom Hayden got involved and tried to raise money to defeat Reagan. Fortunately, their efforts failed. Mondale joined his old running mate, Jimmy Carter, in an exclusive club of those who got their political butts kicked.[5]

So now you've got an idea of why there's all this vitriol coming out of Hollywood. There was a passing of the hatred baton. And it went right from the Great Communicator straight into the hands of the Texas cowboy.

The "I Hate Bush" Club

Alec Baldwin was one of the dozens of Hollywood Republican haters who allegedly threatened to leave the country if Bush were elected. Like the ex-prez, Baldwin played the semantic parsing game, saying that what he meant was that he'd take a "long vacation."

During the 2000 presidential campaign, Cher had a Tinseltown tantrum of the political kind. "Has everyone lost their f—ing minds? Doesn't anybody remember the illustrious Reagan-Bush years when people had no money and no jobs?

What has happened to people's memories? It's like they all have Alzheimer's or something. I don't like Bush. I don't trust him. I don't like his record. He's stupid. He's lazy," the singer-actress screeched.

Continuing with her tizzy, Cher added, "If you're black in this country, if you're a woman in this country, if you are any minority in this country at all, what could possibly possess you to vote Republican?"

Before the final outcome of the election was known, British pop singer Elton John saw the possibility of a Republican in the White House as totally undesirable. Raising money for the Democrats, the singer-turned-prophet of doom said, "I do not want this country to live under George W. Bush. It's back to the Dark Ages if you go with the other guy."

Quirky actor John Cusack, who's starred in films like *High Fidelity, Being John Malkovich,* and *America's Sweethearts,* backed Al Gore in the 2000 presidential election. It seems his support for Gore was mostly based on his dislike for Bush. He declared, "I'm not saying I loved Gore, but I'm saying I don't want that . . . Bush in the White House."

Sean Penn's another one who took some verbal shots at someone he perceived to have a different political ideology. He characterized Fox News Channel's Bill O'Reilly, who's not exactly a fire-breathing conservative, as being more despicable than Osama bin Laden. *Fast Times at Ridgemont High*'s real-life alter ego said, "I'd like to trade O'Reilly for bin Laden." He then compared Bill O'Reilly to Adolf Hitler and called him "an embraced pariah." O'Reilly must have been chuckling as he tried to figure out what Spicoli meant to say with that scrambled phrase.

Speaking of Hitler, in February 2003, David Clennon, star of the hit CBS television series *The Agency,* told nationally syndicated radio talk-show host Sean Hannity that the tone in America under President Bush is similar to the one that existed during Nazi Germany times. "I'm saying that the moral climate within the ruling class in this country is not that different from the moral climate within the ruling class of Hitler's Germany," Clennon snarled over the national radio airwaves.

When Hannity asked if Clennon was comparing the U.S. president to the Nazi leader, the star replied, "I'm not comparing Bush to Adolf Hitler—because George Bush, for one thing, is not as smart as Adolf Hitler. And secondly George Bush has much more power than Adolf Hitler ever had."

There it is, folks. Pure, fiery, crimson-face, vein-popping hatred. Now just imagine that you're an actor who's trying to break into Hollywood. Hearing what Clennon and other celebrity big shots have said, do you suppose you'd sport a re-elect Bush-Cheney T-shirt to your next audition? Unless you're a glutton for ridicule and rejection, it's not likely.

Lawyer-columnist-TV host Ben Stein has spent some time trying to figure out why so many Hollywood folks are liberals. He thinks it has to do with the fact that Democrats used to be more open to immigrants and outsiders than the GOP was. And although Stein thinks things are different now, he notes that Hollywood hasn't caught up with the changes.

Stein describes the lefty majority in the entertainment community as a "Hollywood superstition." He thinks that it's very different when you talk to the working people of Hollywood, meaning the hairdressers, teamsters, grips, and camerapersons. He says, "They're *all* Republicans." And he refers to them as being underground. "Yes, there's a big subterranean group of Republicans in Hollywood, only their names are below the line. Maybe someday their views will percolate to the stars. Maybe not."[6]

Victims of Reverse Blacklisting

Well, there are a few celebrities who buck the political tide, but they sometimes end up paying a price. During the 2000 presidential campaign, Bo Derek appeared on CNBC's *Hard Ball*. Ms. "10" had openly aligned herself with the Republican Party to the point where she stood with party candidates, including the presidential one, George W. Bush. While on the show, Derek remarked that admitting to Republican sympathies can be a dangerous thing in Hollywood, career-wise.

When you think about it, Bo's own professional success hasn't been quite as big as her talent and beauty would warrant. Could this have anything to do with her political beliefs? Actress Sharon Lawrence can give us some insight on that.

Lawrence is best known for the character she played on the long-running cop show *NYPD Blue*. She's also part of the Creative Coalition, a non-partisan advocacy group that, coincidentally, is made up mostly of liberals.

Lawrence was attending a party hosted by the Creative Coalition for the inauguration of George W. Bush. In the February 5, 2001, issue of *People* magazine, a picture of Lawrence happened to be posted on the same page as Dubya's.

Ever since the picture appeared, Lawrence has received hate mail. People have come up to her on the streets of Los Angeles and questioned her about "being a Republican." She was even at a business meeting in February 2001, when, in a very somber tone, a producer said, "I have to ask, are you really a Republican?"

Ironically, Lawrence is not a Republican. She's a lifelong Democrat. She actually worked for Al Gore. As you can imagine, being treated like an outcast didn't sit real well with the actress. She told columnist Liz Smith the following: "If one is even perceived to be a Republican in Hollywood, there can be an excluding reaction and people genuinely resent you!"

To her credit, Smith wrote, "We are ashamed of our fellow Yellow Dog Democrats in Tinseltown who would seek to ostracize others . . . perhaps even deprive them of employment . . . because they are members of the Grand Old Party. That's not the American way."[7]

It may not be the American way, but it is the Hollywood way. Author and activist David Horowitz recognizes the syndrome well.

Horowitz founded the Center for the Study of Popular Culture and the Wednesday Morning Club. The club is one of the places in Hollywood where conservative ideas can actually be uttered out loud. The club's purpose, according to Horowitz's Web site, is to "support diversity of thought and expression within the entertainment community."

Horowitz says that the anti-conservative mood in Hollywood is real. He uses the term *gray-list* to describe its effect on careers. He says that to anyone involved in the entertainment business, the hatred of conservatives is "obvious." And those in the industry who are sympathetic to conservative or Republican goals "are terrified."

When I talked to Horowitz, he gave me an example of the knee-jerk reaction that can occur when one is about to be hit with the Republican label. He said, "Newt Gingrich was the scheduled speaker at one of the Wednesday Morning Club meetings. The introduction was given by actor Kurt Russell. The first words out of Russell's mouth were, 'I'm not a Republican.' No one had asked Russell about his political affiliation."

Politically speaking, Russell's not a typical Hollywood actor. He supports a lot of Republican causes and ideas, but officially, he's a Libertarian. That's a tag that the more conservative leaning in Hollywood are simply more comfortable wearing, along with the "Independent" one.

Horowitz sees gray-listing as being caused by many factors, not the least of which is the predominance of communist and socialist professors in the big-name film schools. He says, "No one wants to admit that there's a gray-list—but there is."

Horowitz lays it all on the bottom line when he describes the Hollywood scene as a marketplace where "there are buyers and sellers. The buyers are the producers. They need the big names. The big names are leftists."[8]

Struggling actors know that the same individuals who discharge leftist dogma in public are oftentimes the most famous names in the entertainment business. These are the kind of people ambitious actors want to become. According to Horowitz, with the power of "all those big names that are out there—no one has to tell you to keep your mouth shut."[9]

Robust Intolerance

Hollywood is a place where people go from waiting for their big break to waiting for their four-story estate to be completed. In order to achieve this kind of professional and financial success, though, you have to get that first movie role or sitcom spot. So people learn quickly how to toe the liberal line.

Here's the way the Hollywood reasoning goes:

TV and film producers need big-name stars; big-name stars lean left; so TV and film producers lean left even if they don't feel like it, and they choose their projects accordingly.

In October 2002, actress Patricia Heaton of the hit TV series *Everybody Loves Raymond* appeared on Fox News Network's *The O'Reilly Factor*. There was some candid discussion about Hollywood's revulsion for Republicans. *Raymond*'s TV spouse was asked whether her peers look down on her because of her beliefs.

Heaton described what is almost a universal experience for any conservative who lacks megaclout in Hollywood. "I vote Republican because of my pro-life stance, and, of course, that was a real hot button issue when Bill Clinton was first elected. . . . I wore a Quayle/Bush button, and literally people would stop and look at the button and look at me and give me dirty looks and, you know, say nasty things to me."

About those welcoming arms Hollywood liberals want you to believe they extend, Heaton had this to say: "Yes. I mean, the thing I found in Hollywood was that the Democrats were supposed to be all inclusive, but they weren't inclusive of my opinion."

The actress doesn't mince words when it comes to the abortion debate. Heaton says she would ban abortion if she were a Supreme Court justice. As to the risk to her career, she admits that there really is a risk of losing jobs, but she answers to a higher authority. "On a personal level, as a Christian, it will not be Barbra Streisand I'm standing in front of when I have to make an accounting of my life." So true, but Judgment Day would be a truly hellish experience for conservatives if, when they got to the pearly gates, they were greeted by St. Babs of Malibu.

Heaton demonstrated her class and courage when she unabashedly proclaimed her pro-life beliefs on national TV. Apparently, she showed off both traits again at the 2003 American Music Awards. The actress actually walked out of the awards event in the middle of the program and took a pass on doing her segment of the show. Why? Well, Heaton told the *Cleveland Plain Dealer* that the swearing and racy jokes of the Osbournes and various other presenters turned the program into a "vulgar and disgusting show."

Heaton was particularly appalled at one of the presenter's references to three-way sex and Sharon Osbourne's joke about Mariah Carey's upper body parts. Ryan Seacrest didn't help things either, when he pulled open Kathy Griffin's shirt and told a young girl in the audience, "Don't worry, honey, you'll have a pair of these soon."

According to the *Everybody Loves Raymond* star, the show was like being "in the Roman Colosseum." She added that it was "an affront to anyone with a shred of dignity, self-respect and intelligence."

The Conservative Closet

In my NewsMax.com column, "The Left Coast Report," I regularly poke fun at the Hollywood crowd and their sometimes insane, almost always wrongheaded, politics. I do it in a lighthearted way, of course, because I know that celebrities have feelings, too. At least that's what I've picked up from watching weepy Barbara Walters specials.

In the LCR feedback I've gotten, I've found that there are more people with conservative beliefs in Hollywood than one would think, and they're working in various places in the industry. I've been personally contacted by producers,

I regularly poke fun at the Hollywood crowd and their sometimes insane, almost always wrongheaded, politics. I do it in a lighthearted way, of course, because I know that celebrities have feelings, too. At least that's what I've picked up from watching weepy Barbara Walters specials.

directors, actors, musicians, and other creative types that run the gamut from staff technicians to well-known celebrities. And they've all verified one thing for me—when it comes to political viewpoints, the oppressive atmosphere that you hear about in Hollywood is definitely real. Here are some of the things people have told me:

- At one Hollywood function, I was approached by a female who's a well-known figure with a legendary name in the entertainment business. She looked around and then whispered to me, "I agree with you, I'm a conservative. Please don't tell anyone."

- A veteran film producer called me one day regarding a story in my column. He told me in confidence that the studio powers that be had forced him to change the story line in a script in order to accommodate a liberal political agenda. He felt that the film lost both artistic content and integrity from the experience.

- A reliable entertainment reporter told me the story of a powerful film company that pressured every executive who worked for it into contributing to select liberal Democrat candidates and causes. It even had a list of quotas for mandatory contributions.

- A young, up-and-coming film star with an impressive track record of roles told me, "You cannot be pro-Republican or conservative if you want to work in the business."

I could go on and on, but you might get the impression that all is lost. It's not. There's some good news on the "free to be me in Hollywood" front. For those who feel the need to keep their political beliefs closeted, there's a new outlet in town, where untouchables can express themselves to their heart's content. It's called the Hollywood Congress of Republicans (HCR).

The group was founded in 2001 as a grassroots organization for those in the entertainment industry who want to further the Republican Party and its philosophy. The group's Web site states that "HCR is built upon the shared Republican principles of individual liberty, genuine economic opportunities and leadership in world freedom."

That sounds pretty doggone Republican to me. So what does HCR think about the Republican moniker and the Hollywood bunch? I spoke to Donovan Weir, one of the founders and the first vice president of the organization, about this. He told me that it's understood by even the rank-and-file folks in Hollywood—the ones who move the sets (grips) and the ones who stand in the correct spots for hours (extras)—that getting fired is a real risk. Weir said, "If you're a grip and you are working on a big star's movie, you could be fired for your political beliefs."

Weir also told me that his group is representative of all parts of the industry and that there are numerous stories his members have *no* desire to tell. I think we can all figure that one out. He did share a few items with me, though. Like the one about the prominent actor who was a presenter at an awards show. The wardrobe and costume guy gave the actor a hard time, asking repeatedly why he wasn't wearing a ribbon. The fellow must have felt like he'd stepped onto the set of that classic *Seinfeld* episode.

Weir told of another star who went from doing prominent TV roles to working behind the camera. He said the fellow "wouldn't go on a local conservative radio talk show because he didn't want to piss anybody off," meaning he was afraid that publicly revealing his political beliefs might damage his career.

Just as Horowitz suggested, Weir said that many of the Hollywood celebs, and wanna-be celebs, would rather use another label like "Independent" or "Libertarian" instead of the "R" word to describe themselves. He explained that the current Hollywood chatter is cluttered with anti-war rhetoric. You know, the "George Bush is an idiot" remarks and the "Bush and Cheney are for big bucks" banter. Weir then offered his analysis about Hollywood's impulse to hate the president, saying, "The ridiculing attitude about Bush is beyond chic. It makes them feel better about themselves."

Weir describes the conventional view in Hollywood as "defiantly liberal," indicating that most would vote for a candidate like Joe Lieberman even if he ends up betraying them. "They don't care whether Lieberman would hurt Hollywood with his policies—as long he is a liberal Dem, he's better than Bush."

In an industry where it's very difficult to move up the career ladder, "people do miss out on opportunities if they have Republican sympathies," Weir said.

In an October 2002 *National Review Online* guest column, Emmy Award–winning comedian and Broadway star Dave Konig wrote the following: "I'm an actor. In New York. I'm also a Republican. For years I was in the closet about my political beliefs—a dark, scary closet filled with shame and back issues of *Policy Review*."

Konig echoes what so many others who have libertarian, conservative, or even moderate views in the entertainment biz say about life in the closet. Those with out-of-step beliefs are not just isolated. They actually expect that they'll be humiliated and made to feel embarrassed if they share their views with anyone.

Konig explains what being a closet Republican is like. "To be a closet Republican in New York show business means spending a lot of time staring at your shoes, giggling nervously, and changing the subject. It means grinding your teeth, biting your lip, and holding your tongue—often simultaneously. It means never having to say you're sorry (because nobody knows you're a Republican)."

He tells a tale of how he was first introduced to the Republican closet. "One of my earliest experiences with the indignant ire of the New York show-business liberal came in the mid-80s. I was young and skinny and performing with a sketch comedy troupe. One night, after a particularly successful show, we retired to the local bar to get drunk and tell each other how great we were (this is also what young, skinny actors do after a lousy show). I was flirting with one of the young, skinny actresses in the troupe and she was flirting with me. The sly innuendo and double entendres were flying briskly until she innocently asked me for my thoughts on President Reagan. (The question was along the lines of, 'Do you think he's evil and malevolent, or the other way around?') I responded just as innocently, 'Well, he was awfully good in *Kings Row*.' That was the end of the flirtation, the end of the evening, and eventually the end of the troupe."

Konig then goes on to explain the repeated reinforcement of the Republican-as-pariah principle. "That was the first of many such incidents. I soon realized, no matter where I went, I was surrounded. At auditions, in rehearsals, on sets, hanging out in coffee shops, wherever I went for the rest of my life, I'd be with fellow actors who view Republicans not simply as people who subscribed to the principles of a political party but as really, really awful people who subscribe to the principles of a really, really evil political party and who ought to be ashamed of themselves, if not actually tarred and feathered (or at least subjected to much glaring, glowering, tongue clucking, and eye rolling, not to mention considerable exasperated sighing and a healthy dose of sneering and smirking)."

As it turns out, conservatives aren't the only ones who feel as if they have to hide in the closet in Tinseltown.

Closet Christianity

I teach in the Radio, Film, and TV School at Biola University in Los Angeles County. The university has been in existence for almost a century. It's a unique Christian institution with a conservative bent to its religious philosophy.

A lot of Biola students hope for future careers in the entertainment and media industries. The school's got a great reputation, so students are able to obtain some coveted internships in the TV, film, and music business. I've had quite a number of conversations with these young people, and they've told me that they realized very early on that their ideas, beliefs, and values had to be kept out of the workplace and, yes, in the proverbial closet.

How are they able to pick up on this—that only certain ideas are welcome in Hollywood? Well, it's actually pretty simple. They see that the bumper stickers on all the cars in the parking lots are from the Democrat or Green Party only. They watch entertainment companies get involved in causes, or get behind candidates, that are as far left as you can get. They witness key executive positions in the entertainment companies being snapped up by people who are known to be avid supporters of high-profile Democrats like Bill Clinton, Hillary, Al Gore, and Gray Davis. That sort of thing.

One of my students at Biola, who for closet purposes I'll call Richard, told me he had come to the United States without really understanding American politics. Richard had gotten a job working part-time as a technician in a production-related company. Even in this peripheral sort of setting, Richard sensed that the political winds were blowing in one direction only. It was easy to figure out. His boss and his boss's boss both had pictures in their offices that flaunted their relationships with liberal politicians. Also, flyers were posted all over the place, but they were for Hollywood-approved type causes only. Richard came to the conclusion that he'd better keep his ideas a secret and his mouth shut tight.

I've come to realize that morality in Hollywood has basically become a convenient set of boundaries, without any of those "troublesome" things that liberals hate, called absolutes. I've also heard Christians and conservatives tell the same uncomfortable story. It's the one about being treated as if you're not really human.

The fact of the matter is, I've experienced it many times myself. Occasionally, the MO used is subtle. But with my personality, things usually just come flying right out of people's mouths. I've appeared on programs, openly, of course, as a Christian, a conservative, and a Republican, sometimes wearing all three hats at once. I've seen the looks of astonishment when I, a person who's supposedly a big fat meanie, crack a joke or just have fun. Some people in the industry have looked me straight in the eyes and said, "Are you sure you're a [choose any one of the Big Three slurs]? You seem a *little* too nice." Guess I'll have to work on that.

The same attitude that Hollywood takes toward Republicans seems to carry over to Christians as well. This is especially true when you're talking about individuals who are traditional in their beliefs and practices. Maybe it's because Hollywood is threatened by a strict moral system. The pedal-to-the-metal approach to having fun doesn't quite fit with a regimen of prayer and fasting. So the same peer pressure that forces people to muzzle it when it comes to talking about their alternate political beliefs is the same one that keeps them quiet about their personal religious faith.

Media Fellowship International is a sanctuary for Christians working in the news and entertainment fields. Its Hollywood office is strategically located in one of the busiest studio lots in southern California. Members include news anchors, stuntmen and women, actors, heads of studios, producers, writers, and editors—virtually all of the media-related vocations. Legendary model and actress Jennifer O'Neill sits on the board of directors.

> The same attitude that Hollywood takes toward Republicans seems to carry over to Christians as well. Maybe it's because Hollywood is threatened by a strict moral system.

O'Neill put into words the sense of prejudice that Christians in the Hollywood community have. "There are a lot of 'closet Christians' in Hollywood because they innately know there exists black-balling and prejudice against professed believers in the entertainment business. It's 'in' to be a Scientologist, Buddhist, or New Age Guru, but all hell breaks loose if one is to say, 'Jesus Christ' . . . (unless of course you are swearing!). . . ."[10]

O'Neill also views the content of Hollywood as something that could actually be improved by organized people of faith. "The people who run Hollywood, for the most part, are not family minded, rather the almighty dollar sits on their throne. If the public makes it clearly known that we want better entertainment with values and inspirational messages that is what Hollywood will produce. We're the consumer, after all."

Flipping Off the Faith

It comes as no surprise when celebrities in Hollywood try to tie Christianity to the evil stereotypes of conservatism. Tim Robbins attempted to blend the two together, while bringing up

Christianity during one of his Clinton defenses. He said, "It's got to have something to do with this radical Christianity. It's got to have something to do with not only morality, but white supremacy and the role of women in the world. It must really bug some of these people that he's [Clinton] appointed so many women, people of color, to his administration . . . the scary thing is that radical Christians have a foothold."[11]

In October 2002, Tim Robbins wrote an article based on a speech that he gave at an anti-war rally in Central Park on October 6. The piece was published in *The Nation*. In the article, he railed against the notion of fundamentalism, and he talked about the necessity for a vigilant resistance. "Let us find a way to resist fundamentalism that leads to violence . . . fundamentalism of all kinds, in Al Qaeda and within our own government. What is our fundamentalism? Cloaked in patriotism and our doctrine of spreading democracy throughout the world, our fundamentalism is business, the unfettered spread of our economic interests throughout the globe." Robbins was basically equating the fundamentalism of militant terrorist organizations with that of the business practices of our major corporations and the love that Americans have for God and country.

The info media are always coming up with articles, specials, documentaries, et cetera, to undermine basic religious beliefs. They especially like to time things so that they coincide with the highest of holy days.

At Christmastime 2002, the BBC came out with a special in which a so-called expert theorized that Mary, the Mother of Jesus Christ, had had an elicit affair or had possibly been raped by a Roman guard.

Jane Fonda's ex, Ted Turner, once mocked some of his Christian employees. They apparently had black marks on their foreheads from an Ash Wednesday service, and Turner referred to them as "Jesus freaks." He also once described Christianity to the *Dallas Morning News* as "a religion for losers."

Moral absolutes seem to threaten the lifestyle, beliefs, and practices of some of the Hollywood libs. For decades now, moviemakers have been trying to sneak in anti-religious messages. Unlike Hollywood's golden era when religious figures were portrayed in a positive light, Tinseltown has somehow switched gears. Films are serving up time-honored convictions with a big old helping of cynicism and hostility.

Over the past few decades, clergy who have gone astray are recurring themes in movies. Here are a few examples of how people of the cloth have been portrayed in cinema:[12]

- 1972—*Marjoe* is a documentary about a charismatic child preacher who's on a southern revival Bible circuit and cons folks out of their money.

- 1976—*Car Wash* features a caricature of a TV evangelist.

- 1979—*The Runner Stumbles* has comedian Dick Van Dyke playing a priest who falls in love with a feisty nun.

- 1980—In *KGOD*, a local TV station is taken from being in the red to making a profit. This is accomplished by having a clergyman, played by Dabney Coleman, steal money from people through a type of televangelism.

- 1981—*True Confessions* shows a corrupt monsignor rigging a church raffle so a local politician's daughter will win a new car. It turns out the priest is a grafter, a former pimp, and a suspect in a murder.

- 1982—*Pray TV* is another televangelist satire.

- 1984—*The Amazing Mr. X* is about a con man–spiritualist who goes after a widow's money.

Mike Farrell, **Martin Sheen**, and **James Cromwell**—Anti-war poster, $2.00. Artists United to Win Without War T-shirt, $15.00. The freedom to make a complete fool out of yourself, priceless!

Martin Sheen dodging the flag with a leftward lean.

AP Photo/Chris Pizzello

Sheryl Crow, other gems in her T-shirt collection include "Support Bombs Over Serbia" and "The Answer Is Not To Have Enemies."

Susan Sarandon showing everybody how many miles to the gallon her chauffeur-driven vehicle gets on the highway.

Reuters New Media Inc./Corbis

Corbis/Amet Jean Pierre

Woody Harrelson, newly elected president of the Hollywood Hemp Advisory Council.

Jane Fonda attempting to convince the North Vietnamese that she really did star in *Barbarella*.

AP Photo/Nihon Denpa News

Suhaib Salem-Pool/Getty Images

Sean Penn, International Dude of Peace, on the job in Baghdad.

Michael Moore trying to remember where he put his NRA membership card.

Reuters New Media Inc./Corbis

Frederic M. Brown/Getty Images

Michael Moore clarifying, "Just because the title begins with the word 'Stupid' doesn't mean it's an autobiography."

Ed Asner wondering aloud, "Something nice about America? Hmmm . . . Let's see . . . I'll have to get back to you on that one."

Robert Redford letting the word out about the number of conservative-oriented movies he's willing to feature at the Sundance Film Festival.

Rob Reiner, simply rub the Magic Meathead and money rolls out to liberal candidates.

CELEBRATE!

Barbra Streisand and **Bill Clinton**
doing the Hollywood/D.C. Hustle.

Bill Clinton checking with **Kevin Spacey**—
"Was that a thong I just heard snapping?"

Jesse Jackson reminding **Barbra Streisand** to
"Mail the check to 555 Shakedown Drive."

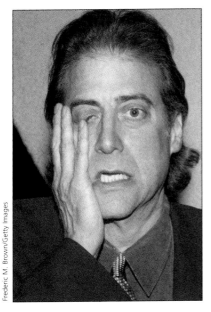

Frederic M. Brown/Getty Images

Richard Lewis telling his therapist that he just realized if taxes go up, he'll have to pay, too.

Rosie O'Donnell reacting to the length of Janet Reno's briefs.

Corbis/Michel Bourquard

AP Photo/Sven Kaestner

George Clooney discovering that eating one's words isn't nearly as enjoyable as dishing them out.

Traci Bingham, in her PETA-perfect bikini, explaining, "This little number comes in romaine, iceberg, and butter lettuce, too."

AP Photo/Jacques Brinon

Corbis/Jason Szenes

Alec Baldwin demonstrating how close he came to wearing a lettuce bikini himself.

Janeane Garofalo asking, "Is that crow I smell cooking?"

Dimitris Kambouris/Fashion Wire Daily

- 1984—In *Crimes of Passion,* Kathleen Turner plays a fashion designer by day and a hooker by night. She gets involved with a deranged preacher who's played by Anthony Perkins.

- 1984—*Footloose* features a hypocritical preacher in the Bible Belt.

- 1985—In *Agnes of God,* an insane nun is accused of killing her newborn baby.

- 1987—*Salvation* has a TV minister who's blackmailed into placing a certain singer on his show.

- 1987—*Dragnet* features another fake televangelist, only this one ends up being a manipulative murderer.

- 1987—*Murder Ordained* includes a promiscuous housewife who meets a clergyman. They commit a double murder together.

- 1991—In *The Five Heartbeats,* a minister thinks jazz and rock 'n' roll are the work of the devil.

- 1992—In *Leap of Faith,* Steve Martin plays a phony faith healer.

Another variation of the anti-faith theme places people of faith in the roles of wackos, hypocrites, and worse.

- 1968—The plot of *Who's That Knocking at My Door?* involves a young Italian Roman Catholic whose faith has made him an emotional cripple.

- 1970—In *The Ballad of Cable Hogue,* Stella Stevens plays a prostitute. She meets up with an old prospector who chats with God. As an added bonus, a disturbed clergyman is thrown into the cast of characters.

- 1976—The movie *Carrie* features a religious fanatic mother who sadistically tortures her own daughter with religious symbols.

- 1988—*Young Guns* has Charlie Sheen playing a Christian who prays while participating in mass killings throughout the western United States.

- 1991—In *Cape Fear,* the villain played by Robert De Niro is covered with tattoos of Bible verses.

- 1994—*Pulp Fiction* features a Bible-quoting hit man who spews scripture before he murders.

Faith itself is often the subject of ridicule and negative portrayal, too.

- 1980—*Wholly Moses* is condemned by Jewish religious leaders as being a mockery of the Bible.

- 1982—In *Sophie's Choice,* passages from the New Testament are quoted by Nazi officials in support of atrocities that were committed.

- 1984—*Swing Shift* includes a strange Bible believer.

- 1988—In *The Last Temptation of Christ*, Jesus is portrayed as a neurotic mess of a man who fantasizes about what his life would have been like if he had been born an average human being.

- 1990—In *Jesus of Montreal,* the story line places the Catholic Church at odds with its own teachings by pitting it against a drifter who spouts the words of Jesus.

- 1994—The chief villain in *The Shawshank Redemption* is the prison warden, who claims to be a Christian.

- 1999—*Stigmata* accuses the Roman Catholic Church of waging a thousand-year-long campaign to keep the true teachings of Christ a secret.

- 2001—*Chocolat* features a good-hearted, salt of the earth, unwed pagan, nonreligious liberal who teaches the restrained, uptight Christians that hedonism during Lent can be fun.

It's safe to say that people of faith aren't being depicted very fairly in Tinseltown these days. But then again, a whole lot of stuff has changed over the years.

The Anti-Code

In what many view as Hollywood's golden days, there was something in place called the Production Code. This code had been issued by the Hays Office. It set down rules that Hollywood used as a guide when making movies.

In the 1960s an unofficial guide took the Production Code's place. It was what you might call the Anti-Code. Hollywood decided to do the exact opposite of everything the original Production Code had told it to do. Anything the Production Code had said to leave out—like nudity, sex, profanity, violence, and drugs—the Anti-Code said to put in. Obviously, as a result, Hollywood movies went through a really, really big change. And it was most obvious in the values that were projected on film.

The contrast between the old Hollywood product and the new stuff was really stark. Claudette Colbert commented on it with a rhetorical question. She asked, "Did you know that when Clark Gable and I made *It Happened One Night* in 1934, there was never a clinch?" She then added, "Much to my sorrow!"[13]

Under the Production Code, twin beds were required. The camera would always pan away just in time to avoid catching any glimpse of a love scene. And a quiet landscape, with passionate music playing in the background, was the most common way of letting people know exactly what was going on outside the scope of the lens.

Under the new Anti-Code guidelines, sexual relations would be shown explicitly—anytime, anyplace, anywhere.

And since the Production Code prohibited "profane or vulgar expression," insults used in the old black-and-white classics were kind of creative. Instead of curse words, terms like *lardhead, four-flusher,* and *crackpot* were used.

Who will ever forget the controversy back in 1939 when Clark Gable uttered the words "Frankly, my dear, I don't give a damn"? Or how about the concerns that arose with *Arsenic and Old Lace,* when Cary Grant's character found out he had been born out of wedlock? Despite the saltier language used in the original play, in the film version, Grant's character exclaims, "Thank, God, I'm the son of a sea cook!"

In contrast to the care that was used under the Production Code to try and avoid offending anyone with foul language, the Anti-Code pretty much made cursing mandatory.

Then there were the issues of drugs and sex. The Anti-Code said, "Bring 'em on!" In the late 1960s, one movie, *The Trip* (1967), had Peter Fonda messing with some LSD while simultaneously stoned on pot. And the film *Bob and Carol and Ted and Alice* (1969) had two seemingly ordinary American couples looking into a little spouse swapping and adultery for fun.

The Motion Picture Association of America set up a board in 1968 to protect kids from the wrong kind of flicks. In checking out the film *Myra Breckinridge* in 1970, more than just a few of the board members were shocked to hear Raquel Welch's character let loose with "Alright, you mother f——s!"[14]

Whenever a taboo is successfully exploited, people immediately look to break even more boundaries. In 1970 *The Boys in the Band* featured a group of homosexuals celebrating a birthday party. In 1971 *Carnal Knowledge* told the story of the sexual antics of two fellows who moved forward in years but backward in morality. And in 1972 *Last Tango in Paris* basically hit the full-on, soft-core porn level.

Of course, limits continued to be exceeded with the Anti-Code in place, and new shockers were vigorously pursued. But pushing the envelope wasn't about to be contained to screens big and small. The trend would eventually become a part of the whole Hollywood way of life.

Pampered to Pieces

What was it that Mick Jagger said—"You can't always get what you want"? Well, apparently that's not true for some of the more coddled celebs in Hollywood. Word travels fast in Tinseltown. And when salaries are driven by massive egos, wages can rise faster than shot glasses at the Skybar.

Some of the more notable libs in Hollywood who qualify as money magnets made the *Forbes* Celebrity 100 List of 2002. Oprah Winfrey ranked second on the list, with $150 million per year in earnings. At $45 million, Tom Hanks took the thirteenth spot. Cameron Diaz and Ben Affleck tied at the twentieth position, with earnings of $40 million apiece. Sandra Bullock, Harrison Ford, and Elton John swung in at thirty-fifth, each raking in $30 million. Coming in forty-second was Rosie O'Donnell at $25 million. And Jennifer Aniston took the forty-seventh place with her $24 million.

Of course, one of the ways success is measured in Hollywood is to see who's making the most money per film. Comedic actor Jim Carrey is apparently neither dumb nor dumber. He took in around $20 million from Columbia for the film *The Cable Guy*. Tom Cruise supposedly got 20 million bucks plus for starring in Paramount's *Mission: Impossible*. And Jack Nicholson was able to capture about $50 million for playing the part of the Joker in the movie *Batman*.

Entourages can really run up a tab. For the *Scarlet Letter*, Demi Moore's bill was $877,000. Julia Roberts needed $841,000 for *I Love Trouble*, and Melanie Griffith hit $589,000 for *Born Yesterday*.

At a typical company, employees might get a bonus every once in a while, or if they're really lucky, they'll win a free trip. When Steven Spielberg made the movie *Always*, key people involved in the film each received a Mazda Miata. Pretty nice token of appreciation, don't you think? And when Paramount came out with *The Firm*, and ticket sales exceeded $100 million, thank-you's to pivotal folks came in the form of Mercedes.

Do stars live in a different world? You bet they do. When Sly Stallone arrived in New York to do some interviews with reporters for his film *Demolition Man*, he was upset about the color of the room where the interviews were scheduled to take place. The room was a light yellow, and Sly didn't care for the hue. Everything was delayed until the walls were redone in peach. Guess the movie title had gone to his head.

> At a typical company, employees might get a bonus every once in a while, or if they're really lucky, they'll win a free trip. When Steven Spielberg made the movie *Always*, key people involved in the film each received a Mazda Miata. Pretty nice token of appreciation, don't you think?

Demi Moore, who's rumored to have dated Slick Willie, may share some of the ex-president's self-absorption tendencies. Once when Moore appeared on David Letterman's show, she had the studio get her two jets and a helicopter to accommodate her crew of cooks, trainers, and assistants. Another time when Moore was lending her voice to an animated film for Disney, she told the studio that she needed transportation to get to a PTA meeting. A limousine was booked to take her there. Apparently, she'd forgotten to tell the studio that the location of the meeting was in Idaho. A $4,500-an-hour private jet was promptly chartered for her.

During the filming of *Mary Reilly*, Julia Roberts had a jet at her disposal 24 hours a day, courtesy of TriStar, in case she got the jones to jet off somewhere.

When Barbra Streisand went to Washington, D.C., to attend then–president-elect Bill Clinton's 1993 inauguration, she put the owners of the hotel in quite a difficult position. You see, Babs was shown her reserved suite of rooms, but the singer wanted to know whether the rooms were the biggest ones in the building. They weren't, so Streisand demanded the super-sized ones. The hotel informed her that the largest suite was already taken. She said that the hotel should relocate whoever was in the room. There was one little problem, though. The current tenants were Hillary Rodham Clinton's mother and father. Streisand allegedly said, "I don't care. Get them out or I will stay in another hotel." In the end, Streisand switched hotels.[15]

In Hollywood, satisfying the appetite for just about everything is a holy quest. Where else but in Babylon West could underground entrepreneurs—big-time madams like Elizabeth "Alex" Adams and Heidi Fleiss—be sustained. How could the hedonistic search by actors, producers, writers, execs, et al., *not* affect their political and philosophical view of the world? The answer is, Of course it does.

How a person views marriage, for instance, deeply affects what that person thinks of serial adultery as a way of life. Being sober may be the more responsible and edifying human condition, but it's inconsistent with the continuous search for mind-numbing highs. The notion that human life is sacred can dampen the rush one gets from instant gratification or an unfettered relationship. Self-restraint and ethical boundaries don't fit easily with the overwhelming lust for material wealth and success.

It's not surprising, then, that traditional faiths with explicit moral teachings are not all that well received in Hollywood.

The Passion and the Prejudice

Mel Gibson stands out in Hollywood like an oak tree in a field of ragweed. That's because he doesn't share the values, beliefs, or lifestyles of the Left in Tinseltown. The man actually makes meaningful films, with messages that celebrate family, faith, and freedom. And worst of all for the entertainment libs, he's super successful at it.

Gibson has really gone and done it this time. Some folks in the liberal establishment are extremely uncomfortable with the producer-director-actor's latest project. It turns out that his company has underwritten a film that Gibson himself is directing. The working title is *The Passion,* and it's about the Crucifixion of Jesus Christ.

This is totally unacceptable to some. Not only is this film *not* going to demean Christianity, as other flicks like *The Last Temptation of Christ* and *Jesus of Montreal* have done, but Mel is actually using Scripture as his guide. And he's telling the literal truth.

"Tolerant" liberals can't stand for this type of material being disseminated. The anti-Christian types have already begun their opposition research. In fact, it appears as if the snoop troops are out in full force.

Gibson went on the Fox News Channel's *The O'Reilly Factor* and indicated that a print reporter is nosing around his friends and family, including his 85-year-old father. There's apparently an attempt to dig up some dirt in hopes of harming Mel and the project.

In answer to O'Reilly's questions, the filmmaker responded with the directness of a faith-filled individual. Gibson referred to Christ's death as a "sacrifice willingly taken." When speaking of those who might appreciate the film, Gibson said, "I think anybody that is in the know about Jesus as God—and they believe in that—realize that he was brutalized and that I'm exploring it this way." That's the statement of an unabashed believer in the deity of Jesus Christ.

Gibson spoke of the actual suffering that will be displayed in the film in this way: "When you look at the reasons behind why Christ came—why he was crucified—he died for all mankind and he suffered for all mankind, so that, really, anybody who transgresses has to look at their own part or look at their own culpability." We all pretty much know this isn't the usual theology of Hollywood.

The film will utilize languages of the New Testament period, Aramaic and Latin. Gibson believes that a filmmaker can "transcend language with the message through image."

Mel anticipated that he'd get flack for his devotion to the project. "I refer to it as the career-killer film. And I was only half-joking at the time. But it's interesting that, when you do touch this subject, it does have a lot of enemies. And there are people sent. I've seen it happening. Since I've been in Rome here, for example, I know that there are people sent from reputable publications—they go about, while you're busy over here, they start digging into your private life and sort of getting into your banking affairs and any charities you might be involved in. And then they start bothering your friends and your business associates and harassing your family, including my 85-year-old father. I find it a little spooky."

I have sources on the set of the film who confirm that Gibson senses he's being attacked for his beliefs. It looks as though the worldview of certain folks is seriously threatened by the combination of Christ's story and Gibson's talent. Whatever the case may be, it's a pretty safe bet that a lot more Americans are grateful to Mel Gibson and won't take kindly to some lefty-led filth-finding expedition. Maybe it's time for these people to get a new hobby. Or maybe even find religion.

CHAPTER SEVEN

Hollywood's Smoke Screen

Sex, violence, alcohol, and drugs are the stock-in-trade of the entertainment mill. Films, TV shows, and music are full of the stuff. But now there seems to be one vice that some in Hollywood are no longer willing to place under the protective mantle of creativity. It's that thin little stick that we thought helped us look cool during the most awkward stages of our adolescent lives, the common cigarette.

According to Tinseltown's anti-smoking fanatics, this habit is an evil unlike any we've ever seen before. They believe the wicked fix has been shoved down the throats of the public by the mighty nemeses of libs everywhere, those ever-elusive and cagey . . . *TOBACCO COMPANIES!*

In Hollywood's mind, tobacco companies are not your run-of-the mill corporate types. No, these business entities have plotted to destroy the lifestyle, lungs, and longevity of every person on the planet. This is why the epithet for the fiends is whispered in somber tones and eerily echoes down the byways of Hollywood—Big Tobacco, Big Tobacco, Big Tobacco, . . .

Now an army of smoke-free storm troopers has invaded Hollywood and convinced some of the top decision makers in town to eliminate "offensive" smoking scenes from films. Profanity? No problem. Blood and guts all over the screen? An artistic necessity. Kids having sex with multiple partners in the school cafeteria? Harmless. But smoking? Now that's way over the line!

For more than a year, a group called Smoke Free Movies (SFM) has wielded its financial and creative clout. It's run full-page ads in the *New York Times* and in Hollywood's own publications, *Variety* and the *Hollywood Reporter*. The ads denounce the use of smoking scenes in movies.

SFM's driving force is Stanton Glantz, a professor of medicine at the University of California, San Francisco. One of the main things that riles Glantz is the use of so-called product placement, where companies pay cash to have their cigarettes put into movie scenes.

In January 2002 an ad sponsored by SFM was rejected by both *Variety* and the *Hollywood Reporter*. The ad had targeted the movie *In the Bedroom*. This particular film was not an insignificant one. *In the Bedroom* had received five Academy Award nominations, including one for Best Picture.

The SFM ad was timed for release during the crucial period of the pre-Oscar promo wars. It contained the following headline: "How many people did it take to put Marlboros '*In the Bedroom*'?" The suggestion was that Marlboro's manufacturer, Philip Morris, had paid for its cigarettes to be featured in the film.

Apparently, actress Sissy Spacek's on-screen character infuriated the anti-smoking brigade by chain smoking through most of the movie. In a scene that really burned activists up, Spacek is seen purchasing Marlboro Lights from a clerk in a grocery store. Miramax denied that it was paid by any of the tobacco corporations to use their cigarettes in the scenes.

The publisher of *Variety*, Charles Koones, felt that the ad was different from the usual sort of lobbying or advocacy, because it had singled out a specific film. Koones even said he thought it was potentially libelous.

Glantz accused Miramax of pressuring *Variety* to drop the ads. After being turned down by *Variety*, SFM tried to place an ad in the *Hollywood Reporter*, but the group's business was turned down once again.

The director of *In the Bedroom*, Todd Field, said that the smoking scenes were a necessary part of the film. "When people grieve they fall back on old habits, especially in an oral way," he said. "My dad was a terrible smoker before I convinced him to quit. But if he lost one of his kids, he would go back in a heartbeat. There is nothing glamorous about this behavior. It's a 52-year-old mother, it's not like the smoking in *Pulp Fiction*. The ad makes all sorts of ludicrous accusations— it feels like cultural McCarthyism to me."[1]

It's strange how, when it came to being bothered by this movie, the focus of activists was on the smoking. After all, the film had some really violent scenes. A human being was shot to death in full gory detail. The vicious murder is why Spacek's character, the middle-aged mother of the victim, is in complete emotional turmoil. Plenty of people would light up a cigarette, or a whole truckload of them, at a time like that, even if they'd never smoked before. Field was absolutely right, and the viewing public could relate.

Smoke Sensitivity

One of SFM's goals is to require that any movie containing a smoking scene, or featuring smoking in it, be given an R rating.

Most studios don't really have a formal smoking approach. Warner Bros. says that it tries to encourage its directors not to portray their characters as smokers, but the final decision is left up to the creative folks. And execs at Universal say they have a "consciousness raising discussion" with their people before film production begins. Can you picture that sensitivity session?

EXEC: Do you plan to have any cigarette scenes in *The King of the Long Island Boxing Ring?*

PRODUCER: Well, yeah, there are a few characters that smoke.

EXEC: Let's talk about it. What can we do to avoid the smoking scenes but still keep the characters believable?

WRITER: We could have Louie be a compulsive Mentos popper. That might work.

EXEC: Sounds good. What about Big Joe McGuff?

PRODUCER: Since he's an ex-con fight promoter, he'll need something a little more consistent with his 43-cup-a-day coffee habit.

WRITER: I think the lollipop thing would fit in nicely here.

EXEC: Perfect. Now what about that bookie in the Bronx? The script calls for him to be taking bets from behind the cage of a smoke-filled room. We can't have secondhand smoke wafting through the air, that's for sure.

WRITER: Hey, we can put one of those air purifiers on the desk. And the guy can have his shirt

> sleeves rolled up so that the nicotine patch
> on his right bicep faces the camera.

EXEC: That'll do it. Thanks, fellas. I think the juice
        truck just pulled up. Let's grab a break.

In April 2001 two other anti-smoking groups, the American Lung Association and Seeking Tobacco Alternatives with Realistic Solutions, invited Hollywood celebs to an event to take a look at smoking in movies. As reported in the April 30, 2001, *USA Today,* virtually none of the Hollywood celebrities showed up. The slight could have had something to do with the hour-long flick scheduled to be shown, which featured some of Tinseltown's biggest names.

The documentary was called *Scene Smoking: Cigarettes, Cinema and the Myth of Cool.* Stars appearing in the film included Ted Danson, Sean Penn, Jason Patrick, Jack Klugman, and Rob Reiner, among others.

In the documentary, author Michael Crichton aligns himself with the anti-smoking crowd. He came up with a novel idea to influence Hollywood that he called the Cancer Awards. He said they could give an award to "the actor who has done the most to kill people with cigarettes by showing smoking in public on film." Crichton went on to say that by implementing his idea, "You can put a stop to this immediately——you can do it in a year."

In the movie, Sean Penn had a different take. He placed smoking scenes in the realm of artistic freedom. "This is strictly a censorship conversation. No question," Penn declared. "This film is about censorship."

He went on to say, "These people who take on a position of creating a homogenous culture . . . are really the source of the cancer in society."[2] Guess there's no consensus yet in Tinseltown on whether cigarettes should stay or go.

Anti-Smoking Crusade

Director Rob Reiner has actually instituted a policy at Castle Rock Entertainment where creative people have to give justification for the smoking scenes they want to include. Reiner told *Time* magazine that any director, producer, or actor who wants to show smoking in a Castle Rock movie has to clear it with him first. "They have to make a really good case," Reiner insists.

Another industry insider who's been trying to snuff out cinema smoke for a while is Lindsay Doran. She was producer of the film *Sense and Sensibility* and a production chief at United Artists. She has given anti-smoking seminars at major production companies and studios all over Hollywood. Her past efforts include convincing filmmaker John Hughes to keep cigarettes away from the title character in the movie *Ferris Bueller's Day Off.*

But the leading anti-cigarette crusader in Hollywood has to be screenwriter Joe Eszterhas. He's battling cancer himself and apparently regrets the prominent role tobacco products played in many of the films that he worked on. Eszterhas penned *Basic Instinct, Jagged Edge, Flashdance,* and *Showgirls.*

In the *New York Times,* August 2002, Eszterhas revealed that he had been diagnosed with throat cancer and had part of his larynx removed by surgery. He wrote that he had "been an accomplice to the murders of untold numbers of human beings. My hands are bloody, so are Hollywood's."

Eszterhas, who began smoking at age 12, quit right after his cancer diagnosis. He thinks that smoking should be looked at with the same seriousness as heroin.

Apparently, Rob Reiner agrees with Eszterhas to some degree. Reiner helped organize California's Proposition 10 in 1998, which added 50 cents to the already high cost of a pack of cigarettes. The money was earmarked for early childhood development programs.

Almost a decade earlier, California voters had passed Proposition 99. It created a 25 cent tax on cigarettes, which was meant to fund an anti-smoking ad campaign. The unfortunate thing is that these campaigns don't seem to work all that well. They do raise money, if the tax stays within a certain range. But sometimes the message backfires.

For example, the ad campaign that resulted from the 1989 California proposition appeared to work between 1990 and 1993. But then, all of a sudden in 1994, smoking dramatically increased. Young people had one of those opposite reactions they're famous for. They thought that smoking enhanced their looks and image. Yeah, we all act the same dopey way when we're teens and probably always will.

I've met Rob Reiner on a couple of occasions, and I have to tell you, he's not your typical Hollywood liberal. He's astute when it comes to matters of government and extremely dedicated to public service. We basically disagree to the max on politics. But I respect this guy for his generosity with his time, money, and resources. Now if I can only get him to shift his political direction on some of those issues.

> Young people had one of those opposite reactions they're famous for. They thought that smoking enhanced their looks and image. Yeah, we all act the same dopey way when we're teens and probably always will.

Reiner would have preferred to garner the money for early childhood development programs by raising the California sales tax by one or two cents instead. But even California voters would probably have resisted that one. Taxing smokers is a much easier sell, and Reiner proved it when he got it by the general voting public.

He understood that the public has a soft spot for programs that help kids, too. His interest in early childhood came from a number of encounters that he'd had with the issue. He was involved with a documentary on ABC-TV, a special-edition issue of *Newsweek,* and a 1996 White House conference on the subject.

Proposition 10 was dubbed the "I Am Your Child Campaign," a name that was meant to send voters into guilt overload if they made a negative choice. It looked as though the thing was headed for a landslide victory. But opposition advertising, paid for by the tobacco industry, slashed its final lead to a narrow victory of 1 percent, with a margin of fewer than 80,000 votes.

But a win is a win. Reiner did have one more hurdle to cross, though. A group of tobacco businesses challenged Proposition 10 in the California Supreme Court on constitutional grounds. In the end, no doubt to Reiner's delight, the court decided in favor of the proposition.

March of 1999 saw Reiner appointed by Governor Gray Davis to head the Children and Families First Commission. The new bureaucracy was formed specifically to dole out the $750 million per year generated by the 50 cents a pack tax on cigarettes. What a deal for Reiner. He got put in charge of distributing the millions that his proposition would continually pull away from people who can't stop puffing.

In March 2002, Reiner appeared on the *Today* show to discuss smoking and the movies. In typical Hollywood fashion, he didn't mention how, during a time when kids are likely watching, a lot of the TV sitcoms give young people the impression that they can sleep around without any care about the consequences. He didn't talk about the excessive use of profanity in movies that usually has nothing to do with the story line and is simply gratuitous. And, of course, he didn't address the detailed and explicit amount of digitally enhanced violence that's being projected on the big and little screen for our young people's absorption. He stuck with the Hollywood line and kept the focus on smoking.

In August 2002, Eszterhas was interviewed by Paula Zahn on CNN. He cited Rob Reiner as his hero. And he publicly apologized for the part he had played in on-screen smoking. "I am haunted by the fact that I may have caused lives to be lost," Eszterhas said. He added that there are other ways than cigarettes to reveal a character's personality and to show someone smoking is "almost a cliché in terms of personal depiction."

Admittedly, Eszterhas is an extremely sympathetic figure. Anyone who has suffered through throat cancer and is in danger of dying is going to have a very special kind of credibility.

But here's the problem. There's a slick sort of diversion being carried out by the Hollywood anti-tobacco gang. They're telling the public, "Look over there. There's a carton of cigarettes on top of that stereo! That's outrageous!" Meanwhile, the fellow in the background who's having his cranium detached with a meat cleaver goes unnoticed. And the nine-year-olds in the basement who are smoking grass and playing a pretty sophisticated version of doctor and nurse don't seem worthy of attention.

The truth is Eszterhas's movies often contain elements of soft porn, which in flyover country tends to set off a lot more alarm bells than ashtrays do. There's actually a doozy of a smoking scene in the movie *Basic Instinct*. But its memorableness has less to do with the presence of a cigarette and more to do with the absence of underwear. The scene's the one where Sharon Stone asks Michael Douglas whether he's going to arrest her for smoking. With the positioning of Stone's clothing, or lack thereof, it's unlikely that a whole lot of audience members had their attention focused on the smoldering ash.

In addition, *Basic Instinct* has a character that in the middle of lovemaking knocks off her romantic interest with an ice pick. Still, Eszterhas worries about the bad influence of the smoking scenes in the flick. Puts a whole different spin on that old saying "What's wrong with this picture?"

The bottom line is if a filmmaker is going to be real, the world will look like the one we live in. And like it or not, ours is a world with smokers in it.

Smoking Superstars

According to Jane Makin of *People News,* October 2002, after being approached by a casting assistant in a shopping mall, a convicted robber was able to bypass all Hollywood security and was given, of all things, an acting role. Unfortunately for Meg Ryan, the guy landed a spot in *Against the Ropes,* the same film that the actress happened to be working on.

If the incident wasn't enough to make Meg feel uneasy, her on-screen persona broke one of Hollywood's biggest taboos. Yes, the movie character did the nasty—she smoked, that is.

James Bond got in trouble, too. He was caught smoking cigars. Britain's *Sunday Times* published an image from the Bond film *Die Another Day.* It showed actor Pierce Brosnan chomping on a stogie.

Bond had kicked the habit, so to speak, over a decade ago. The last time he was seen smoking on the screen was in the

1989 flick *License to Kill*. He upgraded from cigarettes to cigars, but that still ticked off the anti-smoking constables. So they joined with Goldfinger, Dr. No, and the guy with the metal teeth to pound on 007.

Britain actually plans to toughen laws on cigarette ads and may even outlaw tobacco sticks from films and TV dramas in the future. Guess that means Denis Leary can forget about touring the U. K.

So James Bond is a guy who drinks vodka martinis by the pitcher, shaken not stirred, has sex with every female spy he runs across, destroys property with abandon, and is licensed to kill. But let him light up a cigar and look out. In Tinseltown, and now apparently in London town, too, the guy's in deep doo-doo.

Russell Crowe's another star who's been caught with cigarette in hand. The actor smoked during an Aussie TV interview, and that was a problem because Australia's Tobacco Advertisement Prohibition Act rules out any advertising of cigarettes on television.

The Australian Broadcasting Authority conducted an interview with Crowe as part of its *60 Minutes* program. Before the actor lit up, viewers could catch a glimpse of a pack of Marlboros. The channel later challenged a ruling made by Australia's broadcasting watchdog that the network broke the law. It brought the case to Sydney's Federal Court.

In a sort of rewrite of life imitating art, Crowe had previously portrayed a tobacco industry whistleblower in the film *The Insider*. He even received an Oscar nomination for his work. Do you think it may be time for Australia to try lightening up about lighting up?

In the 1997 flick *My Best Friend's Wedding*, Julia Roberts played her usual lovable, sympathetic character. But evidently she also did enough inhaling—of tobacco, that is—to make Hillary Clinton take notice. Hillary ended up criticizing the smoking scenes in the film.

The anti-smoking crowd thinks that when young people see someone who's as admired and successful as Julia Roberts puff away, they're going to be tempted to imitate the behavior. In the words of *Friends* character Chandler Bing, "Duh-uh!"

What's really strange is the way these activists can so easily separate the issues to suit their agenda. Why aren't they worried that kids will imitate the long list of objectionable behavior that's depicted elsewhere on the big screen? Oh, yeah, there I go with that logic thing again.

Some of the biggest female activists in Hollywood have done movie scenes where cigarettes have played a major supporting role. Jane Fonda, Susan Sarandon, Jessica Lange, and Sharon Stone have all left a cinematic trail of cigarette butts behind them.

> Why aren't they worried that kids will imitate the long list of objectionable behavior that's depicted elsewhere on the big screen? Oh, yeah, there I go with that logic thing again.

Sarah Jessica Parker is filling some ashtrays on TV as well. On HBO's *Sex and the City,* Parker's alter ego, Carrie Bradshaw, writes the racy sex column that the program is named after. In countless scenes on the show, Parker is shown with a lit cigarette between her fingers. When she's writing, she's usually sitting at her laptop with coffee in one hand and a cigarette in the other.

Following some of the steamy sex scenes, Parker's character is sometimes seen smoking as she reclines alongside her latest male conquest. Viewers may get the opportunity to be nauseated by the sight of her lover sending well-formed smoke rings in her direction as she playfully pokes her finger in the center of the dissipating circles. The cigarette brand that's occasionally flashed is the same one Sissy Spacek's character from *In the Bedroom* favored—good old Marlboro Lights.

Big Brother Tobacco Cops

Cigarette scenes are so numerous, especially in films, it would be virtually impossible to list them all. Their inclusion goes back to the pre-Bogie days, when a cigarette was pretty much permanently attached to an actor's lip. Still, Hollywood does have a responsibility to pay attention to the content of movies, television, and music, especially when a product is going to be marketed to kids.

Activists may have a valid gripe when they complain about cigarettes getting ember time in films like *Home Alone 2, Honey, I Shrunk the Kids, Kindergarten Cop,* and *The Nutty Professor.* A study published in the fall of 2002 by the Public Interest Research Group sort of supports the premise. It found that tobacco use in movies that appeal to preteens increased by 50 percent since 1998.[3] There was a flaw, though, because the study looked at movies that preteens would likely enjoy, without regard for the ratings of the movies. It lumped together R, PG-13, and PG films.

Many in the anti-smoking movement would actually welcome regulations that would *ban* smoking from entertainment media that's aimed at kids and adults alike. Now emotionally appealing propaganda in the form of advertising is one thing, but government regulation is something entirely different. The idea that government could come in and tell a restaurant or tavern owner that his or her patrons couldn't smoke would have been unthinkable a few decades ago. But today smokers all over the place find themselves shut out of their favorite haunts, thanks to the legal strong arm of the tobacco police. Could entertainment content be too far behind?

In fact, the state legislature of California has held hearings on smoking in the movies. Democrat State Senator John Burton doesn't think that Hollywood filmmakers can handle the matter voluntarily and cited a previous commitment from the Screen Actors Guild that was apparently never met.

Just in case some of the Hollywood creators don't understand what the state senator is suggesting, the opposite of voluntary is *mandatory.* We have another name for what's being discussed, and it's something that ordinarily makes folks in Tinseltown break into a cold sweat. It's called censorship.

Hollywood hackles generally go up at the mere thought of censorship. But in this instance, some in La La Land don't seem to mind the curtailing of expression, as long as it's done for the politically correct reasons.

Fighting Big Tobacco has turned into a whopper of a political game. Tobacco companies traditionally lent their support to Republicans. This piece of trivia didn't go unnoticed by the Democrats. In fact, some people believe it may be the reason why the war against the tobacco industry was waged in the first place.

Similar to other Hollywood causes, those dedicated to seeing cigarettes extinguished forever use statistics and emotional stories to make their case. The tactics have worked in many states and municipalities, where smoking is banned in restaurants, bars, and various other public places.

As a matter of fact, on New Year's Eve 2002, the mayor of New York City, Michael Bloomberg, copied California and signed one of the nation's most stringent anti-smoking laws. The New York law effectively banished smokers from a multitude of public places, including restaurants and most of the city's bars.

The law did have some exceptions, though. The mayor had to cut back on his proposal to exile all smokers because he got flak from the city council. Unlike California and Delaware, which passed sweeping statutes, New York's law included some exemptions. Smoking is allowed in bars that are owner-operated and have no employees, like the so-called cigar bars, those that have separate rooms with special ventilation systems, and private clubs that have no workers.

> If we're going down this road of improving people's health through government regulation, can you just imagine the stuff they're going to try to restrict next? Don't be surprised if chili dogs, spicy chicken, deep-dish pizza, barbecue pork rinds, and cream-filled donuts are suddenly snatched off movie screens.

If we're going down this road of improving people's health through government regulation, can you just imagine the stuff they're going to try to restrict next? The first thing that comes to mind is our weight. Don't be surprised if chili dogs, spicy chicken, deep-dish pizza, barbecue pork rinds, and cream-filled donuts are suddenly snatched off movie screens. Then it wouldn't be long before the food cops were ordered to do neighborhood sweeps. Aunt Millie's triple fudge Bundt cake would be yanked from the picnic table before the crowd finished singing the first chorus of "Happy Birthday." And finally, the Butt Patrol would go after the evil corporations that caused our hips to expand at a geometric rate. Big Oil and Big Tobacco would be joined by the newest member of the rogue's gallery—Big Sweet Tooth.

Hand-Me-Down Smoke

The "if you smoke, we'll choke" crowd has another end-of-the-world scenario with which to scare the general population. It's secondhand smoke.

During Clinton's tenure, the Environmental Protection Agency declared that secondhand smoke was an environmental toxin. The EPA said that hand-me-down smoke was equivalent to asbestos or some other kind of hazardous substance. It classified secondhand smoke as a Group A carcinogen. Once it did that, it was able to tighten regulations in schools and in the workplace. Before long, smoking began to be restricted at more and more sites that were considered to be public, like restaurants, offices, and airplanes. Federal funds eventually had conditions placed on them, so that money would flow only to those places that agreed to be smoker-free.

As reported by CNN on July 19, 1998, William Osteen, a U.S. district judge in North Carolina, ruled that the EPA had based its 1993 report on inadequate science and had failed to demonstrate any kind of statistically significant relationship between secondhand smoke and lung cancer.

Osteen wrote in his opinion that the "EPA publicly committed to a conclusion before research had begun." The judge also wrote that the agency had "excluded industry by violating the procedural requirements" and had "adjusted established procedure and scientific norms to validate the agency's public conclusions."

In other words, the EPA report was a bunch of junk science. And it looks as though the agency basically put together an unscientific, jump-to-conclusion project for anti-cigarette PR purposes.

Recently, anti-smoking enthusiasm leapfrogged from the domestic to the international front. The UN wanted to get in on the action. The global organization called for an effort by the world community to develop some kind of international strategy to control tobacco, restrict cigarette advertising, and, of course, protect the children. Guess freedom stomping is contagious.

It's not as if all of Hollywood is taking this smoking stuff lying down, though. Some folks are taking it lighting up. A project called Hollywood on Tobacco (HOT) interviewed 54 actors, writers, producers, and studio executives who work in TV and film. HOT had its report published by an organization called Tobacco Control. The project was investigating the increased on-screen smoking during the 1990s. Those who were interviewed said they were more concerned about violence on-screen than smoking. HOT determined that there was no real culture of tobacco use in Hollywood. Oh yeah, there's a culture of promiscuity, alcohol use, and drug abuse, but not tobacco.

What HOT did find is that if somebody smoked off-screen, they were more likely to use a cigarette as a prop on-screen. It found that smoking scenes were more likely to be used in independent films to give movies a hipper quality.

HOT wanted to figure out what the most common reason was for putting smoking scenes into movies, and it did. It has to do with the portrayal of a character. Every teen who's ever smoked knows that a cigarette can be a prop to project a certain toughness, coolness, or rebelliousness. Put a lit cigarette in Alan Colmes's mouth and all of a sudden he's James Dean.

Hollywood scriptwriters reacted to HOT's findings saying that smoking could indicate an "inner dissonance," meaning it might create tension between the positive and negative qualities in an individual's character. Hey, the whole Hollywood smoking issue is a source of cognitive dissonance. People who relish free expression would never promote a weenie kind of censorship like this one.

The anti-smoking guards get aggravated when they watch Bruce Willis defusing a bomb with a cigarette hanging out of his mouth or Arnold Schwarzenegger, former presidential fitness expert, posing on the cover of a magazine with a big cigar in his teeth. They believe that when Julia Roberts, John Travolta, Winona Ryder, and Johnny Depp smoke on-screen or off, it influences their fans. But the piece of trash *Pulp Fiction* had a character played by John Travolta who smoked up a storm. And the character was also a heroin addict. From a writer's point of view, wouldn't it be a bit weird for a heroin addict to say, "I'll pass on the cigarettes. I'm trying to quit."

Some of the anti-smoking cops would like to see more realism in movie scenes by having some of the side effects of smoking, like difficulty in breathing and hospitalization, added to films. As Clive Bates, director of the U.K.-based Action on Smoking and Health, said, "The film industry uses the defense that they are portraying realism, but you rarely see someone coughing or wheezing or dying a painful death on a cancer ward on screen."[4]

TV shows and magazines follow the lives of Hollywood stars and show footage and pictures of nightclub hot spots, where cigarettes are basically fashion accessories. And cigar clubs have essentially become growth industries in the nation.

Meanwhile, the tobacco companies aren't passive. They're advertising, promoting, and trying their best to sell their products. No matter how much the anti-tobacco zealots want their own way, people still do have a choice, in movies and in life. That's called freedom, and hopefully *that* will never go up in smoke.

Hollywood Virtues and Vices

Hollywood's a place that stresses freedom. So these are guidelines, not rules, even though they're generally imposed with an iron fist. Hollywood doesn't really consider itself rigid, because the overriding principle in the entertainment capital is "everything is flexible." That means there are absolutely, positively *NO ABSOLUTES!* Got it? Here are the Cardinal Virtues and Deadly Sins, according to the Hollywood handbook.

The Four Hollywood Cardinal Virtues

1. **Inclusiveness.** All genders, races, and species are welcome at the Hollywood table, regardless of biological or planetary origin. But in the name of this virtue, evangelicals, conservatives, and flag-waving patriots are scratched off the guest list.

2. **Biodiversity.** The voiceless, beleaguered beings that live on the planet with us are entitled to our care and protection, with the exception of those pesky little organisms that pop up every now and then in the womb.

3. **Harmony.** Peace with every nation on Earth is the goal. So our country must lead by example and be the first in the world to lay down all of our weapons. Then we will all hold hands and, well, you know the rest.

4. **Free Expression.** Even though the Constitution was put together by dead white bigots, those who call Tinseltown home believe in free speech, as long as it follows the Baldwin brothers' manual of ideas and doesn't criticize would-be Hollywood royals.

The Seven Hollywood Deadly Sins

1. **Sexual Harassment.** A person can have his or her fingernails ripped off for this sin, based on hearsay alone, unless the bad behavior occurs on a casting couch or during film production.

2. **Intolerance.** There's no escaping punishment for this blunder, if it involves race, gender, or religion, except if you're talking about traditional or religious-type folks being pied in the face.

3. **Exploiting the Planet.** This misstep makes you ineligible to consume Ben & Jerry's ice cream for up to six months, unless you can prove that the slip-up occurred because a big-name producer or director ordered you to, or if the planet abuse is necessary to complete the construction of your second, third, or fourth vacation home.

4. **Narrow-Mindedness.** A boo-boo like this breaches the Hollywood code of ethics, which demands that all minds be open to any and every idea, especially those that are anti-American. Infractions will get you kicked off the red carpet until an appropriate period of groveling is complete. And oh, by the way, all penalties for southern white males must be tripled.

5. **Insensitivity.** It's a serious Tinseltown screw-up if you fail to show compassion and caring toward all peoples of the world. But if your lack of sensitivity is directed at a working-class American who is complaining about taxes being too high, don't worry. The offense will not be held against you.

6. **Judgmentalism.** Judging a person on his or her age, clothing, or physical appearance is a no-no, unless you're considering putting the individual in an upcoming reality show or TV pilot, or if you're in need of a hot date for the Golden Globes.

7. **Hate Speech.** To speak ill about another person or group of people is a huge flub-up in Hollywood, and extra punishment is meted out for this offense. But if the speech is hurled at a competing actor, arrogant ex-lover, or Republican adversary, the black mark gets erased from the books.

CHAPTER EIGHT

Hollywood War Games

Americans watched in disbelief. The images of the two airliners careening into the World Trade Center tore through our hearts, minds, and souls like a blazing trail of jet fuel. No matter how many times the tragic scenes were replayed, the reaction would be the same. From the news reporter, to the political leader, to the man or woman on the street, the sense that gripped us was singular. It was one of utter horror.

Later in the day, as we searched for some way to cope with what was happening to us, there it was. That evening, on almost every network and every program, the comparison was being made to December 7, 1941—the surprise attack on Pearl Harbor.

In an equally hideous way, that event caught our government and military by surprise. The devastating blow, which in a span of about 2 hours cost us 19 ships, 188 planes, and the precious lives of more than 2,400 American sailors and soldiers, was delivered via aircraft, too. And through similar means, we were transported from a relatively peaceful state of existence to the dark depths of uncertainty.

Even Americans who don't know much about history, or have forgotten what they learned as kids, have watched enough movies to know that when villains attack our nation, our nation responds. It did after Pearl Harbor and it did after 9/11. On September 16, 2001, media pundit Neal Gabler wrote in the *New York Times,* "Americans believe the nation will triumph. We believe it because we've seen this movie before."

Hollywood Reports for Duty

It was December 1941. A production company was in the process of shooting a film on Catalina Island. The movie was *Rings on Her Fingers.* Two of the stars involved were Gene Tierney and Henry Fonda. Recalling that fateful day, Tierney said, "We had just started our cameras when an assistant came racing down the beach." The assistant apparently told the group about the attack and said they'd have to clear out right away.

Another film was smack in the middle of production. It was *Arsenic and Old Lace,* a movie based on a Broadway play. Even though the film would be completed a few weeks after Pearl Harbor was attacked, its release would be put off until 1944.

And *Across the Pacific,* a film that starred John Huston, Mary Astor, Sydney Greenstreet, and Humphrey Bogart, would shut down production completely. Its plot involved an attempt to foil a Japanese plan to destroy Pearl Harbor. The story line too closely resembled reality.

Hollywood felt vulnerable after Pearl Harbor. After all, the entertainment capital is on the shores of the Pacific. A lot of major aircraft factories were located nearby, including Douglas and Lockheed. To add to the uneasiness, two days after the attack the *Los Angeles Times* ran the headline "Enemy planes sighted over the California coast."

But instead of succumbing to the pitfalls of anxiety, Hollywood enthusiastically jumped in and became part of the military effort. At that time, Hollywood had its studio system intact and could churn out pictures quickly. Stanley Frazen, at 83 years young, was part of the first motion picture unit of the Army Air Forces. The unit recruited Hollywood actors and filmmakers to make movies that would assist the nation during World War II.

You'll recognize one of the recruits—Ronald Reagan. Reagan described the unit as "two hundred million dollars worth of talent on the hoof." Other stars who helped out included George Montgomery, William Holden, Alan Ladd, and Clark Gable. And Irving Wallace was one of the writers who contributed.

In October 2002 the unit was honored for its 60th anniversary. A dinner was held at the Warner Bros. studio, where the whole thing got started with the help of Lieutenant Colonel Jack Warner. The unit produced hundreds of training and propaganda films, which turned out to be effective and appreciated by our side.

In 1942 the Army Air Corps was short of pilots. It needed about 100,000 new recruits, so Jack Warner's help was sought. Warner produced a short film called *Winning Your Wings*. It starred pilot-actor Jimmy Stewart. The movie hit the screens, and in a hardy response, the Army Air Corps got 150,000 new recruits. My own father-in-law, Ralph Brindise, was one of them. He remembers the film as being "an honest one" that impressed him and a number of his buddies to sign up. He added, with a chuckle, "Everyone wanted to be a pilot."

One of the unit's films was actually nominated for an Academy Award in 1944. It showed what would happen to

American pilots if their planes were shot down over enemy territory. It was appropriately called *Resisting Enemy Interrogation.*

The unit even assisted the men who dropped the bombs that ended the war. Special effects experts were used to create models of Japan. In order to give the B-29 crews a preview of what their targets would look like, the models simulated how the terrain would appear from 30,000 feet. And in what must have further enhanced the presentation, Reagan narrated the training films.[1]

If you talk to the men who did the fighting and ask them what they remember about Hollywood at that time, they'll probably mention the pinups. Pinups came in the form of posters, photos, magazine covers, and the like. And they were plastered everywhere. The guys especially liked to put them on the walls around their bunks. Ginger Rogers, Yvonne De Carlo, Veronica Lake, Rita Hayworth, Evelyn Keyes, Marie McDonald, Betty Grable, Marie Wilson, and Jane Russell were all pinup favorites.

> The most famous shot, of course, is the one of Betty Grable looking coyly back over her shoulder at the camera.

At the time, Paramount beauty Yvonne De Carlo spent most of the war as a pinup for love-starved GIs. She was known as the "Sweetheart of the U.S. Mechanized Forces." Her pictures were eye candy in a whole lot of tanks.

In her autobiography, Evelyn Keyes said, "It was our patriotic duty to answer the gallant servicemen . . . with pin-up pictures—the nakedest the Hays office would allow."

The most famous shot, of course, is the one of Betty Grable looking coyly back over her shoulder at the camera.

I spoke to Jane Russell, one of the most popular pinups during World War II. She remembers a very different atmosphere in post–Pearl Harbor America than exists today. "The country was united," she said.

Russell echoed the sentiments of many of the other pinups, saying that her role as a pinup was simply a way of contributing to the war effort. She told me that she "traveled with Bob Hope to Army, Navy, and Marine bases throughout the country to put on shows." But she perceived a big difference in the way the soldiers related to female entertainers back then. She said, "They treated us like queens."[2]

Hollywood helped out the war by contributing to the substance of films as well. The movie *Mrs. Miniver* was just starting production when the Pearl Harbor attack happened. The movie was about a middle-class English family's struggle during the Blitz.

President Franklin D. Roosevelt liked the film enough to urge that the movie be sent out to all of the theaters. The final sermon in the movie, which took place in a bombed-out church, was used for inspiration as well as propaganda. "This is not only a war of soldiers in uniform. It is a war of the people—of all the people—and it must be fought not only on the battlefield but in the cities and in the villages, in the factories, on the farms and in the homes, and in the heart of every man, woman, and child who loves freedom." *Look* magazine reprinted the quote, and Winston Churchill sent a wire to Louis B. Mayer that read, "*Mrs. Miniver* is propaganda worth one hundred battleships."[3]

Hollywood was happy to propagandize, if it would help to defeat the enemy. Charlie Chaplin's 1940 film *The Great Dictator* was an anti-Nazi flick. In 1942 *The Battle of Midway* showed the progress made in the war against Japan, and in 1944 *The Memphis Belle* highlighted a bombing mission over Nazi Germany. Call these kinds of films propaganda if you want, but folks in Tinseltown knew they were positive films for our side.

Hollywood continued to jump in with both feet to assist. Some of the feet turned out to be webbed. In 1943 Donald Duck appeared in a film, *Der Fuhrer's Face,* as an irreverent German soldier duck. Bugs Bunny did his part when he dressed up as Emperor Hirohito and peddled war bonds. The cartoon rabbit also disguised himself as Hitler in *Herr Meets the Hare.* And in 1943 a full-length animated movie called *Victory Through Air Power* was released by Walt Disney.[4]

Yes, Hollywood was a huge player in the war efforts of World War II. But its role in the war on terror is a different story altogether.

Hollywood and 9/11

At first Hollywood didn't really know how to react to the tragedy of September 11, so it fell back on its pattern of holding charity events. In the aftermath of 9/11, most Americans wanted to focus on the real people, particularly the rescue workers who were lost. We're talking about men and women of courage who ran toward the devastation to try and save others, only to lose their own lives in the process.

Maybe the Hollywood decision makers went into a state of confusion, but after September 11 they began pulling products off the shelves. *Pearl Harbor* and *Swordfish* were taken out of the theaters. Arnold Schwarzenegger's film *Collateral Damage* was put on hold indefinitely. The ending of *Men in Black II* was changed because some of the scenes had been shot at the World Trade Center. Jackie Chan's film *Nose Bleed* was halted. And a project called *Flight Plan* was tossed aside.

In the last quarter of the year 2000, there were 68 films in production in Tinseltown. After September 11, there were only

16. Initially, almost anything that had extreme violence, showed large buildings exploding, or had any kind of aircraft in it was delayed. A Jennifer Lopez movie called *Tick Tock,* an Anthony Hopkins film called *Bad Company,* and a Steven Spielberg film known as *Time Machine* were all put on hold. Late-night comedy shows were canceled, and current events–type humor was temporarily yanked off the air.

November 2001 brought President Bush's advisors out to Los Angeles. They came for a meeting with the most important executives in Hollywood. Their purpose was to ask the question, How can Hollywood help to swing the American people and the world public behind the efforts in the war on terrorism?

Jack Valenti, president of the Motion Picture Association of America, described the gathering as a "high powered crowd, top people from top companies." Sumner Redstone of Viacom and Rupert Murdoch, chairman and chief of News Corp., were in attendance. The meeting at the Peninsula Hotel in Beverly Hills lasted 90 minutes. Bush's political strategist, Karl Rove, brought a PowerPoint presentation on the history and reach of Osama bin Laden's terrorist network.

But when Rove arrived in Los Angeles for the meeting with the studio chiefs, Hollywood wasn't exactly thinking about patriotism. Instead, the trade papers were filled with concern. They wondered whether Hollywood would be forced to participate in propaganda. Filmmakers were walking on eggs, trying their best not to use the "P" word in figuring out what they could do to help. They used words like "communicate," "educate," and "inspire."

What came out of the meeting was a group called Hollywood 9/11. There was talk about making documentaries and public service announcements to help in the war on terror. Muhammad Ali was even brought on board as a kind of a salesperson who would explain America, and the war on terror, to the Muslim world.

Still, there was a strong scent of caution in the air about offending Hollywood sensibilities. The Motion Picture Association of America was the organization supervising Hollywood 9/11. Valenti, MPAA president, said that one of the big areas they wanted to get involved in was making "it clear to millions of Muslims in the world that this is not an attack on Muslims. This is an attack on people who murder innocent people."

Valenti suggested public service broadcasts could emphasize that "America has been the most generous country in the world. We have fed and clothed millions of people without asking anything in return."

Although the meeting ended up drawing attention from industry observers all over the news media, about three months afterward nothing much had happened. Some patriotic public service announcements had played in theaters. Some stars like George Clooney, Brad Pitt, and Jennifer Lopez had visited troops overseas. And military bases and aircraft carriers got some free films.

The spirit of support that was evident immediately after 9/11 seemed to have died down, and concrete projects failed to materialize. "Expectations were raised that something big was supposed to happen," said Bryce Zabel, president of the Television Academy of Arts and Sciences. Zabel said that, in reality, it didn't take place.

Sources say the reason more didn't happen was because Hollywood wanted to avoid the impression that the White House was controlling things in any way. It's the "C" word, *content*. According to Zabel, "Everyone was bending over backwards to make sure that content was off the table."

Valenti even remarked that Hollywood 9/11 was "trying not to be the poodle of the White House."[5]

In the November 13, 2001, edition of *Newsday*, columnist Robert Reno called Hollywood 9/11, and its mission, a "World

War II–style propaganda offensive." It's strange that modern-day Hollywood would be concerned about propaganda, when it's the one responsible for shows like *The West Wing* or films like *The American President*.

Apparently, the Hollywood of today has more enthusiasm for politically correct programming than it does for making films that might help out in the war on terror. With the emphasis being on diversity and multiculturalism, patriotism appears to be the odd man out. There's almost an aversion to any overt sign of patriotism in Tinseltown, which carping about the government, knocking the administration, and blaming the United States have all but replaced.

> There's almost an aversion to any overt sign of patriotism in Tinseltown, which carping about the government, knocking the administration, and blaming the United States have all but replaced. In contrast to what we saw during World War II, all that can be said is, This sure ain't your daddy's Hollywood.

There's a loop of anti-American rhetoric that seems to play endlessly in Hollywood. America is racist. America is sexist. America had slaves. America displaced Native Americans. America is greedy. America is wasteful. America is uncaring. America is imperialistic. Blah, blah, blah.

In contrast to what we saw during World War II, all that can be said is, This sure ain't your daddy's Hollywood.

Hollywood Battleground

As September 11 became more and more of a distant memory, Hollywood began to speak out. But as the one-year mark passed in September 2002, and the Bush administration moved toward the invasion of Iraq, the Hollywood anti-war crowd became seriously emboldened.

We started hearing from a lot of the same names that had spoken out politically before, but the rhetoric was becoming a lot more shrill. Stars like Whoopi Goldberg, Danny Glover, Harry Belafonte, Ed Asner, Oliver Stone, Jane Fonda, Mike Farrell, Martin Sheen, Sheryl Crow, Steven Spielberg, Tom Cruise, Susan Sarandon, Tim Robbins, Woody Harrelson, Woody Allen, Dustin Hoffman, Jessica Lange, Sean Penn, Barbra Streisand, the Dixie Chicks, Madonna, George Clooney, Janeane Garofalo, and, of course, Michael Moore, had to let the whole world know just what they thought of the Bush administration and of the war on terror.

Whoops, There She Is

Comedienne-actress Whoopi Goldberg, who said that she supported the administration's war on terror, added that Bush should "finish that job." She also equated the morals of the terrorists, and those of a lunatic dictator, with the ones of sleazy business execs.

In October 2002, while appearing on CNBC's *After Hours,* Whoopi said, "It's kind of frightening, the arrogance with which this has gone down. And, you know, people really trusted and wanted the best and wanted the best for the country only to turn around and see corporate terrorists—because I think these guys are much the same as Saddam. I think they're just as horrific and in terms of, literally, destroying people's lives on a daily basis." Is she saying we're supposed to forget about the spies that look like Osama and be on the lookout for the guys in the Brooks Brothers suits?

Banana-Boat Belafonte and Glover Duck-and-Cover

Harry Belafonte and Danny Glover decided to take a shot at some anti-war repartee. Belafonte's and Glover's comments were reported by Radio Havana. Both were in Havana, Cuba, attending a film festival.

The actors theorized that there was an ongoing effort by Bush and Co. to promote the administration's war machine. They said that because Hollywood is controlled by large corporations, war movies and violent films are shaped by the "interests of the Pentagon and the White House."

Belafonte, who apparently thinks Fidel Castro is fantastico, told the press that September 11 gave President Bush an excuse to implement plans "to control the world militarily, economically and culturally." Looks like Belafonte and Glover were trying to bring back the tradition of Beavis and Butthead.

On another occasion, Belafonte decided to take some of his frustration out on Secretary of State Colin Powell. While on a radio talk show in San Diego, Belafonte said, "In the days of slavery, there were those slaves who lived on the plantation and [there] were those slaves that lived in the house. Colin Powell's committed to come into the house of the master. When Colin Powell dares to suggest something other than what the master wants to hear, he will be turned back out to pasture."

Powell spokesman Richard Boucher told the *Washington Post* that the secretary of state's first reaction upon hearing Belafonte's diatribe was to smile. Powell quipped that the IRS and his accountant both "thought he did better as a field hand."

Showing the class associated with his office, the most powerful black officeholder in American history responded to calypso singer Belafonte's slur on CNN's *Larry King Live:* "If Harry had wanted to attack my politics, that was fine. If he wanted to attack a particular position I hold, that was fine. But to use a slave reference, I think, is unfortunate and is a throwback to another time and another place that I wish Harry had thought twice about using." Do you think it's about time Belafonte came out of his masters' house? Marx, Lenin, and Stalin's, that is.

It's hard to believe Glover was Mel Gibson's partner. On the eve of the first anniversary of September 11, the guy went out and told an audience at the University of Arkansas that terrorism should be fought with dialogue, not war. In his speech, Glover cited poverty as a cause of terrorism and cautioned America not to "govern by anger." The actor apparently doesn't know about the net worth of Osama and his terrorist friends.

In Glover's opinion, the post–September 11 era is a time to reflect on the United States' "over-consumption." He believes that "we're taking a terrible toll on this planet."

Someone ought to remind whoever's listening to this garbage that Glover is the same guy who made millions of dollars, courtesy of some anger-ridden movies called *Lethal Weapon 1, 2, 3,* and *4.* This apparently gives him the right to shoot his mouth off without thinking.

Lou Rant

Perennial activist Ed Asner jumped in the spotlight to give his foreign policy directives. "It's scary, outrageous, the things that are committed in the name of U.S. blood lust. They actually talk about Iraq attacking the U.S. And 55% of the American people now support Bush. How stupid is that? It drives me nuts."

Asner's not one to sit back and let others have all the fun slamming America. He staged a full-on tirade of his own. It seems that Asner has better sources at his disposal than the U.S., the U.K., and Israel combined. Appearing on CNN, the former sitcom journalist gave his assessment on a potential nuclear threat from Iraq. "I think that the idea of Iraq being a nuclear threat is poppycock," Asner said, being careful to use the technically appropriate word. "And if they are a nuclear threat, then they'd have to borrow atomic bombs from Israel."

The stalwart leftist actor explained that America's interest in deposing Saddam was merely because the dictator is a person of color. "There's total Islamic fascism. I also think that there is a strong streak of racism, and whenever we engage in foreign adventures. Our whole history in regime change has been of people of different color." Shouldn't someone tell Asner that his ideas, kind of like his communication skills, seem to be, uh, what's the term? Oh yeah, *poppycock*.

100 Hollywood Half-Wits

In late 2002, packs of protestors for peace came out of the woodwork with Hollywood ready, willing, and able to front for them. Not in Our Name was a group that held gatherings and placed newspaper ads. The typical language used was "Resist the war and repression that has been loosed on the world by the Bush administration." Oliver Stone, Jane Fonda, Susan Sarandon, Danny Glover, Ed Asner, and many others seemed delighted to be part of the gang who couldn't salute straight.

A hundred Hollywood celebrities even signed a letter to President Bush about U.S. military intervention in Iraq. Of course, in Tinseltown, everything's a production. Even the jotting of a celebrity note involves lights, cameras, and action.

To trumpet their little piece of presidential correspondence, the stars called a press conference. The media dutifully showed up. Many of the celebs involved were on Hollywood's list of "B" actors. The collection of characters unveiled a new organization. They thought they'd come up with a clever name for the group—Artists United to Win Without War. The only problem was the acronym, AUWWW, made them sound like a bunch of three-year-olds who'd stubbed their toes.

The letter to the president said that "Saddam Hussein cannot be allowed to possess weapons of mass destruction." But it also stated, "There is no need for war. Let us instead devote our resources to improving the security and well-being of people here at home and around the world." Just makes you want to say "AUWWW" all the more, doesn't it?

> The collection of characters unveiled a new organization. They thought they'd come up with a clever name for the group—Artists United to Win Without War. The only problem was the acronym, AUWWW, made them sound like a bunch of three-year-olds who'd stubbed their toes.

Co-chairs Mike Farrell and Robert Greenwald hit the radio and TV talk-show circuit and filled the airwaves with their harebrained attempts at geopolitics.

So why did the Bush administration need to hang a military threat over the head of Saddam Hussein? Well, faux *West Wing* president Martin Sheen seems to have it all figured out. "I think he'd like to hand his father Saddam Hussein's head and win his approval for what happened after the 1991 Gulf War," Sheen speculated. Apparently, the actor's a faux shrink, too.

This may be just another example of a Hollywood celebrity spouting off, but the implication is truly monstrous—that the president, along with Cheney, Rumsfeld, Rice, Powell, and others, would sacrifice human life for petty pride. Strange how the haughty hundred didn't seem to have anything to say when Serbia was bombed into the Stone Age and Iraq was mottled with "Monica" bombs.

Bowling for Big Bucks

Michael Moore reportedly sent out e-mails to his fans stating that the best way to protest the president's plans for war on Iraq was to see his latest movie, *Bowling for Columbine*. "Dear friends, fans, and fellow evildoers," the e-mail began. The movie is "the last thing the Bushies want projected on the movie screens across America." Entrepreneurial little radical, isn't he?

Cackling Crow

These were the words of Sheryl Crow as she introduced patriotic country singer Toby Keith during the 2003 American Music Awards: "Hey everybody, I know this is an award show but I just want to encourage everybody to get involved in some kind of movement for peace."

Crow was wearing a specially made T-shirt that bore the slogan "War is not the answer."

The singer later told the press, "I think war is based in greed and there are huge karmic retributions that will follow. I think war is never the answer to solving any problems. The best way to solve problems is to not have enemies." Wonder if in her next life Crow will come back as Xena the Warrior Princess.

Hem and Haw

While promoting the film *Minority Report,* Steven Spielberg and his collaborator, Tom Cruise, made some comments about Iraq, something along the lines of Iraqis would probably be better off without Saddam. This gave the press, and eventually the world, the sense that the two supported the Bush administration. After all, wasn't one of them the maker of *Saving Private Ryan* and the other the star of *Top Gun?*

But the powerful Hollywood peer pressure caused both Spielberg and Cruise to *clarify* matters. "I did not say I support a war with Iraq," Spielberg said in a statement issued by his production company, DreamWorks. "I do not have access to information that only the President has which might cause me to take a different position. In any case, it was never my intention to give an endorsement of any kind."

Separately, Cruise told an interviewer he had been misquoted in the statement that had him supporting a military incursion into Iraq. Guess the stars have to keep those invitations to the A-list cocktail parties coming in. The lesson to up-and-comers in the entertainment world—go left young man, or woman, whatever the case may be.

Princess of Prattle and Director of Drivel

Susan Sarandon has that way of transporting us back to the 1960s. She showed up at an anti-war protest. The handheld signs illustrated the level of intelligence present with phrases like "Bush Sucks." The mob of America haters waited intently for chief foreign policy expert Susan Sarandon to begin her speech.

The words flowed freely out of the left side of the actress's mouth. Sarandon condemned Bush for having "hijacked our losses and our fears." She told the adoring crowd that terrorism could not be fought with violence.

As the crowd yelled in approval, Sarandon proclaimed, "Let us hate war in all its forms, whether the weapon used is a missile or an airplane." Demonstrators chanted in lilting lockstep, "George Bush, you can't hide. We charge you with genocide." Makes you wonder how these 21st-century hippies are going to handle things when a red alert disrupts their next peace parade.

In 2002 Sarandon's guy-pal, Tim Robbins, accused President Bush of encouraging war with Iraq for mundane political reasons. "I'm against this whole, 'Let's bomb a new country because things aren't going our way,'" he said. Things must have really been going Clinton's way when Monica Lewinsky was testifying.

Sarandon and Robbins were in Scotland appearing in a play about the attacks of September 11. While speaking to the press about their roles in the production, somehow they got the notion it would be a good time to bash the United States and the war on terror.

Ananova reported that Sarandon offered a geopolitical analysis. "First you have to ask the right questions, and we haven't formed the right questions on what's going on in the world right now."

The actress also gave her perspective on the post–September 11 American attitude. She told a Scottish newspaper, "In about the third week, a cut-out of John Wayne showed up and a jingoist kind of thing started taking over, and nobody could ask questions anymore."

The seldom-restrained celebrity activist said that one of the constructive things about the attacks was how they gave our nation something in common with countries that have had terrorism committed against them. She claimed that she told her kids they have "joined the rest of the world now."

But the real clincher was when Sarandon uttered the words "You're so lucky in Ireland, England and Spain. Everyone there already knows what it's like to have inexplicable terrorist violence." Wonder if next Sarandon will suggest that for really good fortune, the U. S. might try engaging in some agonizing famine, wretched poverty, and an incurable disease or two.

Woodyheaded

Guess white men can jump—to conclusions, that is. In what seemed to be a rant on America and the world, Woody Harrelson published a freelance column in the left-leaning British newspaper the *Guardian*. The actor wrote, "I'm an American tired of American lies."

Harrelson characterized America's war on terror as a "racist and imperialist war" and described our leaders as "the warmongers who stole the White House." He claimed that the current occupants "have hijacked a nation's grief and turned it into a perpetual war on any non-white country they choose to describe as terrorist."

The guy must have had some amazing sources because he made the following claims: The CIA helped Saddam Hussein to power; Bush 41 kept Saddam supplied with nerve gas and technology even after he used it on Iran and the Kurds; and the economic sanctions against Iraq have caused the death of 500,000 children.

Harrelson went on to note that he would handle things a lot differently if he were in the White House. He would legalize drugs, cut defense spending in half, close all nuclear power plants, and provide fuel from wheat straw, rice straw, and hemp. Can't you just see a third political party forming around Harrelson's ideas? Too bad the jackass logo is already taken.

Woody Pile

Not to be outdone by Woody Harrelson, another famous Woody decided to chime in with his own attacks on our president while abroad. Director, actor, writer, and all-around basket case Woody Allen demonstrated his mastery of the subtleties of the English language while in Paris. According to the French newspaper *Journal du Dimanche,* Allen said that Bush had allowed America's post–September 11 goodwill to slip away, because the president "has no idea about anything."

Guess Woody's kind of an expert about having no idea about anything.

Allen went on to share his opinions about America's potential war with Iraq. "Like the majority of Americans, I think Bush has not advanced convincing reasons for war. So one has the disturbing impression that he is persisting for personal and political reasons." With questionable behavior and comments like these, Woody Allen's genius seems to have slipped away about the same time his sense of decency did.

Raging Rain Man

During an acceptance speech for the Empire Film Awards in the United Kingdom, Dustin Hoffman apparently thought it was the right time to launch a verbal missile at the president. Hoffman said that the Bush administration was "manipulating the grief of the country" after September 11.

He went on to say, "I think that's reprehensible . . . the President's real motives for going to war are power and oil." Anyone know if Hoffman's back in character and working on a sequel to *Rain Man?*

Poison Penn Pal

Sean Penn had to let the president of the United States, and the rest of the world, know just how simple the entire geopolitical situation really is. And he was apparently willing to shell out $56,000 for an ad in the *Washington Post* to do it.

In an open letter to the president, the star of *Fast Times at Ridgemont High* pleaded, "I beg you, help save America before yours is a legacy of shame and horror."

On good and evil, the former husband of Madonna opined, "I do not believe in a simplistic and inflammatory view of good and evil. I believe this is a big world full of men, women, and children who struggle to eat, to love, to work, to protect their families, their beliefs, and their dreams."

Even fans on the Left must have been scratching their heads as they read "You are a man of faith, but your saber is rattling the faith of many Americans in you." Raise your slice of pizza if you think the world might be better served if Penn kept his advice on weapons to himself and stuck with the bombs he knows best—his movies.

> Raise your slice of pizza if you think the world might be better served if Penn kept his advice on weapons to himself and stuck with the bombs he knows best—his movies.

Squealing Overseas

While over in Spain, Jessica Lange blubbered, "I hate Bush. I despise him and his entire administration. . . . It makes me feel ashamed to come from the United States—it is humiliating."

King Kong's main squeeze informed all of us that an attack on Iraq would be "unconstitutional, immoral and illegal."

After hearing this, a lot of Americans probably agreed with Lange on one point. They're ashamed she comes from the United States, too.

Typing Tirade

Barbra Streisand sent some misspelled and mistake-ridden instructions to then–Minority Leader Dick "Gebhardt," claiming that there was a Daddy Warbucks–type motive behind the war plans of the Bush administration. She informed "Gebhardt" that industries "run by big Republican donors and insiders, clearly have much to gain if we go to war against Iraq."

Between the typos and/or misspellings of "Gebhardt" and "Sadam," Streisand insisted that Richard Gephardt and his cohorts "get off the defensive and go on the offensive."

Babs handled the highly publicized gaffe by blaming an underling and bragged about being a former spelling bee champion. A Streisand "Truth Alert" from her Web site said, "A Republican/Conservative candidate . . . blatantly misquoted Barbra Streisand, fabricating outrageous quotes and completely misrepresenting Ms. Streisand's deep opposition to the Iranian dictator, Saddam Hussein." Iran, Iraq, hey, what's the difference? Guess if Babs were in charge of the military, there's no telling who might get hit with a cruise missile.

Besides providing a good laugh, the memo illustrated how far Hollywood's influence on politics has gone. In a response to the story, Gephardt spokesman Erik Smith told the *Washington Post,* "We take advice from many people. People who need people are the luckiest people in the world." Actually, it's more like political people who heed advice from Hollywood people have got to be the dopiest people in the world.

Dive-Bombing Dixie Chicks

What do you do when you're a red-hot bluegrass group in danger of losing airplay? Apologize fast. During a concert in London, Dixie Chicks lead singer Natalie Maines reportedly told an audience, "Just so you know, we're ashamed the president of the United States is from Texas."

Before you could say "Goodbye Earl," country stations across the U.S. started pulling the Chicks off their play lists. A few hundred protesters in Louisiana expressed their sentiments by crushing Dixie Chicks CDs with a tractor. And a Kansas City radio station held a "chicken toss" event, where the group's CDs and concert tickets were dumped into trash cans.

Maines attempted to explain her comments made abroad. She said, "We've been overseas for several weeks and have been reading and following the news accounts of our government's position. The anti-American sentiment that has unfolded here is astounding. While we support our troops, there is nothing more frightening than the notion of going to war with Iraq and the prospect of all the innocent lives that will be lost."

But apparently Maines couldn't resist adding that "the president is ignoring the opinions of many in the United States and alienating the rest of the world. My comments were made in frustration, and one of the privileges of being an American is you are free to voice your own point of view."

Maines did end up apologizing for her comments. She said, "As a concerned American citizen, I apologize to President Bush because my remark was disrespectful. I feel that whoever holds that office should be treated with the utmost respect." But then she and her sister Chicks started pecking away again, this time on home turf, and many of the group's fans took offense at the squawking.

So how did the Dixie Chicks try and reconcile with disaffected fans? They got naked on the cover of a magazine. Thank God for small favors—at least Michael Moore didn't go the same route. Did these country croonettes and/or their handlers really believe that devotees were going to flock back to the Chicks ranch just because they showed some skin? Well, apparently that was the plan.

Along with the buff strategy came a worried-faced Diane Sawyer and her fact-altering unreality show. On an April 24, 2003, ABC *Primetime Thursday* program, the Dixie Chicks paused, sighed, sobbed, and sniffled their way through a softball interview. Noticeably absent from the scene were any signs of contrition. What was evident in the patter, though, particularly on the part of Maines, was defiance. Her admissions were usually either qualified or countered by some further inappropriate pap.

She owned up to "wrong wording" but claimed that her erroneous message was made "with genuine emotion and questions and concern." At one point, Maines moaned, "Am I sorry that I asked questions and that I just don't follow? No."

But let's look at the actual sequence of events. Maines was on a concert stage. She was overseas in the U.K. Contrary to whatever she says was going on in her head, she didn't ask any questions during her performance. Instead, what the British audience heard on the eve of the war was a *statement* of her embarrassment that the U.S. commander in chief hailed from the same state that she did. Wrong time. Wrong place. Wrong words.

It's pretty clear that the lead chick is no fan of the president. Maines told Sawyer that she "felt there was a lack of compassion every time I saw Bush talking about this [the war]. . . ." And when asked whether she had anything to say to the president, the singer wisecracked, "Your show's not long enough."

Her statements seemed to emanate from that time-honored liberal value of ducking responsibility. The message the public got from Maines was that, no matter what, she was not going to change. She was not seeking forgiveness. She didn't think she needed it.

The Chicks seem to follow a familiar political pattern— moving from the half-cocked attitude to the scrambled explanation to the hurried apology to the naked ego.

Madonna's Legally Blonde Ambition

On an April 16, 2003, VH1 special, Madonna bellyached, "Anybody who has anything to say against the war or against the president or whatever—is punished, and that's not democracy—it's people being intolerant."

The P.T. Barnum of pop then gave a lesson on constitutional law, saying, "That's what our constitutional rights are supposed to be, that we all have freedom to express ourselves and to voice our dissent if we have that."

Yes, Madonna, there is such a thing as free speech. But there's also such a thing as the free market. And the rule is, in a free market, free expression has real consequences. Just ask John Rocker, Trent Lott, Al Campanis, Bill Maher, Jimmy "the Greek," Rick Santorum, Fuzzy Zoeller . . .

Commander Clooney

Apparently, the ex-*ER* doc did some serious blabbing when he was in Berlin. George Clooney went on a TV program and launched a little attack of his own. It seems that the actor decided to take on the role of military strategist.

Prior to the whopping success of Operation Iraqi Freedom, Clooney had some words of un-enlightenment for Defense Secretary Donald Rumsfeld. He said, "I believe he thinks this is a war that can be won, but there is no such thing anymore."

Clooney went on to offer his assessment of the U.S. armed forces, saying, "We can't beat anyone anymore."

Rumor has it that Clooney's gearing up to hit the motivational speaking circuit with Alanis Morissette. The seminars will incorporate the age-old French philosophy "Give It Up Now, You're Gonna Lose Anyway."

Garofalo Buffoonery

Next to the face of Martin Sheen, Janeane Garofalo's mug is the one often seen leading the Hollywood anti-war orchestra.

As reported on NewsMax.com, Garofalo came up with an explanation for why Hollywood never protested Bill Clinton's military adventures in Haiti, Iraq, and Yugoslavia. The comedienne quipped, "It wasn't very hip."

Echoing the views of Mike Farrell, Garofalo argued that anti-war celebrities were being targeted for their beliefs. Farrell apparently had told the *Hollywood Reporter* that he believed there was a backlash taking place. He also claimed that it was an "organized attempt by the right wing." He must have been having another Art Bell moment.

Garofalo put the blame on the media for creating the so-called backlash. She thought the media focused attention on Hollywood celebs to try and lessen the effectiveness of the appeasement movement.

Apparently, after witnessing the overwhelming reception that the Iraqi people gave the coalition forces, Garofalo still didn't feel any urge to apologize for her speech or her actions. According to NewsMax.com, she said, "I have nothing to apologize for." But back in March 2003 on *The O'Reilly Factor*, Mr. "No Spin Zone" himself asked Garofalo, "If you are wrong, all right, and if the United States—and they will, this is going to happen—goes in, liberates Iraq [with] people in the street, American flags, hugging our soldiers, all right, we find all kinds of bad, bad stuff, all right, in Iraq, you gonna apologize to George W. Bush?"

Garofalo replied, "I would be so willing to say, 'I'm sorry.' I hope to God that I can be made a buffoon of, that people will say, 'You were wrong. You were a fatalist.' And I will go to the White House on my knees on cut glass and say, 'Hey, you and Thomas Friedman were right. I shouldn't have doubted you.' But I think to think that is preposterous."

So far no one's spotted any Band-Aids on Garofalo's knees.

Moore Dumb Remarks

The nerve of the president to start a war just as Hollywood was about to host its most self-absorbed event of the year. Despite the heavy military distractions that were taking place on March 23, 2003, the 75th Annual Academy Awards show went on as scheduled. Things did have to be adjusted, though.

Peter Jennings had the job of interrupting the festivities with regular Operation Iraqi Freedom updates. The anchor was careful to include a bit of the old French blasé for "balance."

Oscar organizers were concerned about celebs engaging in excessive Bush-bashing, since plenty of it had occurred the day before at the Independent Spirit Awards. Dubious documentary filmmaker Michael Moore sported a badge that read, "Shoot movies, not Iraqis." Moore may have been going through a dress rehearsal for what could easily have been called "the acceptance speech from hell." Even though the Academy had let it be known political speeches were verboten, Michael Moore's massively inflated ego seemed to get the better of him.

Maybe the guy had a little too much French wine on his way over. Or maybe the tuxedo just threw him off his game. Whatever the case, Michael Moore apparently thought his mindless rant would be accepted by the Hollywood glitterati. He was wrong.

Maybe the guy had a little too much French wine on his way over. Or maybe the tuxedo just threw him off his game. Whatever the case, the filmmaker apparently thought his mindless rant would be accepted by the Hollywood glitterati. He was wrong.

Upon cinching the Award for Best Documentary, Moore walked confidently up to the podium and said, "I've invited my fellow documentary nominees on the stage with us. . . they're here in solidarity with me because we like nonfiction. We like nonfiction and we live in fictitious times."

Moore continued, "We live in a time where we have fictitious election results that elects a fictitious president. We live in a time where we have a man sending us to war for fictitious reasons. . . . We are against this war, Mr. Bush. Shame on you, Mr. Bush. Shame on you and any time you've got the Pope and the Dixie Chicks against you, your time is up."

Although the word "shame" is obviously part of Moore's personal lexicon, one had to wonder whether it had ever been part of his own emotional repertoire. If it hadn't been, that condition may have changed after he watched the replay. Almost immediately after the words "fictitious president" dribbled off Michael Moore's lips, the Oscar winner was hit with something that he most likely never expected to hear from a Tinseltown crowd. The *"No!"* *"Boo!"* and *"Hiss"* shouts that came at him were so loud that the cacophony nearly drowned out any applause. What the cries of disapproval didn't take care of, the music summarily did. Graciously, the orchestra spared the public any Moore pap and cut off the juvenile outburst.

Judging by the look on his face, Moore was surprised by the response. As he was shuffled off backstage, he undoubtedly was trying to figure out how things had gone so awry.

Steve Martin then proceeded to downsize Moore. Martin was able to spotlight Moore's hyper-hypocrisy with a devastating one-liner. The lightning-quick host said, "Oh, it was so sweet backstage . . . you should see it. The Teamsters are helping Michael Moore into the trunk of his limo." As the audience let loose with a burst of laughter and applauded with approval, it was the hope of many that some Teamsters would act on the first-rate idea.

Following the Awards show, Moore seemed to snap into heavy-duty damage control mode. The accidental Academy Award winner tried to use figures of authority to justify the lack of class, wisdom, and decency that was on display during his acceptance speech. Wielding the name of the president of the Motion Picture Association of America, Inc., Moore said, "Jack Valenti told me backstage afterwards that he wouldn't have expected any less."

In an editorial published in the March 27, 2003, edition of the *Los Angeles Times*, Moore touted his attendance at a Roman Catholic Mass indicating "that is where I found myself this past Sunday morning, at the Church of the Good Shepherd on Santa Monica Boulevard, at Mass with my sister and my dad."

Believe it or not, Moore also invoked the name of the Pope. At the same time, he seemed to lend support to an anti-Catholic position on abortion. The docu-fictionary maker wrote, "The majority of Americans, according to polls, want stronger environmental laws, support *Roe vs. Wade* and did not want to go into this war without the backing of the United Nations and all of our allies."

But the biggest spin of all came in the form of a claim by Moore that the reason the boos were so loud at the Oscars was because "the majority in the balcony—who were in support of my remarks—started booing the booers."

It makes one wonder how the supposed champion of the working man happened to stumble on the one Catholic Church that's located smack dab in the middle of Beverly Hills 90210.

Neocinematic Warfare

On March 2, 2002, Fox News Channel's *The Beltway Boys* did an interview with Hollywood writer-filmmaker Lionel Chetwynd. Mort Kondracke asked Chetwynd whether September 11 had returned Hollywood to a World War II mind-set.

Chetwynd responded, "Well, yes, certainly they cheered the war effort. The mind-set of World War II is a little more difficult. Since the 1960s there's been a kind of an incipient underpinning in the community that unless you are critical of your country, almost to the point at times of ridiculing institutions like the CIA and the FBI, then you are not fulfilling your duty as an artist."

Fred Barnes questioned Chetwynd about the movie *Collateral Damage*. In the film, the villains are depicted as a group of terrorists, but the U.S. government is also shown to be at fault for the deaths of women and children.

Chetwynd commented on the film by bringing up another example—Robert Redford's *Spy Game*. "That may have seemed like harmless fun before 9/11, or—now I think we realize that throughout many parts of the world, these kind of things are taken as gospel truth . . . demonstrations that, that we are a corrupt people."

Spy Game is set in Beirut. In the movie, our people set off car bombs. The implication is that the CIA's out of control. Chetwynd appropriately admonished Hollywood by saying, "I think there's a greater sense now that we should be circumspect about how we present our government."

But Hollywood can't seem to help itself. It's obsessed with portraying the military in a negative light. Take the movie *Courage Under Fire*. It featured cowardice on the battlefield. George Clooney's *Three Kings* showed soldiers attempting theft. And *The Thin Red Line* was hostile toward the armed services.

The attitude that liberals display toward the military is at times just plain bizarre. When *Saving Private Ryan* was released, Steven Spielberg gave an interview where he talked about World War II. "I think it is the key—the turning point of the entire century. It was as simple as this: the century was either going to produce the baby boomers or it was not going to produce the baby boomers. World War II allowed my generation to exist."

So let's see. When we think about World War II, the most prominent thing that should come to mind is not fighting the Nazis. It's not working to crush an evil despot. It's not preserving liberty for our children and grandchildren. It's producing *BABY BOOMERS!* How weird is that? Spielberg gives a whole new dimension to the word *egocentric*. Maybe that was the hidden message in *A.I.*

Hollywood wasn't exactly economically enriched from the war films that were supposed to ride the wave of post–September 11 sentiment. Bruce Willis's *Hart's War* and Nicholas Cage's *Wind Talkers* had so-so numbers. Mel Gibson's Vietnam War movie, *We Were Soldiers,* did a little better, but it didn't come close to typical Mel Gibson numbers.

Hollywood sometimes has difficulty with the truth. It is, after all, a bastion of political correctness, and we all know what that means. Truth gets put through the heavy-duty wash cycle and comes out looking faded in color and five times smaller.

PC Villains

Basically, Hollywood is neurotic about stepping on multicultural toes. This is especially true when it comes to representing bad guys. Oh, it's perfectly fine to have TV and movie fiends who are white. But if they're of a minority persuasion, it makes Tinseltown very, very uncomfortable. Hollywood has even gone as far as postponing the release of a movie when the film has featured terrorists or villains who actually resemble real-life ones. So how is Hollywood dealing with this dilemma?

Well, it's been sort of sidestepping the issue. In the 1996 film *The Rock,* the bad guys were American military renegades. In the 1997 film *Con Air,* creative heads used an airplane full of whacked-out escaped prisoners to convey evil. And in the 1998 film *Die Hard,* the beasts were made up of European ex-terrorists who became international thieves.

Hollywood hypersensitivity to ethnic groups, though, is having an impact on the projects themselves. In 1998 a prophetic film called *The Siege* was released. The reaction to the film surprised longtime Hollywood dweller and director Ed Zwick.

I got to meet and talk with Zwick when we appeared together on a TV show. The two of us had a chance to talk about *The Siege.*

The movie featured Denzel Washington, who plays a top FBI counter-terrorism agent who has to deal with a terrorist attack in New York City. Annette Bening plays a CIA agent and Islamic specialist. And Bruce Willis plays a sort of quirky army general who ends up imposing martial law.

Zwick's film is thoughtful and, as it turns out, visionary. He himself describes it as "a cautionary tale." It's possible that if members of the U.S. intelligence community had had the opportunity to watch the film prior to 9/11, it may have served as a useful harbinger.

Hollywood often uses the ethnically equivalent good-guy sidekick technique. This is where the main character's closest companion is of the same ethnic background as the bad guys they're after. We saw the technique used in the TV series *The Untouchables,* where Elliot Ness's trusted pal was an Italian-American. We saw it even farther back with the Lone Ranger, who always seemed to have his Native American buddy, Tonto, at his side.

Well, the sidekick technique was used in *The Siege.* The villains in the film were militant Muslims, so Denzel Washington's character routinely had his indispensable Arab-American friend at his side, who was played by Tony Shalhoub.

Shalhoub told CNN that as an Arab-American, the role was an unusual one. "I have never seen a role like this of an Arab-American that's seen in such a positive light—a really well-rounded character with a sense of humor, a professional life, a family life," Shalhoub said. "Not a goodie-goodie—a person who has his flaws and his shortcomings—but a real character, not a stereotype."

But the positive character wasn't enough to please everyone. After all, the movie still showed Arab Muslims blowing up New York City and killing innocent people. Zwick tried to explain that he wasn't trying to malign either Arabs or the Islamic faith. Rather, he was using actual events to tell a cinematic tale. "There have been bombings by extremists," Zwick said. "They are not representative of Islam. They're not representative of the vast majority of people who love this country, but nonetheless, they exist. The response to that is what I am interested in."

Zwick was taken aback by the anger and the charges of racism the film generated from the Arab-American and Muslim communities. He first found out about the flak when there were only a few weeks of filming left. He received a letter from the Council on American-Islamic Relations (CAIR) asking for a meeting.

Zwick accommodated the request. He tried to listen to the concerns that were reasonable, like those that had to do with the portrayal of Islam in the film. But then he was asked to change the premise of the movie. He refused. So CAIR held an official protest of the film. The protesters wrongfully accused Zwick of stereotyping Arabs and Muslims. After 9/11 Zwick was completely vindicated.

A similar brouhaha took place when the film *True Lies* was released. The film was attacked as unfair by the same groups you'd expect. *True Lies* was directed by James Cameron and starred Arnold Schwarzenegger and Jamie Lee Curtis. The character of Harry Tasker, an agent for an ultrasecret organization known as the Omega Agency, was played by Arnold. Tasker's job was to stop some Arab terrorists from launching a massive nuclear attack against the United States.

The fact that the flick was comedic in nature didn't stop the negative charges from flying. PC police called the film "racist." Having movie rascals with ethnicities that resemble any historical reality other than white was unacceptable. It violated the industry's handbook of cinematic redress.

In April 2002 Hollywood got its boxers in a twist at an episode of the CBS series *JAG*. It's the one that showed an al-Qaeda leader who had been captured, brought before a military tribunal, and charged with planning the September 11 attacks.

In the episode, a hearing took place inside an aircraft carrier. Arguments involved the Fifth Amendment and whether a confession that had been yanked out of a suspect would be admissible in court. The producers of the series said that they wanted to show how military tribunals could offer fair justice to terrorist suspects. But Hollywood was concerned that the Pentagon had controlled the episode. The Pentagon confirmed that they had seen scripts and "weighed in on them."

Creator and executive producer of *JAG*, Donald Bellisario, happens to be a former Marine. He stated, "Personally, I think they [the terrorists] should all be taken out and blown up." Someone ought to work with Bellisario and try and get him to say what he really feels.

The Hollywood elite and their media chums were apparently displeased that the producers of *JAG* furnished the scriptwriters with a detailed account of how military tribunals would operate. The thing that probably bugged them the most is that they didn't get to the information first. They ended up coming down with a bad case of intelligence envy.

By the summer of 2002, Hollywood thought that enough time had passed for the public to be ready for a Tom Clancy movie. It chose *The Sum of All Fears*. Clancy had actually written the book in 1991, and the plot involved terrorism. In Clancy's original version, the bad guys were militant Muslim terrorists. Apparently, the ethnicity of the characters made the PC media moguls sort of squeamish. Things ended up being adjusted, so to speak, and the villains emerged as neo-Nazis instead.

In the flick, a neo-fascist group buys a nuclear weapon from a South African man. The villainous leader of the group is a wealthy neo-Nazi who wants to start a nuclear war between the United States and Russia. Eventually, the neo-fascists detonate a nuclear bomb in Baltimore during the Super Bowl. The U. S. suspects that Russia is responsible, so America decides to attack Russia with nuclear weapons, and a countdown begins.

The hero, CIA agent Jack Ryan, is able to communicate with the Russian president and talk him into stopping his plans to launch a nuclear strike. The American president is so moved by the turn of events, he stops his nuclear plans as well. The movie ends with the perfect liberal Hollywood conclusion—the leaders of the two countries sign an arms control agreement.

On *The Sum of All Fears* DVD, director Phil Alden Robinson tries to justify his decision to substitute white European terrorists into the film adaptation of the book. He says, "I had less than two hours of screen time to tell a story, and I couldn't put together such a complex group of villains."

Robinson remarks, "We needed a villainous conspiracy that was very quickly and easily understood. It couldn't just be Arabs." Oh, yeah, after 9/11 that would be way too hard a sell.

The director continues on. He says, "I know that a lot of people will assume that this was all because of political correctness, and we didn't want to offend Arabs. It really wasn't. It had to do with the needs of the plot." Translation: We really didn't want to offend Arabs.

Author Tom Clancy made his opinion clear, though, during a commentary on the DVD. While the chief neo-Nazi terrorist invokes the name of Hitler as inspiration for his diabolical plan, you can hear Clancy quip, "Does anyone really believe this except Hollywood?"

In February 2002 the ABC network announced that it was coming out with a Pentagon-approved reality show. The program was based on the premise that it would follow U.S. troops around the world, observing them in action in the war on terror. The show was called *Profiles from the Front Line* and aired in the summer. One of the show's producers was Jerry Bruckheimer, who also brought us *Pearl Harbor* and *Blackhawk Down*.

Apparently, public sentiment had changed enough by December 2002, though, that the *Hollywood Reporter* said the series had "hit a snag." ABC had to cut down its order from 13 one-hour episodes to six. But eventually executives gave the green light for the episodes to begin airing in the second half of the season.[6]

Reportedly, Dan Rather and other journalists whined that Bruckheimer and his associates were getting better access to the Pentagon than reporters covering the war on terror were.

Unfortunately, as the memory of 9/11 softens with the passage of time, we see that the anti-war rhetoric coming out of Hollywood becomes more harsh. Tom Clancy put things back in the proper perspective when he appeared on the Fox News Channel's *Hannity & Colmes* on February 8, 2002.

In response to a question from Sean Hannity, which referred to the relationship between our freedom and the military, Clancy said, "Well, the reason we have the ability to read the newspapers and watch all the TV we want and go to the church of our choice is that those rights have been won for us by people carrying guns and wearing uniforms. It's really that simple." He added, "For that reason we ought to show a little respect for them once in awhile."

Amen to that.

The Ultimate PC TV Show

Meet Maria Liu-Flanagan. She's a Mexican-American Asian gal whose husband is a blind African-American Irish tenor named Patrick.

Patrick lost his sight while visiting his ancestral homeland of Belfast, when a militant who had been ousted from the Irish Republican Army threw horse manure laced with drain cleaner in his face, because he thought the thin, fastidiously groomed, smartly dressed redhead was gay.

Maria and Patrick live in an integrated urban village. They have four children: one set of twins whose arrival was carefully timed with the assistance of Planned Parenthood, and a brother and sister combo who were adopted from the Ivory Coast. They live in an environmentally friendly HUD house, ride bicycles to work, and have a hybrid car parked in the garage for use in emergencies.

The Liu-Flanagans grow their own organic vegetables on a co-op farm that's run by reformed gang member Poochy

Running-water. Weekends are spent with neighbors, organizing rallies and hosting 5K fun-runs to fight tobacco giants,
fast-food chains, and big oil companies. But the most important moments of the week are dedicated to keeping all of the
children in the local school district safe from the imminent
danger of the Christian Right.

Highlights of several upcoming episodes from this exciting
TV series include the following:

- The Liu-Flanagans' adopted daughter, Badger, begins
dating a young man who owns a firearm. Badger tells the
boy that she cannot continue the relationship until he
brings the evil piece of instrumentality over to the Annual Sharon Stone Cookies-for-Guns Bazaar.

- A relative of Maria and Patrick's next-door neighbor,
who had flown in from Kentucky for a visit, slips out
onto the patio to have a cigarette. Halfway through his
smoking break, the man is startled by the Anti-smoking
Swat Team, which surrounds him and carries him off in
handcuffs. The Liu-Flanagans called 9-1-1 to report the
incident because their secondhand smoke detector had
been triggered.

- Maria enters a charity fashion show and is looking forward to strutting down the runway in her homemade
pleather raincoat and boots. To his shock and horror,
Patrick hears that one of the other models in the show
plans to wear some alligator shoes that match the elbow
patches on her spring blazer. Patrick tells his son, Condor,
to quickly pogo-stick home and fetch the container of
fake pig's blood, which is stashed in the hallway closet.

- The Liu-Flanagans find out that a Chinese restaurant around the corner has failed to update its outmoded exhaust system. As a result, mu shu pork fumes have been wafting through the atmosphere and ruining the scent of Maria's freshly hung laundry. The EPA is called to the scene, and the restaurant is hit with a stink citation.

- The Liu-Flanagans' youngest child, Pollen, is in second grade. Pollen comes home and tells Maria that a classmate wore a T-shirt to school with the words "God Bless America" printed on it. Maria and Patrick call the ACLU for help. An emergency PTA meeting is held the next day to try and get the principal fired for not immediately insisting that the child go home and change.

- Patrick notices that a nearby mission doesn't list the contents of the free lunches it distributes to the needy in Braille. He files a complaint with a nonprofit public interest law firm, which in turn files a lawsuit on his behalf. Since the mission can't afford to make the necessary changes in its program, it closes down the charitable operation. Patrick takes the money he receives in damages and donates it to the Save the Roof Rat Foundation.

With values like these, anyone can see that the show is sure to be a hit. But if for some reason it doesn't work with the general public, the Hollywood honchos will say it was just ahead of its time. And they'll keep it on for multiple seasons anyway.

CHAPTER NINE

Celebrity Greenies

The Tinseltown crowd's gone green. We're not talking about the emerald shade that creeps up when someone else gets the lead in the *Harry Potter* sequel. Or the waxy pallor that sets in when a sitcom star compares his or her weekly monetary intake to that of *Friends*. It's that broccoli-colored hue of environmental mania that's taken over the minds and hearts of the hotshots in Hollywood.

There's nothing more satisfying for stars and starlets these days than when they stand up in public and champion the cause of the Earth. They preach to us about the urgency to address the environmental problems of polluted Perrier, a pot-holed ozone layer, and a global thermostat that's on the fritz. We can tell from the sounds of their voices and the looks on their faces that their hearts and souls are in the right place. It's just that their brains have turned into lime Jell-O.

Gang Green

When it comes to the environment, a lot of Hollywood activists are wearing leftist goggles. They hold a view on the environment that's embodied in the former veep Al Gore's cure for insomnia called *Earth in the Balance*. The thesis goes something like this:

A massive conspiracy exists between evil corporate types in the nation and their Republican buddies. These schemers hold secret meetings, where they sit around and dream up ways to get their stinking hands on every bit of the world's cash that they possibly can. While they hoard the wealth that's meant to be distributed equitably among all of the people—with the exception of the Democrats and the news and entertainment elite, who deserve to have gobs of money because they're the smartest people on the globe and know what's best for everyone else—they intentionally try and wreak havoc on the environment.

They're all right-wing capitalists who use code words like "free market" and "entrepreneurial spirit" to disguise their wicked intentions. Their long-range plan is to have all of the suckers who are not part of their cabal die of illnesses related to environmental poisoning. Then they'll use all of the dough that they stole from us to clean up the mess that's been created. And they'll live happily ever after without us.

The fear that results from belief in this conspiracy theory makes Hollywood greenies act a little nuts. They say and do ridiculous things, but they often don't realize they've made major fools of themselves until after they hear the audiotape or see the video footage. Then they're embarrassed, and so they either go into hiding for a little while or appear on *Larry King Live*.

Back in 1989 the Natural Resources Defense Council was able to convince CBS's *60 Minutes* to put on a program designed to scare approximately 40 million Americans out of their wits. The public was told that a chemical, which had been used on apples to control growth and add color, was a dangerous carcinogen.

> We can tell from the sounds of their voices and the looks on their faces that their hearts and souls are in the right place. It's just that their brains have turned into lime Jell-O.

Hollywood quickly jumped into the act. Meryl Streep went before Congress and talked about the terrible threat alar was to children. A celebrity warning of Streep magnitude, of course, caused political pressure to mount. Public schools started pulling apple juice bars and apple crumb cakes from cafeteria menus faster than the tweezing frenzy that occurred after the inexplicable hairy eyebrow phase was over.

In a 1995 piece in the *Smithsonian* magazine, John F. Ross called the *60 Minutes* program with the alar segment "perhaps the most dramatic example of erroneous public perception of unnatural and involuntary risk." He referred to it as a controversial report of "questionable science." That's another way of saying it was all a bunch of hooey.

The *Washington Post* reported that the levels of alar present in apples were lower than federal standards required. The *Post* also charged the media with exaggeration. The FDA, USDA, and EPA ended up issuing a joint statement assuring the public that apples were safe.[1]

In the same year, Democrat Congressman Henry Waxman, a U.S. representative with ties to the Hollywood community, introduced the Pesticide, Safety, and Right to Know Act. This legislation required that a warning label be placed on foods treated with potentially carcinogenic pesticides. But it also targeted pesticides that were considered safe. This waste of taxpayers' money occurred despite the fact that the findings on alar indicated a child would have to chow down 10 to 15 thousand apples per day for several years in order to be at risk, based on the amount of the stuff that's present in alar-treated apples.

There's been a whole host of health scares that the media have tried to create hysteria with. Back in the 1970s, there was a panic about red M&M's, causing them to be plucked out of the color mix because red dyes were believed to have a possible cancer link. It took several years before the little crimson discs returned and the media announced that they were as safe as any other lump of sugar.

Then there was the scare about power lines. Studies from the 1970s suggested that living near the lines might increase the risk of childhood cancer. Although the connection was never scientifically confirmed, the frightful talk created so much apprehension that we ended up having electric blankets tagged with warning messages for pregnant women. It took more than a decade to find out that there was no mysterious tie between wired blankies and childhood malignancies.

In the early 1980s, a study came out linking coffee drinking to pancreatic cancer. Suddenly, it was tea party time all over again in America, but, in this instance, the beverage wasn't limited to the Boston area. People all over the country were switching from java to the British brew. The disease connection later turned out to be a statistical screw up.

More recently, we heard stories about cell phones possibly being responsible for brain tumors. Although there's been no scientific evidence hooking the two together, rumors still saturate the airwaves.

And remember back in the 1990s when we learned how scary the substance that some dentists used to fill cavities was? Once again *60 Minutes* had a woman claiming she got rid of multiple sclerosis after she had her silver fillings pulled out. This caused a lot of people to contemplate using the old string on the doorknob technique with their teeth. Thankfully, the ADA, the World Health Organization, and the U.S. Public Health Service saved us all the discomfort. They concluded that there is zero risk from having silver fillings in your mouth, unless, of course, they're located in your front teeth and you're going in person to meet your Internet chat date.

It's not surprising that the environmental scaremongers want to preach doom and gloom with every fable they can concoct. Hey, it gets them a lot of press coverage, and, if they're lucky, there may even be a movie or two in it for them. Let's take a little trip down eco-disaster lane.

Eco-Baloney

Some of you may recall the frightening scenario about acid rain. And you may be wondering why you haven't heard too much about it lately. Well, in 1980 the EPA claimed that acid rain, which is caused by sulfur dioxide emissions, had increased the levels of acid in Northeast lakes by 100 times over the previous 40 years. It claimed the increase was killing fish and trees. And the National Research Council predicted that the number of lousy lakes would double by the year 1990.

Congress responded. When it reenacted the Clean Air Act, it cut sulfur dioxide emissions. But in 1987 research showed that the whole acid rain matter was a lie. And scientists found out that by applying lime to lakes that were acidic, the problem would be solved at a fraction of the cost of the Clean Air Act provisions. So how did environmentalists respond to all the good news? They quit talking about the issue.

Then there was that unforgettable scare about depletion of the ozone layer. That goblin seems to have vanished into thin air, too. In January 1992 a Harvard University chemist named James Anderson scared the heck out of the nation by warning of a hole in the ozone just above Santa Claus's home. It only took four months for Anderson to admit the dreaded ozone hole had never materialized.

Hollywood has almost unanimously embraced the latest environmental craze of global warming. The theory was first advanced in the 1890s and reemerged in the 1950s. In the 1970s global cooling theories came into vogue, and there was talk about a new Ice Age. Then we swung back to global warming conjectures again just for fun.

While we're on the subject of global warming, here's an intriguing recipe for a new flavor of ice cream. Blend one ice cream company run by first-class liberals and one rock band with a receptive front man. Add a double-crossing U.S. senator. What do you get? "One Sweet Whirled" dessert to fight global warming.

Apparently, Ben & Jerry's teamed up with the Dave Matthews Band and Senator Jim Jeffords to promote the frozen dairy treat. The confection's name is a takeoff of the band's single from the early 1990s called "One Sweet World." The group promoted the One Sweet Whirled campaign on one of its concert tours.

This wasn't the first time that the Dave Matthews Band was motivated to become socially active. The rockers previously initiated a program to encourage bicycle riding as an alternative form of transportation. The group donated $4,500 to Charlottesville, Virginia, to set up a bike program where, in theory, people could borrow bikes, use them, and return them to designated drop-off points. But the plan didn't exactly work. Bikes were scattered all over the place. Some were vandalized. Others were lost.

Now it seems as though we're seeing a similar lack of understanding of humans, and of nature. Guess some libs believe that if enough ice cream is distributed, the Earth will cool off. Yep, this kind of reasoning is just about as scientific as the global warming theories that are out there.

Guess some libs believe that if enough ice cream is distributed, the Earth will cool off. Yep, this kind of reasoning is just about as scientific as the global warming theories that are out there.

These kinds of doomsday predictions, which Al Gore and the various environmental organizations make regarding global warming, have actually been debunked. Even though continued emissions of "greenhouse gases" tend to aid the warming process, there's virtually no scientific evidence that says cutting back on emissions will stop a trend that appears to be natural. But you see, time-tested global warming horror stories bring in billions of dollars for environmental organizations. Why would anyone ever want to give up that kind of fund-raising power?

In reality, these types of groups look, smell, and operate exactly like the corporations they profess to loathe. They have CEOs who make huge salaries and receive tons of perks. They house their offices in high-rise buildings where they pay exorbitant rent. And they bring on a big old support staff so they can pay them hefty salaries, too.

Sometimes an average member of one of the high-profile environmental groups will pay a visit to an organization's headquarters. When the person does, he or she is usually in for a real shock. A fellow named Jack Shipley decided to visit the headquarters of the Wilderness Society. When he got there, he saw what looked to him like "a giant corporation." Shipley described the place that housed the Wilderness Society as "floor, after floor, after floor—just like Exxon or AT&T."

And about that Superfund legislation that was supposed to clean up toxic waste, the only people who cleaned up were a bunch of hungry attorneys.

In 1997 a newly elected Sierra Club board member named Chad Hansen attended a group-sponsored event that was held at one of San Francisco's glitziest hotels. The board member was stunned when he found himself sipping martinis in the penthouse of the Westin St. Francis. Hansen came up with a new name for the Sierra Club. He dubbed it "Club Sierra."

Environmental activism has become big business. Maybe it ought to be called Big Green for all of the money that's involved now. Annual salaries for environmental CEOs are well over $200,000. In 1997 one group fired a president and gave him a severance package of more than $760,000.

Competition for enviro-bucks is fierce, too. In 1999 the amount of cash flowing into the organizations was approximately $3.5 billion. That's a whole lot of eco-loot.[2]

To promote the religion of environmentalism—and pay homage to its deity, the almighty state—the news media along with allies like *60 Minutes, Nightline, 20/20,* and other infotainment programs interview Hollywood types because they're much more intriguing and telegenic. And besides, they draw a lot more viewers than boring scientists do.

As it turns out, much of what Tinseltown naively accepts as true is actually the result of deceptive practices, where the end justifies the half-baked means. In other cases, real concerns are just plain exaggerated, with the help of the media and the Hollywood mouthpieces.

What better way to create new, burdensome environmental restrictions than to get a whole bunch of celebrity Chicken Littles to shout, "The sky is falling!" So many catastrophes to choose from, so many dollars to rake in. Scary scenarios about polluted air, toxic topsoil, endangered species, vanishing wilderness, escalating crow's feet, and ballooning behinds can be used to get the attention of the public, and that of insecure politicians.

For 200 years population growth has been used to make people believe that a widespread famine and staggering death toll were in our immediate future. Paul Ehrlich put out a doomsday forecast in the 1970s. It was around the same time that a lot of so-called experts were predicting we'd be running out of natural resources at any moment. What do you know, they were *WRONG!*

Even though Hollywood seems to view Uncle Sam as being a kind of environmental savior, government hasn't done too well handling its own property. The feds have around 2 million acres of forests, but the government's so bad at managing the trees, it's lost money—our money. And about that Superfund legislation that was supposed to clean up toxic waste, the only people who cleaned up were a bunch of hungry attorneys.

The Hollywood Left loves to use environmentalism to argue for collective solutions, despite the fact that the free market offers better paths to take. Here's how the free marketplace really works:

> When goods become scarce, prices go up. When prices go up, people who are always looking for ways to make money become very interested in locating more of the

goods that people want. Libs call people like these money-grubbing capitalists, but noncommie and nonsocialist types call them entrepreneurs.

Sometimes entrepreneurs find ways to make substitute or synthetic versions of the products that are scarce. Or they might find ways that products can be used more efficiently than in the original manner. Then prices go down.

The free market tends to stop shortages from happening, too. Maybe *that's* why there were all those long lines in the Soviet Union.

Whether it's because of the ignorance about free market economics, the general disdain for businessmen and women, or some other wildly illogical reason, Hollywood lefties just seem to want to ignore private sector solutions, especially when it comes to the environment. Ideas like privatizing federal timber and rangeland, or establishing private property rights for water, are simply left out of their environmental hymnals.

Green Themes

Hollywood has had a long fascination with story lines that focus on environmental threats. There were early science fiction movies like *Them* (1954), where atomic testing in the Southwest causes ants to mutate into NBA-sized insects. The giant ants, in their search for a giant picnic, kill everyone in their path. The overgrown bugs finally die in the sewers of Los Angeles, presumably because residents of the town had eaten giant beans.

The year 1957 brought us *The Incredible Shrinking Man*. A cloud of radiation causes the lead character in the film to become diminutive. He starts out resembling Hulk Hogan and ends up looking like Ross Perot.

Baby boomers were raised on this kind of fare. This may help to explain why a number of those who weren't crazy about the idea of having to grow up moved to Hollywood to make message films instead.

Soylent Green brought the doomsday predictions about overpopulation to the big screen in 1973. The film illustrates what New York City will supposedly look like in the year 2022, if we fail to heed the warnings of anxiety-ridden liberals. In the movie, New York's an overcrowded place with horrible air and bad water, sort of the way it was before Rudy Giuliani was mayor. Everybody eats this food called soylent green that's supposed to be made from soybeans. Charlton Heston plays a cop who's investigating the death of a businessman. Heston's character finds out, much to his shock and the audience's horror, what soylent green is really made of. We can almost hear Barbra Streisand singing, "People, people who eat people. . . ."

In 1979 perennial lefty Jane Fonda starred with Michael Douglas and Jack Lemmon in *The China Syndrome.* In this flick, the usual evil corporate bad guys try to cover up an accident that takes place in a nuclear facility. Because of their incredibly huge lust for money, the villains want to get things running again so they don't lose big bucks. The movie turns out to be prophetic in a way. It was released just days before a real nuclear plant accident occurred in Pennsylvania at Three Mile Island. Fortunately, there were no giant ants or shrinking guys that resulted from either the film or the real-life incident.

In 1983 Meryl Streep took a break from her apple polishing to play the lead in the true story of Karen Silkwood. The movie, *Silkwood,* is a tale of someone who works in a nuclear plant, has concerns about worker safety, and ends up blowing the whistle on the joint. The character later dies under mysterious circumstances. The twist is that her death occurs just as she's on her way to meet a Bob Woodward–style reporter.

The 1998 film *A Civil Action* gives us an inside look into the sad state of litigation in the environmental field. It was produced by a trustee of the Natural Resources Defense Council named Robert Redford. Yes, we're talking about *the* Robert Redford.

The movie tells the story of a 1980s lawsuit that's filed against W. R. Grace and Beatrice Foods over water pollution. The icky water is thought to have contributed to the deaths of children. In the trial, the jury lets Beatrice Foods off the hook, but not W. R. Grace. W. R. Grace ends up settling for $8 million. The final legend of the film says this: "Fifteen years after Jimmy Henderson's death, the Massachusetts's Department of Health made it an official finding that the contaminants in the water were indeed responsible for causing leukemia in the children."

In reality, the icky water wasn't known as the cause of leukemia, and none of the victims had contact with the polluted sites. Redford accomplished what he wanted to, though— he furthered the green cause.

In the year 2000, Julia Roberts found a superstar vehicle in *Erin Brockovich*. The film features a twice-divorced, single soccer mom who discovers that a cover-up involving more icky water is going on in a local community. The water is creating weird illnesses among the town's residents. Brockovich is able to obtain the largest settlement ever paid in a lawsuit in U.S. history up to the time—more than $300 million. And she establishes a signature cleavage while she's at it.

In 2001 director Tim Burton must have been listening to a Joni Mitchell record when he did a remake of *Planet of the Apes*. The film takes place in the year 2029. A space station is hit by an electromagnetic storm, so the captain—as captains are inclined to do—sends out a genetically engineered chimpanzee in a little monkey rocket to check out the storm. The rocket and its hairy passenger are lost in the storm. The captain puts himself into another spaceship but, unfortunately, it crash-lands on a jungle planet.

Much like the original version of this film, the captain finds himself in the middle of a crowd of panicky humans. They're fleeing hunters that just happen to be apes. The captain gets captured and is sent to Ape City, where he's purchased by a young female ape. She, of course, is an ape who's a civil rights advocate that fights for "human" rights. The captain ends up working as a servant in the female ape's house. On the occasion of a dinner party, a poignant debate about the human race takes place. "We can't just keep throwing money at the problem," one of the apes spouts. But the heroine ape speaks out on behalf of humans. She says they should have equal rights, and she tells of her concerns about equality, environmentalism, justice, and animal rights. Anyone ready for a gorilla-sized barf bag?

When it comes to environmental manipulation, Hollywood wouldn't be so shortsighted as to leave out the kiddies. In September 1990 a show called *Captain Planet and the Planeteers* muscled its way into the minds of our little ones under the guise of a cartoon show. To call this an agenda-driven, politically correct piece of poop would be an understatement.

In the now-defunct show, Captain Planet is a being that possesses the powers of Earth, Fire, Wind, Water, and Heart. He uses his powers to stop other beings from messing with the environment. The characters in the episodes are always yakking about Gaia, the pagan spirit of the Earth. Any rational adult who's watching could easily get the impression that the whole thing is a veiled attempt to move kids away from traditional religion and into a New Age belief system. Funny thing, but Gaia's voice sounds an awful lot like Whoopi Goldberg.

Of course, the characters on the show come from all over the world and display the proper multicultural faces. But the most flawed kid in the bunch is the one from America. He's your typical, over-consuming ugly American who always seems to want food to satisfy his voracious appetite. And the names of villains are crafted to help vent some animosity toward the stereotypical environmental abuser. Children in the audience root for Captain Planet to kick the respective butts of eco-bad guys like Hoggish Greedily, Looten Plunder, Doctor Blight, and Verminous Skumm.

Do you remember hearing fans of the *Captain Planet* program sing the show's obnoxious ditty? It's the one that had you longing to hear the droning Barney classic. The anti-melodious aggravator went like this: "Captain Planet, he's our hero, gonna take pollution down to zero."

This contribution to the culture was the creation of the tried-and-true lefty Ted Turner. Turner also put together a Save the Earth Week extravaganza that included a special called "The Great Plains." The program turned everyday farmers into vicious exploiters of the land. Turner had a Save the Earth campaign on his TBS station that encouraged children to pressure their parents into supporting environmental causes. He also created a nonprofit organization called the Captain Planet Foundation, so he could continue his infiltration into our kids' psyches.

Captain Planet really gave voice and image to what appears to be inside a lot of Hollywood activists' heads. These birdbrains envision corrupt business execs yipping like nervous hyenas as they try and come up with new ways to dump oil into the ocean. Children who were unfortunate enough to watch *Captain Planet* learned that corporations are rotten to the core and are intentionally out to destroy the Earth.

Wouldn't it have been healthier to fill their little noggins with *Howdy Doody* reruns?

The Enviro-Media Lobby

There's a ritual that goes on in Hollywood that's similar to the one that takes place in the nation's capital each day. It's called lobbying.

Organizations truck on over to Washington, D.C., and meet with members of Congress to push for legislation that they think might serve their particular cause. Well, in Tinseltown, just like in D.C., "media lobbyists" hit the studio circuit and try to influence creative professionals in the TV, film, and music industries. And environmental advocates are right in there with the rest of them.

These green media lobbyists are well organized and extremely well financed. The Earth Communications Office is one of the more significant players. The group gave birth to the Environmental Media Association (EMA), which is frequently responsible for the eco-friendly messages you see in your favorite movies and TV shows.

You may be watching a particular show when, all of a sudden, out of the blue, environmental talk pops into the dialogue. It might sound something like this:

MARGE: Homer, what's this trash doing in the kitchen?

HOMER: I'm recycling pizza.

MARGE: You know you're not supposed to be eating that stuff. You're supposed to be exercising!

HOMER: No can do, Marge. I'm conserving energy.

If anyone wants to know how to lobby special interests in Hollywood, all they have to do is look at the way the EMA operates. It's laid out a virtual road map.

The EMA is actually the brainchild of three Hollywood leaders' wives. They were apparently tired of the usual charities, so in 1989 they started the organization in the hopes of transforming creative decision makers into environmental activists. They knew when they needed funds that a lot of celebs would be there to help.

For example, in 1990 the EMA and a group called the Rainforest Foundation needed some additional cash, so a few rock 'n' rollers came to their rescue. Sting, Bruce Springsteen, Paul Simon, Don Henley, and Bruce Hornsby all showed up to help. They raised a quick million dollars at a Beverly Hills bash. Hollywood luminaries in attendance included Ted Danson, Chevy Chase, Goldie Hawn, Billy Crystal, Norman Lear, and Don Johnson.

The group gives executives, producers, writers, and actors materials that highlight its environmental concerns. It holds briefings for writers and producers to advise them on how to slip environmental messages into a story line. Like the time it provided the underlying data that Michael Douglas's character in the film *The American President* used in his speech.

The EMA exists to encourage the entertainment industry to put green themes into its products. And in Hollywood, where self-adulation is practically one of the Ten Commandments, a lobbying technique that works well is the awards ceremony. Since 1991 the EMA has been using this one to the hilt. It holds awards ceremonies and gives out trophies to film and TV shows that tow the green line.

On its Web site, the EMA describes what it takes to win an Environmental Media Award. It says, "The Awards recognize writers, producers, directors, actors, and others in the entertainment industry who actively expressed their concern for the environment through their work. The Environmental Media Awards have also honored people in the entertainment industry who have gone above and beyond their peers in consistently including environmental practices and story lines in their work."

Awards are given for feature films, TV movies, comedies, dramas, and kids' shows, as long as the environmental message is delivered in the EMA-approved way. The EMA gives the following instructions to those hoping to win an award: "Please keep in mind: environmentalism today isn't just about recycling or saving trees. It's about people in a consumer culture learning to say, 'I have enough.' It's about people of color fighting against hazardous waste dumps, which end up in their neighborhoods more than anywhere else. It's about courageous individuals fighting to protect the health of their families and friends. It's about humans and nature coexisting in a myriad of ways."

The organization even hands out a special award for the TV episode that best deals with the issue of population growth. It's called the Turner Prize, in honor of Jane Fonda's ex.

The whole reason for the EMA's existence seems to be to sway the media in the greenies' favor. The group says, "We believe in the power of the media and here at EMA, we use that power to the environments' advantage." *Home Improvement, Baywatch, Hearts Afire, Lois and Clark, All in the Family, Murphy Brown, Ellen, The Simpsons,* and *The X-Files* are just a few of the shows that have succumbed to the EMA's lobbying efforts.

To this end, the EMA has suggested the following environmental story lines for writers and producers:

1. **Population.** Because there are "too many people chasing too few resources," the EMA believes these ideas

might get people thinking differently: "A family elects to adopt rather than have another child; a poster for 'Zero Population Growth' appears in a teenager's bedroom; a couple decides to stop after having two children and debate vasectomy vs. tubal ligation." Yeah, this sounds like the stuff to use during sweeps week.

2. **Consumption and Waste.** According to the EMA, people in the United States consume too much. Apparently, we're supposed to feel bad because a child born in America eats better and dresses nicer than a child born in the Third World.

To address the consumption problem, here are some TV show suggestions from the EMA: "A family simplifies its life and finds more satisfaction in a less-is-more lifestyle; a teenager insists on bringing reusable canvas bags to the supermarket; a garbage collectors strike shows how much trash can pile up in just a few weeks." I don't know if any of the networks have followed the advice, but the Garbage Collectors Union would probably like it.

3. **Climate Change.** The EMA thinks of global warming kind of like this: There's something called a "greenhouse effect." It causes the Earth's surface to get hotter. This makes the polar ice caps melt. Then ocean water levels rise and droughts or floods occur. Food production is hurt as a result, and the weather really gets crazy. You know the rest of the story. It's the "end of the world as we know it" tale.

And here are some of the riveting plotlines that have been suggested: "A record breaking blizzard traps a family in its home; a science project on climate change has a young student turning off every light in the house; a family decides to buy an electric car to reduce their own greenhouse gas emissions." The plot about the young student turning off every light in the house sounds familiar, but I'm pretty sure global warming isn't the motive behind a voluntary blackout.

4. **Endangered Species/Biodiversity.** "As humankind pushes into all corners of the world . . . we routinely push plants and animals aside, making room for larger farms, bigger mines, more homes." So says the EMA. Exactly when did farms producing food, mines producing energy, and homes providing shelter become bad things in society?

   To help promote awareness of the biodiversity issue, the EMA suggests that TV shows should consider including the following scenes: "A medical cure applied in an urban hospital is traced back to a tropical rainforest; the planned construction of a new mall will destroy habitat of migratory birds whose annual arrival has become part of a family's history; aliens abduct humans to preserve our DNA before this species becomes extinct." That last plot sounds intriguing. Of course, it all depends on which human is abducted. Take Hillary, please! And don't worry about preserving that DNA stuff.

5. **Water Quality.** The EMA came up with this interesting piece of trivia: "The amount of water is constant, and is recycling throughout time . . . it is actually possible to drink water that was part of the dinosaur era." Hmmm, Pterodactyl Spring Water. Just the kind of H_2O I want in my dispenser.

   The water suggestions from the EMA for TV scriptwriters include these: "A local beach is closed due to storm drain pollution; tap water causes a series of illnesses in a small town near a chemical plant; plans for a new dam would put a family's summer cottage under 100 feet of water." Is the EMA sure this isn't the plot of *Erin Brockovich, the Sequel?*

6. **Air Pollution.** The EMA cites studies conducted by Harvard Medical School, the EPA, and the American Cancer Society that say air pollution kills 64,000 U.S. citizens each year. So the EMA has these suggestions for TV scriptwriters: "An American Lung Association poster featuring their slogan, 'When you can't breathe, nothing else matters,' appears in the background; a couple climbs to a spectacular viewpoint to share a romantic moment, but the view is obliterated by smog; an asthmatic child is rushed to an emergency room due to unusually bad air quality." The EMA's suggestion regarding the couple that goes to a spectacular viewpoint to share a romantic moment may not work. Hey, chances are the two who go up to Inspiration Point aren't going to care about the smog obscuring their view, because it's doubtful that they're there to look at the landscape.

7. **Land Conservation.** The EMA actually cites a Republican on this one! It's Teddy Roosevelt, and he's noted for his tradition of protecting land for "its scenic beauty, abundant wildlife, or recreational pleasure." Here are some of the script suggestions the EMA has to pitch conservation: "An inner city family raises money to build a park; a field that was home to picnics and softball games is purchased by a developer; a group of teens holds a benefit to raise money to save the rainfor-

est." How about starting a fund to bring back TV's family hour?

8. **Transportation and Energy.** The EMA talks a lot about new sources of energy but, as always, environmentalists have the wrong idea about where the new sources come from. They don't come from *government*. Here are some of the EMA's energy suggestions for TV scriptwriters: "A family starts a carpool; a dad installs solar panels to reduce energy cost and pollution; a five-year-old wants to live on a 'wind farm' and plant wind." That wind farm idea might work really well in Washington, D.C.

9. **Food Pesticide.** The EMA says, "Many foods are now made with genetically-altered components with the long-term effects of this 'Frankenstein food' still unknown." Here's what the EMA suggests as TV food topics: "A family decides to go organic to avoid pesticides and other dangers; an individual has an allergic reaction to a food he (or she) was not allergic to because of genetically-engineered components; a teenager swears off meat to help protect the rain forest." Gee, if we'd only known sooner. Getting teens to swear off meat is the way to save the rain forest. You think if we got them to swear off nose rings we could save the spotted owl?

> Gee, if we'd only known sooner. Getting teens to swear off meat is the way to save the rain forest. You think if we got them to swear off nose rings we could save the spotted owl?

10. **Environmental Justice.** It seems as though the EMA has discovered a whole new way to play the race card. It's invented something called "environmental racism." It makes the claim that "the more people of color you can find in a given community, the greater the chance you'll find a toxic dump nearby." Here's what it suggests for scriptwriters in Hollywood who want to play the environmental race card, too: "Inner city residents end up in an emergency room due to a toxic spill in their neighborhood; a gang problem is solved when a park opens and a soccer league replaces gang war; plans for a new oil pipeline would take it right through the heart of an urban housing project." My favorite is the gang problem that's solved by a soccer league. Wouldn't it be a riot to watch that soccer tournament?[3]

Eco-Celebs

There's a pretty lengthy list of environmental activists in Hollywood. Mary Tyler Moore, Paul McCartney, Susan Sarandon, Patrick Stewart, Alicia Silverstone, and Kevin Bacon all appear to be distant relatives of Captain Planet.

Meryl Streep founded a group called Mothers for a Livable Planet. The actress campaigns against the dangers of pesticides. Hey, just because the alar scare didn't stick doesn't mean she can't keep trying.

Harrison Ford has taken on the real-life role of enviro-cop. In an effort to assist Bobby Kennedy Jr.'s Riverkeepers, the megastar decided to patrol the Hudson River, using his own specially equipped chopper. The helicopter of choice happens to be outfitted with high-tech cameras, so Ford can detect any polluters of the waterway. Wonder if while Ford is up there, he can swing past a certain house in Chappaqua and check for hot air and muddy waters.

Ed Asner, who always seems to be campaigning for environmental issues, is actually a member of the board of directors of the Defenders of Wildlife. Among other things, he's gotten involved in trying to save the gray wolf.

Valerie Harper has a group called Actresses for Animals. No, it's not an organization made up of friends of hers who are looking to meet some bad boy types. Harper actually tries to find homes for abandoned pets.

Pierce Brosnan wants to keep whales alive. Not that he necessarily wants to see any of them in his next 007 flick waiting for him in a nightie when he arrives at his hotel room. He has, however, partnered with the International Fund for Animal Welfare to Save the Whales.

Leonardo DiCaprio spoke out at a rally organized by Global Green USA, an affiliate of Green Cross International, whose founder and president, incidentally, is none other than ex-Soviet leader Mikhail Gorbachev. The international gathering of enviro-fascists, otherwise known as the Earth Summit, was just about to begin, and DiCaprio was trying to persuade President Bush to go to Johannesburg, South Africa, to attend it.

The actor cried about the rejection of the Kyoto Protocol and muttered that "we are the biggest economy and the biggest polluter." Too bad Leo didn't do his homework. If he had, he'd have found out that, more than anything, the folks behind the summit wanted to sink American liberty and sovereignty just like the *Titanic*.

These days Dennis Weaver, star of past TV hits *McCloud* and *Gunsmoke,* is promoting alternative fuel sources. Weaver and his wife set up a nonprofit environmental group 10 years ago to study how the needs of the economy and the environment could be reconciled. Their group is called the Institute of Ecolonomics. Easy for them to say.

In a speech, Weaver mused, "I want people to become aware of the importance of relating to the Earth, to become aware of what we're doing to it now." Then he got into some doomsday stuff, saying, "Scientists are telling us in no uncertain terms that we are now in the process of destroying what we have." He went on to say that "we have the technology to make a veritable Garden of Eden in this place we live."

In spite of his touchy-feely ramblings, the actor does appear to practice what he preaches. In 1989 the Weavers built a home in Ridgway, Colorado, from materials that included recycled tires and aluminum cans. Rumor is that *MTV Cribs* is going to do a spot on Weaver's recycled beer can bonus room.

One of the most unusual celebrity greenies is actor Ed Begley Jr. Begley actually lives in a simple, solar-powered, energy-efficient house. And he's been known to show up at Hollywood events riding his 10-year-old bicycle. Even I've got to give a guy like this some points for sincerity.

Ever wonder how aging Hollywood enviro-libs entertain? With cocktails, hors d'oeuvres, dinner, and—some nuclear waste. Not too long ago Paul Newman and Joanne Woodward decided to have some people over to their Manhattan apartment for "drinks, simple dinner and an off-the-record discussion about nuclear power and the disposal of nuclear waste."

The legendary film couple invited reporters, nuclear power advocates, and environmentalists to their home to try and solve the thorny environmental problems that come with nuclear power.

Representatives from *Time, Newsweek,* and the *New York Post,* which covered the story, were all included on the guest list. The question I have to ask is, With a radioactive entrée, do you serve white wine or red?

Kevin Richardson is a member of the Backstreet Boys. In addition to dancing around with fellow boy-banders, Richardson set up a nonprofit entity called Just Within Reach. Not to be outdone, Backstreet Boy Nick Carter went out and started his own group called Nick Carter's Oceans Campaign.

Richardson decided to appear at a venue that was a little bit different from his usual. He showed up at a Senate hearing on mining. Supposedly, he was there to testify about the damage being done to wetlands, rivers, and streams, etcetera. But as long as he was in D.C., he decided to take the opportunity to criticize the Bush administration's whole approach to the mining industry. One senator was prompted to go into a dance routine of his own at the thought of a singing teen giving expert testimony. In response to Richardson's presentation, Ohio Republican Senator George Voinovich said this: "It's just a joke to think that this witness can provide members of the United States Senate with information on important geological and water quality issues."

Voinovich ended up boycotting the session. He remarked, "We're either serious about the issues or we're running a side-show."[4] Hey, senator, I'm pretty sure it's the latter.

We can't leave the subject of eco-celebs without mentioning the money machine for this, and just about every other, leftist cause. It's Barbra Streisand. The singer did a fund-raiser in 1986 for Democrat Senators Tom Daschle, Tom Harkin, Pat Leahy, and the late Senator Alan Cranston. It brought in $1.5 million. When the thing was shown on HBO, Babs got another $6 million. She used that money to set up the Streisand Foundation. The Streisand Foundation goes around hosting conferences on the environment in Washington, D.C., and handing out big lumps of cash to the most radical environmental groups out there.

Hip Hip Hypocrisy

When it comes to eco-ethics, Hollywood types don't always practice what they preach. As a matter of fact, billionaire entertainment executive David Geffen, singer-actress Julie Andrews, Andrews's husband producer-director Blake Edwards, and other Hollywood figures are battling a group called Access for All. Access for All is an environmental organization that seeks to make the Malibu beaches available to ordinary folks.

Malibu is where the mansions of Barbra Streisand, Tom Hanks, Robert Redford, and others are located. In California, just like in many other states, citizens have been given the right, according to various environmental regulations, to walk, swim, or plunk down a beach towel just about anywhere along the shoreline. This makes the celebs in the extremely elite and wealthy area worried, because it means that the ordinary public, a.k.a. riffraff, is free to blemish their scenic beaches.

Malibu has a coastline that stretches 27 miles. Of that long stretch, there are only four paths that allow ordinary commoners to get to the beach. And even these paths aren't the easiest to navigate because there's not a lot of parking available and it's fairly dangerous to get across the highway. If you visit the area, you'll see loads of signs that say "Private Property." Other signs say "No Trespassing" or "Beware of roving packs of pit bulls and rottweilers." There are even some properties where illegal fences or other questionable barriers have been constructed. So the California Coastal Commission, the organization that's supposed to protect the environment along the coast, has proposed 10 public right-of-ways to the Malibu shoreline.

Other coastal towns are going ahead with plans to give ordinary citizens access to the beaches, but not Malibu. Steve Hoye, the former president of the Malibu Democratic Club, is trying to get his Malibu friends to be more consistent with their rhetoric. Hoye is apparently the one who formed Access for All. But it looks like the idea behind the group's slogan is going to be a tough sell, at least in this suburban Hollywood haunt.

David Geffen, a billionaire contributor to all causes Democratic and liberal, has brought a big-time lawsuit against the group. The suit is purportedly based on some studies about public safety, environmental impact, and traffic. But it seems like the goal of Geffen's legal action may be to deny Access for All the access it wants to the land next to his beachfront property.

Environmentalists, local officials, and homeowners are all set to fight it out. This thing may even go all the way up to the U.S. Supreme Court. Robert Garcia, who is director for the city project for the Center for Law and Public Interest, says this: "The California coast belongs to all people, not just entertainment moguls and rich movie stars." Even in a Tinseltown world? We'll just have to wait and see.

Julie Andrews and Blake Edwards live in the area, too. They've come up with a unique way to try and stop beachgoers from getting too close to their place. It's called big bucks. Apparently, the couple paid the state $338,000 to place a staircase in a public access path that was near another home, which belonged to the head of MGM Pictures, Frank Mancuso.

Then Mancuso came up with his own plan. He offered to pay for a busing program. Yeah, that's right. A busing program! The buses would likely move scummy non-celebs to beaches farther away from his home.

Hoye made a statement that sent chills through the Malibu crowd. He said, "It ain't your backyard, buddy. It belongs to the people."[5] Sounds like the leftists are beginning to be victimized by their own liberal ideology.

There's apparently some hypocrisy going on in the European suburbs of Hollywood, too. Looks like Mrs. Ritchie, better known as Madonna, is teed off over plans to place a public right-of-way through her and her husband's lavish estate in Britain. It seems some U.K. environmental land access laws allow for "areas of mountain, moorland, heath and downland" to be granted to the public.

Guy Ritchie's mom told the *Daily Express* that Madonna and her director-spouse "feel the legislation has put them and their two young children in a potentially dangerous situation." Guess this is where the real material girl shows through.

Michael Douglas and his wife, Catherine Zeta-Jones, have been busy building a new home in Wales. The residence is purportedly in an area that's named after Senator Joseph Lieberman called "the Mumbles." The location is very close to Swansea, where Zeta-Jones was born.

Douglas and Zeta-Jones have not exactly been acting like Mister Rogers. In fact, they've ticked off their neighbors before even moving in. The couple has changed the plans of their new abode from two stories to three. The opulent design overlooks a bunch of other properties, and neighbors are especially disturbed about the number of windows. As one said, "We will lose our privacy—it will be like living in a goldfish bowl."

The Swansea Council approved the plans and indicated that the proposed structure "is considered suitable for the site." Like so many of their Hollywood buddies, Mr. and Mrs. Douglas are champions of peace, harmony, sensitivity, and cooperation— except when it comes to their multistoried mansions.

Even Hollywood filmmakers occasionally lock horns with folks who would typically be considered allies. A while back some filmmakers wanted to shoot a scene off the coast of Florida, but they ran into a little snag. The area is home to a bunch of sea cows. When environmentalists got wind of the movie plans, they had a cow of their own.

Sea cows, otherwise known as manatees, are beloved in this part of the world, so much so that protective rules were developed to safeguard the creatures. One of the rules bans high-speed boats in the Biscayne Bay area.

That's where the problem came in. *Bad Boys 2,* starring Will Smith and Martin Lawrence, had a high-speed water chase scene that was supposed to be shot in the protected habitat. Columbia Pictures hired lobbyist Ron Book to help get around the sea cow protective rules. Florida state environmental officials rejected a request to waive the rules. So producer Barry Waldman decided to meet with Governor Jeb Bush.

According to the *St. Petersburg Times,* the state agreed to allow the shooting to go ahead, as long as provisions for sea cow monitoring were met. Lookouts would be posted to spot any sea cows that might be in danger of harm during the boat chase.

Still, environmentalists were not happy. Patti Thompson, director of science and conservation for the Save the Manatee Club, told United Press International, "I've never heard of any emergency waivers for manatee rules, period, and I certainly know there's never been an emergency waiver for something like this." Once again, it looks like liberal elitists in Hollywood embrace strict enviro-maniac rules, as long as they apply to someone else.

What Would Norman Lear Drive?

A portion of Hollywood has declared war on the SUVs of the nation. Now most of us know that Americans all over the United States love SUVs because they're great vehicles for towing around kids, pets, and equipment, and they're tons of fun to drive. The auto dealers have the phenomenal sales records to affirm the affection. Currently, there are about 20 million of the sporty metal boxes on the roads. The trend is supposed to continue, with a doubling of the combination auto–truck–sports cars in the next few years. Analysts say the vehicles have really helped give the U.S. car industry a megashot in the arm.

But some Hollywood environmentalists see the SUV as a huge enemy, because the vehicles tend to burn more gas and chug out more smog than something like a Honda Civic does. These anti-SUV advocates tried to tie SUV driving to the war on terror. Author Arianna Huffington, the lukewarm conservative-turned-frothy liberal, and her Hollywood friends tried to guilt the public into seeing the SUV light. Patriotism was what was in question, according to Arianna's Detroit Project, if you chose to drive a gas-guzzling SUV. Apparently, the crowd was convinced that when you opted for the added safety of a sport-utility vehicle, you were somehow aiding and abetting terrorists.

Huffington, who is a quasi-Hollywood celebrity herself, worked with activists to raise money for the advertisements. Essentially, the publicity spots were designed to humiliate SUV owners into getting rid of their vehicles and going back to driving sensible sedans. One of the TV ads showed an SUV driver filling his tank. The scene abruptly changes to show the face of an evil oil executive. One more switch and the audience is transported to a terrorist training camp. Similar to the drug ads that tied use of the illegal substances to terrorism, the anti-SUV ads had an announcer saying, "Without your SUV gassing up, terrorists could not kill people." The underlying message was that if you drive an SUV, you're basically a low-level terrorist.

In reality, SUVs don't come close to the typical energy-sucking lifestyles of most celebrities. Huffington, whose ex-husband made big bucks off of oil and gas, lives in a big home in Brentwood, California. You know, O.J.'s old stomping grounds. One of Arianna's backers, producer Norman Lear, founder of what ought to be called "People for the Soviet Way," lives in a palatial pad, too. His garage holds 21 cars. Wonder how many Third Worlders that motor space would bunk? Presumably, though, no terrorist-funding vehicles are stored there.

When it comes to extravagance, Hollywood has certainly not been known for putting on the brakes. Stretch limos, private jets, Olympic-sized bathtubs, and spas for all house and staff members are the norm. But these same folks want ordinary families, who are looking for transportation that makes them feel safe and is able to handle a Colorado snowstorm, to scoot around in an "It" mobile.

In this town of make-believe, the script that has celebrities themselves living a truly austere lifestyle for the sake of the environment can be filed under fantasy.

CHAPTER TEN

The Lefty Awards

No book that's pried open the political back door of Hollywood would be complete without an—*AWARDS SHOW!*

Although the names and faces should be familiar to you, these winning categories represent what can only be described as the best of the ludicrously lame, laudably laughable, loony Left Coast.

Best Performance by an Actor in Propping Up a Lunatic Dictator

While searching for illegal arms in Iraq, Hans Blix thought that he'd discovered a weapon of mass narcosis. As it turns out, it was only an actor. But this particular actor's been known to induce sleep as rapidly as a Tom Daschle press conference.

He recently paid a little visit to Saddam's stomping grounds. He claimed that he wanted to get an inside look.

"By the invitation of the Institute for Public Accuracy, I have the privileged opportunity to pursue a deeper understanding of this frightening conflict," he said in a written statement.

From Baghdad, the sometimes actor, sometimes director told Reuters that he thought war could be avoided, "but obviously it's going to take enormous commitment on the part of the Iraqi government as well as the United States."

While in Iraq, he took a tour of a Baghdad children's hospital and met with the former Deputy Prime Minister Tariq Aziz. The usually cagey Aziz must've spilled his guts. After all, the defrocked deputy PM was able to report back to Saddam, "Hey, the guy was married to Madonna!"

In a related story, a rumor was circulating that General Tommy Franks was tracking the actor for his own safety. To keep tabs on him, Franks was apparently using the technique of locating the spot on the terrain where there was no brain activity.

In what must have been a disappointment, the self-appointed celebrity ambassador returned to the U. S. only to discover that the Iraqis had used him like Tiger Woods uses a Scotty Cameron putter. The Iraqi News Service told the world that he'd pronounced Iraq "completely clear of weapons of mass destruction."

After all of this, his PR people were left with a pretty tough job. They had to figure out a way to help him recover some cool. So they booked him on *Larry King Live*.

The only problem was, he talked just enough to display his unparalleled talent for incoherent thinking.

He'll always be the irrepressible and generally daffy Spicoli. The winner is . . . *Sean Penn.*

Best Performance by an Actress Abroad in Pandering to a Foreign Audience

She's done it over and over again. Like an emissary from Hades, she uses her celebrity power to push a bone-headed political agenda.

She was the announcer on the ill-conceived anti-war TV ad that aired on the same day as the president's 2003 State of the Union Address.

She's been front and center at some of the screwball peace rallies that seem more like outtakes from the miniseries *The Sixties.*

While at the premiere of *The Banger Sisters* in London's Leicester Square, she took some verbal shots at British Prime Minister Tony Blair's relationship with President Bush.

"What's happened to Blair? I don't understand his reasoning or his logic. I don't understand his evolution. I can see him being seduced by Clinton, but don't understand what him and Bush speak about," she told the British press.

One can only imagine that her favorite ex-prez, Bill Clinton, was seduced by the title of the movie she was in and rushed out to see it. He must have been pretty disappointed to find out that *The Banger Sisters* was about two aging ex-groupies and, to top it off, the thing was only rated R.

She's the excessively outspoken roommate of actor-director Tim Robbins. The winner is . . . *Susan Sarandon.*

Best Piece of Celluloid Propaganda

It was unveiled at the Cannes Film Festival.

Like fact-ignoring, agenda-driven projects that preceded it, the film uses exploitation to undermine the rights of honest people to defend themselves.

A scene in the movie lampoons a Michigan bank, which as a business incentive gives out rifles to new account holders.

Another scene shows a grieving father who wears on his person a photo of his son who is a victim of the Columbine tragedy.

Footage of the Columbine shootings that was captured on surveillance cameras is displayed, while 9-1-1 tapes from panicked callers inside the school are broadcast.

There's even an ambush-style interview of Charlton Heston that's designed to humiliate the legendary actor.

Lastly, two survivors from Columbine are taken to the headquarters of Kmart, so the boys can show the executives their scars. Kmart announces that it won't be selling bullets any longer.

It's a so-called documentary about guns and violence in America, but it's really a *Michael Moore* mega-slice of manipulation. The winner is . . . **Bowling for Columbine.**

Best PC Costume Design

Traffic recently came to a halt in Berlin.

A Playboy model and former *Baywatch* lifeguard was trying to promote animal rights and vegetarianism. The problem was she was doing it in a lettuce bikini.

The actress donned the green-leafed bikini, with a sign that read "Go Vegetarian," for a PETA-sponsored event.

She made her way toward a steak restaurant, which had apparently sponsored a meat industry congress in Berlin.

But when the bikini-clad beauty crossed the threshold of the restaurant with a crowd of reporters in tow, she was asked to leave.

Although activists may not know, almost everyone else does. When guys see an attractive woman in a bikini, regardless of the substance the bathing suit's made of, animal rights is the furthest thing from their minds.

Still, fashion and cuisine found a way of coming together in a delectably creative way. The winner is . . . *Traci Bingham in a lettuce bikini.*

Best Animated Makeover

The proliferation of plastic surgery in our culture is changing the way men and women look, even in the cartoon world.

In one episode of a popular animated series, the leading lady decides she's going to get liposuction after she becomes envious of the younger women she thinks are distracting her hubby.

The cartoon mom goes in for liposuction on her tummy and is accidentally given breast augmentation. Initially, she wants the breast implants removed but later changes her mind because of all the attention she's getting.

Homer Simpson may now have no choice but to have some surgery of his own—maybe a fifth finger on each hand. The winner is . . . *Marge enlarged.*

Best Political Apology

A cable TV program called *Clone High, USA* recently featured an animated character named G-Man. G-Man is a clone that wears dangling earrings, eats junk food, and is a party animal. He's a dead ringer for Mahatma Gandhi, too.

The show itself hasn't aired in India, but a newspaper report about it has. And that's put a lot of Indians in a lather.

In a statement faxed to news media, the cable giant said it was sorry. It apologized if it had "offended the people of India and the memory of Mahatma Gandhi."

Clone High, USA parodies historical figures from around the world. But the Gandhi spoof irritated political activists and lawmakers so much, they went on a hunger strike to protest.

The network certainly missed an opportunity to solve the problem quickly. It could have said that the character was really a parody of G. Gordon Liddy. The winner is . . . *MTV US's apology for the great Gandhi goof-up.*

Best Limousine Liberal

He was in the nation's capital for the premiere of his so-called documentary. He took the opportunity to attack both of the major political parties.

According to the *Washington Post,* he accused the Democrats of protecting the interests and people in the top 10 percent of the income bracket.

The offbeat filmmaker was asked whether he was a bit embarrassed about being driven to and from the event in a Cadillac stretch limousine. The response sounded very much like a politician. "I asked for the biggest limo they could find in Washington, D.C., but it had to be a GM car. There's a special reason for this: I travel with a lot of exotic birds, all on the endangered species list, and as part of a special diet I eat one of them each day."

While he criticizes Dems, he sure knows how to act like one. It's done like this: When accused of a double standard, change the subject.

He's the pseudo-champion of the working man. The winner is . . . *Michael Moore.*

Best Crony Casting

It wasn't bad enough that the Clinton cronies have been running for office, invading the networks, and generally threatening to never go away. Now they're infecting our kids' cartoons.

It seems that serpent-head himself is about to make the cartoon scene. He is set to lend his voice to an animated Disney flick.

The upcoming movie is described as an Appalachian tale with bluegrass music. Its working title is "My Peoples," and the release date is scheduled for sometime in 2005. Dolly Parton, Lily Tomlin, Lou Rawls, and Travis Tritt also have roles in the project.

Most adults aren't going to be too happy about having to explain to the young ones why a Clinton defender's voice is coming out of a cartoon character.

Guess he just keeps slithering from one cartoon to another. The winner is . . . *James Carville.*

Best PC Adaptation of a Classic

One of the world's most beloved novels has undergone a name change. Striving to reach absurd heights of tolerance, a touring production company tampered with the title of a classic.

After discussions with a disability advisor, Oddsocks Productions decided to call its version of Victor Hugo's 1831 novel *The Bellringer of Notre Dame.*

The story of deformed bellringer Quasimodo and his love for a beautiful gypsy girl, Esmeralda, has been translated into 20 languages and adapted many times for stage and screen. But never has the book's title created this kind of a stir. If the trend continues, we'll have to look more closely at a lot of the classics and make the necessary tolerance adjustments.

Guess in the future we'll be reading Samuel Taylor Coleridge's "The Rime of the Young-at-Heart Mariner," Rudyard Kipling's *The Rainforest Book,* Charles Dickens's *A Happy*

Holiday Carol, Hans Christian Andersen's *The Everybody's Beautiful Duckling,* and the just-can't-wait-to-read Dostoyevsky's *Crime and Rehabilitation.* The winner is . . . **The Hunch-Blank of Notre Dame.**

Best Petition to TV Execs

It looks as if more than 10,000 women wouldn't mind busting CBS in the chops.

Apparently, a sizable number of ladies have a petition going on the Internet, demanding that "CBS provide equal time to plus-size women in America and air the Lane Bryant lingerie fashion show."

The letter argues that CBS could bring in a whole new audience and help the self-esteem of plenty of folks at the same time. It notes, "It is widely believed that media images of very thin women have a significant effect on body image in young girls. This feeling of inadequacy can lead to excessive exercise, starvation diets, drug abuse, and deadly eating disorders. By depicting real, healthy 'average' women, CBS could have a substantially positive impact on the body image of millions of women across the country."

The show in question is Lane Bryant's *Intimate Apparel Runway Show.* The program features models of a more realistic variety, wearing similar outfits to those of a while back that were also seen on CBS.

You may recall that the network aired models of the more svelte kind in the *Victoria's Secret Fashion Show* that was billed as "the sexiest night on TV."

In an industry dedicated to diversity, this idea seems like an enormously good one. The winner is . . . *The petition from the buxom beauties of America.*

Best Exploitation of a Children's Show

It looks like the numero uno globalist just can't stop hanging out with puppets. The Nobel Peace Prize winner tried to give Elmo and friends a lesson in the art of diplomacy.

It seems the puppets were arguing about who would get to sing the alphabet song when the global leader came up with his suggestion—Why not sing the song together?

The secretary-general said that he agreed to make the appearance on the show because "it is wonderful to be able to reach the young to try to give them the spirit of the United Nations."

He's a guy who is used to dealing with dummies. The winner is . . . *UN Secretary-General Kofi Annan's appearance on Sesame Street.*

Best Anti-American Music

In the entertainment world, country music has long been considered a bastion of patriotism. But one fellow is breaking with tradition in a big way.

He's a Grammy-nominated singer-songwriter, and he's written a tune called "John Walker's Blues." In the song, he sings the praises of John Walker Lindh, the young man many folks think of as "traitor-boy."

His warped words speak of fighting a "jihad" and praying for "martyrdom." He refers to the capture and return of John Walker Lindh to the United States as "dragging me back . . . to the land of the infidel."

He's the crooner who sounds like he's fallen off his show horse. The winner is . . . *Steve Earle and his musical cowpie.*

Best Left-Handed Compliment

First the guy tried to get Ball State University to change the name of its football stadium and christen it after him. Then he implored Indianapolis to use his name for the highway that encircles the city.

So what happened? The late-night talk-show host got an alley named after him.

Muncie, Indiana, the place where he lived while attending college, decreed that the name of one of the city's busiest alleys would be officially known as "Dave's Alley Open 24 Hours."

According to the Associated Press, not everyone was happy about the name change. Some protesters showed up at the alley. They turned out to be fans of Garfield the Cat.

The cartoonist who created Garfield, Jim Davis, lives in the area. Two of the more dedicated protesters were dressed in Garfield and Odie the dog costumes. They had signs that read "Dave Bites," "Cats Rule, Dave Drools," and "Alleys Are for Cats."

Maybe an alley should've been named for someone you'd expect to find in one—like a UN inspector. The winner is . . .
Right down David Letterman's alley.

Best Hollywood Political Matchup

They recently showed signs of interest in the political big leagues.

Although both celebs have amused themselves with political pastimes before, there's a scent of more serious aspiration in the air. Each has hired election strategists.

If things play out as indications suggest, the race would be for the governor of the state of California. The year would be 2006. And the rivals would be none other than Archie Bunker's son-in-law, Meathead, and the unceasing cyborg, the Terminator.

It is expected that in this matchup, when the Terminator's done, his opponent will be known as Mincemeat-head.

They're two of Hollywood's most colorful characters. The winners are . . . *Rob Reiner and Arnold Schwarzenegger.*

Best Hollywood Influence on Foreign Law

A Hong Kong woman lost her case against the New Idol Hair Salon.

It seems that the gal wanted to look like Julia Roberts. Instead, she claimed she wound up looking like Osama bin Laden.

After the judgment was given, the hair victim refused to leave the Small Claims Tribunal. Following a standoff with the court staff, which lasted more than an hour, she was taken away by ambulance. So says the *South China Morning Post.*

"Do you mean you did not get the Julia Roberts look after the perm?" adjudicator Yuen Chun-kau asked during the proceeding.

She answered, "Not just that. It was like a broom. Every hair stuck out and it looked like an open umbrella which could not be shut. It was horrible. I looked like Osama bin Laden."

Yuen Chun-kau dismissed her claim, but the woman felt that Yuen was not sympathetic to her predicament.

"He's bald. Of course he would not know the pain of having damaged hair," she exclaimed.

The least the court could have done was given the lady some money for a Magic Turban. The winner is . . . *Chu-Ieu and the Bin Laden Hairdo.*

Best Duo for Redistribution

A couple of deluded do-gooders in Hollywood demonstrated once again just how out of touch a celebrity's life can be.

Apparently, they've forgotten how tough it is to work your tail off, only to have the government grab the bulk of your already insufficient wages.

The two wrote a letter to Governor Gray Davis and the leaders in the California legislature pleading with them to raise taxes.

Although the actors asked for an increase on the state's top income earners, socialist-minded suggestions like these always seem to have a way of biting the average guy in the rear wallet.

Whenever fiscal irresponsibility causes deficits, we can count on the usual gang of Hollywood simpletons to come up with the higher-tax solution. What about trimming some of the excess spending that's rampant in the state instead?

Former California Democrat Assemblywoman Helen Thomson told the *Los Angeles Times* that if the proposed Republican cuts were made, there would be "so little left in terms of health care, parks and education."

This sounds way too familiar—celebrities advocating the taking of somebody else's money to give to politicians so they can squander it away.

They're two of Hollywood's most liberal stalwarts. The winners are . . . *Richard Lewis and Ed Asner.*

Best Unoriginal Score

Being a star has its advantages, but one actor has apparently used his fame in some not-so-notable ways.

The actor, who is actually being touted by the Left as a possible presidential candidate, told *Details* magazine what he thinks of President Bush. He labeled him a hypocrite who is going to "do a lot of damage."

He said, "Bush means Dick Cheney, Tom DeLay, and all these . . . crypto-fascists are gonna get in and start carving up the pie and handing in all their markers to the Republican Party that's been itching to get back into power."

The *New York Post* reported that he's fond of a practice he calls "celebrity looting." In an interview with *Black Book* magazine, he explained what the activity entails. He pointed out a clothing store to the interviewer and said, "We did celebrity looting there. . . . They asked me to come over, patronize the store, pick up some stuff. So I took all my friends over, and we went straight for the $8,000 rack of leather coats and took a bunch. The managers, they get all nervous and twitchy. They freak. But you just look at 'em really hard and walk out. That's celebrity looting."

Having to shell out cash to watch this guy's movies—now, that's celebrity looting. The winner is . . . *John Cusack and his pointers on pilfering.*

Best Unsound Editorial

He recently wrote an editorial, which the *Los Angeles Times* dutifully published. The piece claimed that the Bush administration showed a lack of leadership in not reducing the nation's dependence on fossil fuels.

"Prolonging our dependence on fossil fuels would guarantee homeland insecurity," he wrote. Then he added, "If you are worried about getting oil from an unstable Persian Gulf, consider the alternatives: Indonesia, Nigeria, Uzbekistan."

The actor-director praised San Francisco's $100 million bond initiative, which earmarks money for solar panels, wind power, and energy-efficient public buildings.

"American rooftops can be the Persian Gulf of solar energy," he lectured.

Maybe there is a new alternative energy source. Why not harness all of the hot air coming out of this guy's mouth?

He's the founder of the "Sundunce" Film Festival, and he's penned the top piece of recycled trash. The winner is . . . *Robert Redford's eco-Pulp Fiction.*

Best Response to a Shakedown Artist

Have you heard about the new American pastime—asking for an apology? Everyone's doing it, especially liberals.

It seems that a feud took place not too long ago, and it had to do with requests for apologies. You may recall that a famous reverend asked the makers of the mega-hit comedy *Barbershop* to apologize for jokes about black leaders.

Then a group of Los Angeles barbers from the National Association of Cosmetologists asked the parson to apologize for his criticism of the film. The CEO of the association, James Stern, told Reuters that he screened the film for more than 100 African-American barbers, and they had zero problems with the movie.

Stern had a strong message for the preacher. He asserted that members of his organization lost business due to his comments. Stern said he "did not consider the future of black filmmakers. We, as blacks, have to let the movie studios know that when he is wrong, we're willing to speak out for ourselves."

Because the minister decided not to apologize, the group sued him for negligence, among other things.

Here's a bit of advice for the reverend. Next time you're in the barber's chair, you might think about skipping the shave. The winner is . . . *Barbers give Jesse Jackson a trim.*

Best Unhumanitarian Award

He's apparently not content to just sit around and hurl tired, hackneyed anti-war phrases at the president, like when he was on the Charlie Rose show. No, he also seems to have the need to kick around an American icon when he's down.

According to Liz Smith of the *New York Post*, while accepting an award from the National Board of Review, he wisecracked, "Charlton Heston announced again today that he is suffering from Alzheimer's."

When asked about his statement, he told Smith, "I don't care. Charlton Heston is the head of the National Rifle Association. He deserves whatever anyone says about him."

Heston wasn't about to let the indignity go unchallenged. According to the World Entertainment News Network, Heston walloped the actor by contrasting his demeanor with that of his late aunt, singing legend Rosemary.

"It just goes to show that sometimes class does skip a generation," Heston shot back.

It's ironic that this actor, who liberally spouts compassion, tolerance, and sensitivity, would use a man's illness as material for a joke. But if he keeps on talking, he may end up where he belongs—next to Alec Baldwin on *Hollywood Squares*.

He's the out-of-control actor who drew the ire of Moses. The winner is . . . *George Clooney*.

Best Maker of Conspiracy Theory Movies

His film *JFK* has imaginary scenes where American officials plot the murder of the president. Certain sections of the movie are made to look like a documentary, but their content is fantasy.

In another one of his films, he tries to create a link between the Kennedy assassination and the Nixon resignation.

Then there's the cable flick he made, *The Day Reagan Was Shot*. In this project, though, you can tell that his usual amount of conspiracy curiosity is lacking. Maybe it has to do with Reagan's brand of conservatism.

It's been rumored that he plans his films on a grassy knoll, at Area 51, while chasing after Bigfoot and playing a Beatles album backward.

We may never know if he's really an extraterrestrial being who's posing as a Hollywood director. But we do know the name he goes by.

He's the primary purveyor of paranoia. The winner is . . . *Oliver Stone.*

Best Opening Act

Concertgoers were ready to rock. They were at the Staples Center in Los Angeles, waiting to see the aging dons of rock 'n' roll, those maestros of quasi-rebel boomer music, the Rolling Stones.

Then the opening act was announced. And who came in to do a speech on global warming, of all things? It was none other than the superintendent of sleaze himself. Never mind that the famed rock group burns enough fossil fuel on its concert tour to power a Third World country for a year.

Stones fans got to hear some real doomsday gems from this politician, like the warning that we'd all better hurry and "stop the planet from burning up."

One can just imagine that the crowd was mesmerized by this bit of preaching: "The old energy economy that's cheating us as a planet is very well organized, highly centralized, rich as can be and very well politically connected."

And no doubt, they were further wowed by this sermonizing: "And the new energy future is decentralized, entrepreneurial and needs people like you to say, 'Give me a clean car, give me solar shingles to put on my roof—give me a clean future.'"

Lisa Kudrow, Leonardo DiCaprio, Pierce Brosnan, and Rob Reiner were some of the celebs who were in attendance and were probably nodding at the Slick One in approval.

His speech was followed by a Stones set, which featured "Start Me Up," "Street Fighting Man," and "You Got Me Rocking."

For his next act, he's thinking about opening a Michael Jackson concert with a lecture on parenting.

Everyone always knew that this "X"-prez wanted to be a rock star. The winner is . . . *Bill Clinton doing "Start Me Up, Bubba."*

Tinseltown's Election Connection

Ever since stardust was invented politicians have been making regular pilgrimages to Hollywood. The trek is taken for various reasons, but it's usually done to try and bag some valuable commodities, two of them being star names and celebrity cash. The names are gathered for endorsement purposes. The cash is collected to fatten campaign coffers.

It's clear why a pol might pursue capital, but why would he or she do a backflip for a celebrity endorsement? Well, it's because celebrities can turn a what's-his-name into a headliner overnight. And that kind of clout can provide enough forward motion to propel a candidate to electoral victory.

It's undeniable that political libs in Hollywood are as bountiful as bikini waxes in spring. Almost 80 percent of the entertainment dough from the 2002 election cycle went to the Democrats, according to the Center for Responsive Politics. And the entertainment industry is the fourth-biggest source of cash overall for politicos seeking federal office. For years the

Dems have turned to the Left Coast to beef up their campaign biceps, and 2004 was no exception.

The "I Really, Really, Really Hate Bush" Club

The Dems know that nothing energizes lefty celebs quite like anger. More than ever, the glitterati's gone bitterati over the commander in chief. Former practicing psychiatrist and current op-ed writer Charles Krauthammer identified a new disorder in December 2003. He called it Bush Derangement Syndrome, or BDS.

The condition seems to have ravaged a lot of left lobes in Tinseltown. In fact, by 2004 scads of star libs were apparently experiencing episodes of BDS-related hysteria. Michael Moore publicly stated on cable TV that he thought the Bush administration was hiding Osama bin Laden. Janeane Garofalo mused aloud on the national airwaves that the president and Saddam Hussein were morally indistinguishable. According to *Us Weekly,* Cher voiced a peculiar sort of preference, saying, "I would rather stick needles in my eyes than be a Republican."

Then there was Sean Penn. The guy just can't seem to break free from Spicoli. In February 2004, Penn took a jaunt to South America to promote his Oscar-winning performance in *Mystic River.* Somehow the politics of dude took center stage. Penn was asked whether he thought of himself as a patriot. According to MSNBC's Web site, he replied, "I am more patriotic than this president we have, who I consider a traitor of human and American principles." As if insulting the commander in chief during wartime wasn't gnarly enough, Penn threw some pepperoni at his colleagues, too. When asked if the criticism of his trip to Iraq surprised him, Penn went for the Hollywood hook. He said, "I'm not surprised with the fact that there are many comfortable cowards in my profession."

Gwyneth Paltrow seemed to be suffering from BDS as well. From her British haunt, Paltrow accused the president of misleading the public and not paying attention to the rest of the world. Translation: Bush doesn't kiss enough UN, French, or German keister. The *Shallow Hal* gal said, "I think George Bush is such an embarrassment to America in the way that he doesn't take the rest of the world into consideration." Paltrow also appeared to be reading from greenie cue cards when she said, "It all seems to be for him and his friends to keep getting richer at the expense of a nation, at the expense of the environment. It's like a full-scale assault on the environment."

On a separate occasion, the Oscar-winning new mommy had sort of an anti-U.S. tizzy. "I worry about bringing up a child in America," Paltrow told World Entertainment News Network. "At the moment there's a weird, over-patriotic atmosphere over there, like, 'We're number one and the rest of the world doesn't matter.'"

Another serious BDS case was Margaret Cho. In an interview with BuzzFlash, the standup comic tried to justify MoveOn.org's ad contest entries that compared President Bush to Adolf Hitler. BuzzFlash asked Cho, "What do you think specifically upset so many of the bigot 'freepers' that they sent you hate mail?"

"I think it was because I said that they were stupid, which they are," answered Cho. "I actually respect a lot of conservatives. And I understand there are people that actually are smart on the right, but they're totally embarrassed by the dummies out there in the right wing. And when you call people stupid, if they are stupid, they get so mad that all they can do is just implode."

Cho gave her theory about why she was criticized after saying this about the RNC and the president: "Despite all of this stupid bulls— that the Republican National Committee, or whatever the f— they call them, that they were saying that they're all angry about how two of these ads were comparing Bush to Hitler? I mean, out of thousands of submissions, they find two. They're like f—ing looking for Hitler in a haystack. You know? I mean, George Bush is not Hitler. He would be if he f—ing applied himself."

Cho chattered on about members of the GOP, saying, "I think this last year has just proven how stupid Republicans are." According to the comic, people singled her out either because she's Asian or because she's female. She said, "I don't think that anybody else had the same kind of backlash from being involved with MoveOn.org as I did. And partially it's racial, of course, and it's gender-based. And it's that people just don't see that Americans are of other ethnic backgrounds." Frankly, it's disappointing to see Cho dealing from the bottom of the deck and, when criticized for it, playing the race and gender card.

Barbra Streisand appeared to have one of the worst cases of BDS ever. The singing activist displayed her symptoms in Los Angeles in March 2004. While speaking to a crowd of gays and lesbians, Streisand let out a sort of Howard Dean/Al Gore yell, saying, "The Bush Administration wants to change the positive inclusive direction of our Constitution by calling for an amendment that authorizes discrimination on the basis of sexual orientation. Well, I say, no way."

Streisand also vented her frustration about hubby James Brolin's miniseries on Ronald Reagan, which had to be punted over to Showtime from CBS. "I've seen [the right wing's] ferocity up close. . . . They attacked that movie and drove it off network television before any of them had ever seen it. The right wing is very well-organized. They fight dirty."

Uma Thurman was apparently a BDS sufferer, too. The samurai sword–slashing star of *Kill Bill* took a swipe at Dubya in the December 2003 issue of *GQ*, saying "I really wish he wasn't running the country. . . . I didn't want him to be elected, but I hoped he wouldn't do a bad job. I have to say it's been less than impressive."

In my own humble opinion, two years without a repeat of 9/11-style terrorism, an economy on the mend, some cash in our pockets instead of Uncle Sam's, condemnation of partial-birth abortion, and an Oval Office draped in dignity again is pretty darn impressive. Then again, never having experienced the syndrome firsthand, I can't really relate to the pain and humiliation that victims of BDS regularly undergo. And sadly, there's not even an ointment or suppository available to provide relief.

A couple of other BDS-related stories deserve mention. Apparently, a group of women in Michigan took to calling themselves Babes Against Bush. The ladies said they wanted to "promote political awareness in the most unlikely of audiences: men whose cultural tastes tend toward centerfolds and the swimsuit issues of sports magazines." One livid lady named Eleanor Vast-Binder explained to the *Washington Post*, "What better way is there to get guys to notice that the president is a bozo."

Another batch of BDS sufferers was known as the Radical Cheerleaders, who reportedly had squads around the globe. These young female activists tried to draw attention to their cause by doing cheerleading routines at left-wing protests.

I have a few words to say about cheerleaders who do cartwheels and splits trying to get the attention of the White House: Creative concept, wrong White House.

Bushwhacking Wares

Sometimes Hollywood's Bush hatred, and its parallel political agenda, has ended up right smack in the middle of the entertainment product. Take, for instance, the project that filmmaker George Butler, of *Pumping Iron* fame, was working on in earnest in 2004. Butler was producing and directing a documentary called *Tour of Duty*. The flick, based on Douglas Brinkley's best-selling book, would deal with the story of John Kerry's military service in Vietnam. Butler was planning to time the film's release for the most favorable Kerry bounce, right at the peak of the fall campaign season.

Michael Moore's *Fahrenheit 9/11* was targeted for release around the same time. The film was purported to be about Bush family relationships with the Bin Laden clan and was supposedly going to expose the ways in which the Bush administration used the events of September 11 to push various agendas. There was no word as to the degree of input coming from Oliver Stone's head or the amount of money budgeted for black helicopters.

Then there was *The Hunting of the President*, a film adaptation of the revisionist piece by Joe Conason and Gene Lyons. Hillary Clinton's cuckoo's nest concept of a vast right-wing conspiracy was going to make it to the silver screen. Not a big surprise considering that one of the film's codirectors was Harry Thomason. He and wife Linda Bloodworth-Thomason, you may recall, were two of Bill Clinton's closest Tinseltown buddies.

Dubya drubbing occurred on the little screen, too. In the spring of 2004, NBC's *Whoopi* had a Bush look-alike walk into Whoopi Goldberg's character's hotel to use the restroom. Whoopi's hotelier declared, "I can't believe he's in there doing to my bathroom what he's done to the economy!" When a *New York Times* reporter asked Goldberg whether her show might help bring about a Bush loss in the election, she replied, "I would like that."

In another of TV's cheap shots at the president, one of the detectives on NBC's *Law & Order* described the commander in chief as the "dude that lied to us." The character added, "I don't see any weapons of mass destruction, do you?"

And on a Bush-bopping episode of HBO's *Curb Your Enthusiasm,* an affair involving Larry David's character turned sour because the object of the guy's affection had a portrait of President Bush on top of her dresser.

We hadn't seen Hollywood this ticked off since Heidi Fleiss was forced to take down her shingle.

Tinseltown Bares Its Bias

With many Hollywood players out screaming about how much they hated Bush, it was only natural that they would get involved when it came time for the Democrats to pick a presidential candidate for 2004. In this election, though, things unfolded a bit differently. Big-money players appeared to be holding back through most of the primary season. Compared to the amount of entertainment money seen in previous campaigns, the season seemed to produce a smaller Tinseltown cash flow than normal.

Part of the drop had to do with campaign finance reform, which led to new election regulations that limited "soft money" contributions. But there also seemed to be another trick in play, one where slush-type funds were being used to bypass the law. And Hollywood personalities took some lead roles in the ruse.

Remember how the Dems told us that the way to stop Al Gore from partying with Buddhist nuns was to institute campaign finance reform? Well, they found loopholes. With the help of Hollywood, the Democrats basically skirted the regs they had previously championed.

One group that surfaced is called America Coming Together (ACT). Although its name sounds warm and cuddly, the group is actually sort of cold and prickly. It was formed under a section of the tax code that essentially allows soft money to exceed those pesky $2,000 limits set by McCain, Feingold, and friends. So unlimited amounts of soft money from corporations, unions, and individuals can pour in with a vengeance. Case in point, by early 2004 Bush-whacking billionaire George Soros had already pledged $10 million to ACT. There was every indication that the charade would continue.

Laurie David, wife of enthusiasm-curbing *Seinfeld* creator Larry, organized a pair of star-studded gatherings called Victory Campaign 2004. The events were held at East Coast and Left Coast venues. *Seinfeld* alum Julia Louis-Dreyfus, among others, cohosted the L.A. portion, which according to the Drudge Report was being called a "Hate Bush" meeting. The *New York Daily News* reported that a man in the Midwest had merely added the "Hate Bush" characterization on an e-mail subject line, but Republican National Committee communications director Jim Dyke put it well when he said, "I doubt that anyone who is going disagrees with the e-mail title." The New York event, meanwhile, drew hundreds of lefty activists, including celebs like Susan Sarandon, Tim Robbins, Harvey Weinstein, Meryl Streep, Glenn Close, Kyra Sedgwick, Nora Ephron, and Al Franken.

Harold Ickes was the featured speaker on both coasts. The Clinton administration veteran unveiled something called the Media Fund to the Hollywood crowd. By some estimates the Media Fund would raise as much as $80 million for "independent" advertising and, ultimately, election influence in 2004.

Before getting fired in the fall of 2003, Jim Jordan was John Kerry's first campaign manager. In 2004 Jordan headed up a consulting firm that just happened to represent the Media Fund and ACT. The Media Fund was using bucks from Soros, Hollywood producer Steve Bing, and others to fuel a $5 million campaign against Bush in seventeen battleground states. The Republican National Committee complained that these ads and those aired by MoveOn.org, which was also funded by Soros, violated federal law because they attacked the president rather than advocated an issue. Senator John McCain even threatened to sue the Federal Election Commission if it failed to enforce the law against groups that used soft money to influence presidential and congressional races.

Left Coast King Makers

Months before the Victory Campaign 2004 events were held, the Democrats had begun targeting Tinseltown royals. After Al Gore announced that he would spare the country from another of his personal runs, Dem presidential wanna-be's-in-waiting knew who to phone—director Rob Reiner of Castle Rock Entertainment and "Meathead" fame. Reiner received a triad of calls from John Kerry, Joe Lieberman, and Howard Dean. In less than a week, Reiner had spoken with the three and also chatted with John Edwards and Dick Gephardt.

Early on, Gephardt rendezvoused in Beverly Hills with former film studio owner Marvin Davis. Howard Dean made the scene with Warren Beatty. And John Edwards schmoozed at the Pacific Palisades home of Larry David.

John Kerry was already pretty close buddies with Sherry Lansing, who runs Paramount Pictures, and her husband, director William Friedkin. Lansing and Friedkin sponsored a Beverly Hills birthday bash for Kerry at their home in December 2003. Singer-songwriter Carole King melodically spoke for the bunch when she let the senator know that he's "got a friend" in Hollywood.

Some names of other Left Coast campaign operatives may not be as familiar. But this doesn't make the gamesters any less important in the Tinseltown power lineup. We're talking about the folks who can bring more to the table than some stacks of perfectly flipped flapjacks. They can deliver the deep-pocketed donors.

One of the more obscure bigwigs is Andy Spahn. Former senator and new Disney chairman George Mitchell knows his name, though. So does former senator and presidential candidate Gary Hart. In the past, Spahn raised money for the two Dems. But his latest job is running a foundation for DreamWorks SKG. The SKG stands for Spielberg, Katzenberg, and Geffen. Basically, if someone wants to get ear or face time with Steven Spielberg, Jeffrey Katzenberg, or David Geffen, he or she has to first go through Spahn. You can bet that a lot of candidates and political organizations began hovering around Spahn in 2004.

A fellow named Chad Griffin has a similar gig to Spahn's, but his boss is Rob Reiner. Griffin worked with Reiner on the liberal fluff piece *The American President.*

Another lib power broker is Margery Tabankin. She's an advisor to Barbra Streisand. Tabankin was really a pioneer in the biz. She was executive director of the Hollywood Women's Political Committee, which from 1986 to 1996 raised more than $6 million for the Democrats.

Then there's Laurie David. A dyed-in-the-grass celebrity greenie, Laurie is a board member of the Natural Resources Defense Council, which has lobbied the studios to use hybrid cars on television and in film. The TV shows *Alias* and *24* are both lobby success stories with hybrid-driving characters. Of course, Laurie's husband, Larry, drives a hybrid on his show, *Curb Your Enthusiasm,* and in real life as well. Mrs. David was involved with Norman Lear, Arianna Huffington, and producer Lawrence Bender as they concocted an ad campaign that suggested SUV owners were terrorist supporters.

Most important for aspiring Dems, her Pacific Palisades home is a mandatory stopping place for any serious candidate.

Endorsement Roulette

In 2003 and on into 2004, the Dem primary endorsement game proved to be an interesting one. John Kerry captured the political hearts of Jamie Lee Curtis, Kathleen Turner, Dennis Hopper, Aaron Sorkin, Moby, James Taylor, Bradley Whitford, Jerry Seinfeld, Michael J. Fox, Penny Marshall, Peter Yarrow, Kenneth "Babyface" Edmunds, Quincy Jones, Carole King, and Uma Thurman. Dick Gephardt brought Barry Manilow, Courtney Cox, and Chevy Chase into his fold. Dennis Kucinich got the backing of Ben Affleck, Deepak Chopra, Ed Begley Jr., Casey Kasem, Ed Asner, Linda Blair, Jerry Springer, Jeff Bridges, Elliott Gould, James Cromwell, Willie Nelson, Bonnie Raitt, and Castro lover Danny Glover. John Edwards attracted Glenn Close, Ashton Kutcher, Glenn Frey, Ali McGraw, Hootie, and the Blowfish, too. Sadly for Joe Lieberman, it looks as though he paid a price for pointing out the virtue void in Tinseltown, because Hollywood seemed to say no-go to Joe.

Wesley Clark had a little more luck than Lieberman, snagging the support of Madonna, Michael Moore, Alan Alda, and Christopher Guest. But in pandering to the Tinseltown crowd the general looked anything but presidential. The endorsement from Madonna, for instance, seemed to turn Clark into an "I'm not worthy" *Wayne's World* character. Not long after the Material Girl endorsed him, he began listing her favorite religious organization alongside the world's great faiths. In a speech to Florida Democrats, Clark said, "There's one common principle to every faith that I've ever studied, whether it's Catholicism, Protestantism, Christianity, Buddhism, Islam, Judaism, Kabbalism, or every other, and it's this: that those who are the most fortunate help those who are less fortunate." Kabbalists everywhere applauded their sudden rise in stature.

Throughout his campaign, Clark's religious background seemed to grow more interesting by the hour as he revealed to select constituents that he was raised Jewish, had converted to Catholicism, now attended a Presbyterian church, and may have even been willing to shave his head for the Buddhist vote.

The Michael Moore endorsement caused even more problems for General Clark. Moore stood on stage with Clark and called the president of the United States a "deserter." When confronted with the fact that he had remained silent while the outrageous charge was hurled, Clark replied that Moore was just exercising his right to free speech. The general actually blew a couple of opportunities to distance himself from Moore—first in a January 2004 debate and later on NBC's *Meet the Press*. Each time, he stood by the mudslinging movie maker, even calling Moore "a man of conscience."

Perhaps Clark was desperate to hang on to the few Hollywood endorsements he had managed to corral. After all, it was pretty obvious that at that early stage no one was able to float Hollywood's boat quite like former Vermont governor Howard Dean. After William Jefferson Clinton took his final White House bow, Hollywood was on the lookout for a new liberal hero. Dean seemed to fit the Bill, as he went after President Bush in pit-bull fashion.

He bagged endorsements from the likes of Rob Reiner, Martin Sheen, Susan Sarandon, Michael Douglas, Paul Newman, Mary Steenburgen, Ted Danson, Mel Brooks, Carl Reiner, Whoopi Goldberg, and Robin Williams. Reiner and Sheen even went to Iowa to campaign for Dean during the January caucuses. On CNN, Reiner described Dean as "the only Democratic candidate that can stand toe-to-toe with George Bush," while Sheen proclaimed, "I assure you, he will win."

It just goes to show that political predictions can be dangerous, especially when they come from the mouths of hopeful Hollywood lefties.

Left Coasters remained enthusiastic about Dean until he committed one of Tinseltown's cardinal sins. It wasn't the one where he said we weren't any safer after Saddam Hussein's capture and transfer from spider hole to jail cell. And it wasn't the famed screech during his Iowa concession speech. No, Dean's Hollywood capital offense was his criticism of the Clintons.

Dean let it be known that he planned to get rid of Bill Clinton's money maven, DNC chairman Terry McAuliffe. In January, Dean broke away from the Clinton direction that the Democratic Party had previously taken. "Bill Clinton was a master politician . . . but that was a different time," Dean told supporters. He proclaimed that Clinton's philosophy of governing from the middle was no longer the right thing to do. "I think this is a time to fight," Dean snipped.

Reportedly, Clinton was peeved and let his friends in Hollywood know about it. Dean should have known that in La La Land, Bill Clinton ranks right up there with FDR, JFK, and Cher impersonators. You just don't dis the icons.

Hollywood John

After Howard Dean's campaign imploded, Tinseltown lefties had to scramble to find a Democrat pinch hitter. John Kerry would ultimately be the one.

Actually, Kerry had been cozying up to Hollywood for years. The guy's got a natural affinity for the film capital, and for its endless schmooze potential. The late 1980s were what Kerry's current wife, Teresa Heinz Kerry, refers to as his "gypsy period." It was during this time that Kerry had a puberty flashback. He engaged in one of the more popular Left Coast pastimes—the celebrity dating game.

Kerry usually clams up when it comes to his Tinseltown trysts. When a reporter brings up the subject, Kerry ducks the question and simultaneously smacks Dubya. He typically moans, "If George Bush can run around and say, 'When I was young and irresponsible, I was young and irresponsible,' I can say, 'When I was young and single, I was young and single.'"

During his roving days, Kerry lingered a bit with Morgan Fairchild, Michelle Phillips, and Catherine Oxenberg. He also courted Dana Delany, who wore a black rubber bustier long before Janet Jackson sported one at the 2004 Super Bowl half-time show. Apparently, Dana's outfit was built a bit sturdier than today's theatrical garments.

During the 2004 primary campaign, rumors surfaced that Kerry had reverted to his wildhood days. But those who were aware of his present wife's perspective also knew he best never go there, unless he wouldn't mind being known as John Kerry Bobbitt. Mrs. Kerry told *Elle* magazine that she had made it crystal clear to her first husband, mega-empire heir Jack Heinz, that he'd better be faithful. She warned, "If you ever get something, I'll maim you. I won't kill you. I'll maim you." Wonder if anyone thought to tell John.

Kerry didn't limit his Hollywood activity to starlet hopping. As a matter of fact, he once had a brief stretch in front of the camera. No, it wasn't for the 1991 big-screen version of *The Addams Family*. According to the Internet Movie Database, the Frenchy who would be president was in a film called *The Last Party*. The flick is a documentary about the 1992 Democratic National Convention. It features Robert Downey Jr. interviewing fellow stars and various Dem personalities. Squeezed in between interviews with Bill Clinton, Spike Lee, Roger Clinton, and others is Kerry himself. Evidently, he got to play one of his own body doubles.

When Senator Kerry began getting serious about making a run for the presidency, he set his sights on Hollywood gold. In March 2001, while at a Beverly Hills bash, Kerry let his Hollywood friends know about his presidential aspirations. By 2004, as it began to seem that Kerry was a lock for the Democratic nomination, the Hollywood money started coming in.

Once people in Tinseltown realized that the election was shaping up to be a choice between Bush and Kerry, Hollywood's money engines revved up for the Dem prez hopeful. In February 2004, Teresa Heinz Kerry spoke at the home of actress Cynthia Sikes Yorkin, wife of Norman Lear's partner, Bud Yorkin. Sherry Lansing was one of the cochairs of the event. The guest roster included Maria Shriver, Rita Wilson, Laurie David, Michele Reiner, Melanie Griffith, and Heather Thomas, among others.

DreamWorks' Jeffrey Katzenberg sprung into cash-cultivating action, too. He circulated a letter that invited people to a March 30, 2004, Kerry fund-raiser. Lawrence Bender lent a left hand in organizing. Celebs lined up to pay between $1,000 and $2,000 to attend a Beverly Hills moolah-mustering gala at former food store magnate and billionaire Ron Burkle's five-acre mansion. The 1,500 luminaries included Barbra Streisand, Jennifer Aniston, Jamie Lee Curtis, Dustin Hoffman, Ben Affleck, Tom Arnold, Lucy Liu, Sharon Stone, Meg Ryan, Kevin Costner, David Spade, Martin Short, Richard Lewis, Christina Applegate, Ted Danson, Daryl Hannah, Jon Lovitz, Oliver Stone, Helen Hunt, Ben Stiller, Danny DeVito, Warren Beatty, Don Henley, Ed Harris, Angelica Huston, and Jason Alexander. Guests had the chance to listen to a Bush-clobbering commentary by Larry David before singer James Taylor performed for the group.

"I am a natural-born nincompoop," David quipped. "Not only am I one in life, but I play one on TV. And this I can promise you: I will deliver the nincompoops. They are comfortable with me—comfortable—they love me! Go ahead, ask me who is the president of Japan—I don't know. Ask me what was in the newspapers today—I don't know. You know why? I don't read the newspaper."

The Kerry campaign raked in $3.2 million, with an additional $1 million for the Democratic National Committee, and solidly secured the nincompoop vote.

Interestingly, though, Kerry's "It Guy" status has posed a bit of a dilemma. His voting record is as liberal as it comes, but he's a consummate insider with a teeter-totter take on the issues. Here are some examples of his biggest wobbles:

- He voted against the Gulf War in 1991, but when things started to look good, he claimed he had backed it all along.

- He voted for NAFTA, but as a presidential candidate he said he opposed it.

- He voted for the Patriot Act, but he suddenly condemned it when he set his sights on the White House.

- He voted for the Iraq War Resolution in 2002, but then he voted against its funding.

- He voted for the No Child Left Behind Act, but by 2004 he was against it.

- He has said he opposes gay marriage, but he voted against the Defense of Marriage Act.

- He has said that he's dedicated his entire political career to combating special interests, but he's the number one recipient in the Senate of campaign money from paid lobbyists, according to the Center for Responsive Politics.

The lefties in Tinseltown rallied behind their man in 2004, but few could have predicted that the most spirited debates in the election would take place between John Kerry and himself.

Tinseltown's D.C. Dream Team

Chief of Stiff—Al Gore

Secretary of the Ulterior—Al Franken

Secretary of the Posterior—Jennifer Lopez

Secretary of Agriculture—Paris Hilton

Treasury Secretary—Mike Tyson

Director of the Consumer Product Safety Commission—Janet Jackson

National Insecurity Advisor—Dr. Phil

No Justice No Peace Corps Coordinator—Jesse Jackson

Head of the Office on Aging—Keith Richards

General Unaccountable Office Director and Chief Inspector of Billings Records—Hillary Clinton

Coordinator for the White House Travel Office—Matt Lauer

Miscommunications Director—Terry McAuliffe

Limousine-Liberal Licensing Bureau Chief—Norman Lear

Internal Revenue Service Supervisor—Willie Nelson

Director of the President's Council on Physical Fatness—Calista Flockhart

Head of the Bureau of Alcohol, Tobacco, and Alcohol—Ted Kennedy

Undersecretary of the Oval Office—Monica Lewinsky

Central Unintelligence Agency Director—Frank Rich

Head of the Environmental Perfection Agency—Ed Begley Jr.

Administrators for the U.S. Kiss and Wildlife Service—Madonna and Britney Spears

A Political Glossary
of Hollywood

additional Democrat voter   1. An existence-challenged individual who resides in a Chicago cemetery. 2. A senior citizen in Miami with election dyslexia. 3. An undocumented immigrant who's been bribed with a glazed donut and shuttled in so that he or she can vote in a Los Angeles, Phoenix, Houston, or New York election.

air pollution   A press conference given by Hollywood liberals.

big sleep   What overtakes you when you're listening to an Al Gore speech.

Bill of Rights   1. A collection of ideas drafted by old, dead white guys who owned slaves. 2. The stuff in the Constitution about freedom of speech, assembly, and the press that was meant for actors, artists, and other creative types only and can mean anything a Hollywood celebrity wants it to.

campaign finance A rotten activity that deals with one of the most evil commodities and corrupting influences—money; the activity is forbidden unless it involves a concert or performance given by a high-minded celebrity and raises lots of dough for a liberal Democrat.

diverse The most important thing that an institution, community, or locale can be, as long as it doesn't apply to ideas.

drugs Substances that lead to an improved level of consciousness; used in ample amounts by celebrities whenever it strikes their fancy.

Earth Day A sacred, high holy day set aside to honor Gaia, the goddess of Earth, and to plant hemp seeds.

ecology The organizing principle behind the web of life that's meant to guide all choices, except if a celebrity needs to go a few miles in a limo or helicopter, or needs to do a movie with a high-speed car chase.

family Any collection of people or animals that occupy the same space for more than a minute.

hate speech Speech that's considered racist, sexist, xenophobic, misogynistic, jingoistic, or specie-centrist; banned under all circumstances except when talking about white males.

investment A means of raising taxes while sounding noble; usually used with phrases intended to persuade, like "improve education," "eliminate poverty," and "recycle those old Vera Wang wedding dresses."

left The only political direction allowed in Hollywood.

Marx 1. The brother who was not quite as funny as Groucho. 2. A wonderful, caring leader who had some great ideas about sharing one's personal material wealth with everybody else.

morality A flexible code of ethics that can be bent like an aluminum can and conform to any situation you want it to.

Ms. White and the Seven Vertically Challenged Individuals A classic children's tale whose language has been changed so that the story matches contemporary psychobabble.

open mind The state of mind that every Hollywood liberal strives for, which turns out to be the one that forgets about logic and allows the emotional side of the brain to take over.

political jokes The slate of candidates supported by Hollywood liberals.

political slogan "You can fool some of the people all of the time, so focus your attention on the ones you can fool easily."

powerful interest For men, it's the enraged ex-wife or ex-girlfriend. For women, it's the boyfriend who holds the nude pictures of you. Otherwise, it's the madam, studio boss, or mega-agent who'll take your call.

profanity The hippest form of artistic expression.

right The direction that leads to the place of eternal punishment, where creatures that come between "reptile" and "repugnant" are sent.

sex   1. The most essential thing to include in any screen-play, TV sitcom, or music video. 2. The activity that takes precedence over everything else, except for drugs, and should be engaged in wherever, whenever, and with whomever a celebrity so desires.

smoking   The most embarrassing thing one can be caught doing, unless the tobacco-related behavior looks cool and is featured in a movie that's designed for kids or teens.

Notes

Chapter 1

1. Victor S. Navasky, *Naming Names* (New York: Penguin Books, 1991), 202.
2. Interview with George Putnam, 15 December 2002.
3. Interview with Jane Russell, 15 February 2003.
4. In 1995 Harvey Klehr and John Earl Haynes published *The Secret World of American Communism,* a collection of documents they stumbled across in the Soviet Union, followed in 1998 by a second document collection.
5. Stephen Koch, *Double Lives: Spies and Writers in the Secret Soviet War of Ideas Against the West* (New York: Free Press, 1994).
6. See generally Kenneth Lloyd Billingsley, *Hollywood Party: How Communism Seduced the American Film Industry in the 1930s and 1940s* (Roseville, California: Prima Publishing, 2000).
7. Arthur Koestler, *Darkness at Noon* (New York: Bantam Books, 1981).
8. Ibid.
9. Victor A. Kravchenko, *I Chose Freedom: The Personal and Political Life of a Soviet Official* (New York: Charles Scribner's Sons, 1946).
10. www.discovery.com, TLC, "The Ukraine Famine."

Chapter 2

1. Fred Goodman, *The Mansion on the Hill* (New York: Times Books, 1997), xi.
2. Robert Shelton, *No Direction Home: The Life and Music of Bob Dylan* (New York: William Morrow, 1986), 75. Dylan explained his need for a new identity to a few close friends.
3. David Hajdu, *Positively 4th Street* (New York: Farrar, Straus and Giroux, 2001), 212, 213.
4. Shelton, 287.
5. Blair Jackson, *Garcia* (New York: Viking, 1999), 85 and editors of *Rolling Stone, Garcia* (New York: Little, Brown and Company, 1995), 10.

6. See Tom Wolfe, *The Electric Kool-Aid Acid Test* (New York: Bantam, 1999).

Chapter 3

1. Spielberg's office wrote to NewsMax in May 2003 claiming that the director never made the statement and blaming Castro's state-run press for its origin. The quote appeared between November 2002 and June 2003 in *The Wall Street Journal, The Boston Globe, The Washington Times, Providence Journal-Bulletin, Washington Monthly,* and *Deutsche Presse-Agentur.* It was also broadcast on CNN's *Crossfire,* MSNBC's *Scarborough Country,* and Fox News Channel's *The O'Reilly Factor.*

Chapter 4

1. *Time,* 4 March 2002 cover.
2. Tom Giliatto, "Bono's World," *People,* 25 February 2002.
3. Other quotes for Bono section, Madeleine Bunting and Oliver Burkeman, "Pro Bono," *The Guardian,* 18 March 2002.
4. *Sacramento Bee,* 12 August 2002.
5. Lawrence Goodman, "Celebrity Pill Pushers," Salon.com, 11 July 2002, and "Stars Profit from Covert Drug Pitches," CBSNews.com, 29 August 2002.
6. "Stars Profit from Covert Drug Pitches," CBSNews.com, 29 August 2002.
7. Melody Petersen, "Heartfelt Advice, Hefty Fees," *New York Times,* 8 August 2002.
8. Ibid.
9. Lawrence Goodman, "Celebrity Pill Pushers," Salon.com, 11 July 2002. All quotes in this section that are not referenced are from Mr. Goodman's article.
10. "Famous People Pair Up with Charities," *Market Place,* Minnesota Public Radio, 10 October 2002.
11. Ibid.
12. Ibid.

Chapter 5

1. *Washington Post,* 13 November 1983. See also Deroy Murdock, "PETA Puts Rats First & People Last," *National Review Online,* 22 June 2000.
2. Dean Schabner, "New Front on Ecoterror?" ABCNews.com, 26 February 2002.
3. As per Jeff Getty, interviewed by Norma Bennett Woolf for www.naia.org.

4. Ibid.

5. Baldwin told this to KCAL TV, 14 December 1996, as reported by Cal Thomas, "Will Radicals Rule and Humans Suffer?" *Los Angeles Times,* 24 June 1997. Also reported by *New Orleans Times—Picayune,* 21 June 1997.

6. Judy Wieder, "Melissa Etheridge," *The Advocate,* 23 January 1998.

7. Sarah Ferguson, "Strike a Pose," *New York,* 7 November 1994. For animal research quotes, see generally www.fbresearch.org.

Chapter 6

1. *The Nation,* "Under the Cloud of Clintonism," 5 April 1999.

2. Ronald Brownstein, *The Power and the Glitter: The Hollywood—Washington Connection* (New York: Pantheon Books, 1990), 278.

3. Ibid, 279.

4. Ibid, 284, 285.

5. The section "Bashing Republicans," relies in part on Brownstein, chapter 8.

6. *E-Online,* 14 February 2001.

7. *Newsday,* 15 February 2001.

8. Interview with David Horowitz by telephone, 27 January 2003.

9. Ibid.

10. Media Fellowship International Web site, www.mediafellowship.org.

11. Peter Biskind, "On Movies, Money, and Politics," *The Nation,* 5 April 1999.

12. Most of the anti-religious film titles are from a manuscript by John W. Cones, *Patterns of Bias in Motion Picture Content* (Los Angeles: Rivas Canyon Press, 1996), as excerpted on the Web site of the Film Industry Reform Movement.

13. Enid Memy, "Broadway," *New York Times,* 28 June 1985, 17, as found in Paul F. Boller, Jr. and Ronald L. Davis, *Hollywood Anecdotes* (New York: Ballantine Books, 1987), 383.

14. One board member is said to have pointed out that Welch seemed to have her own ethical code because she had never appeared nude in her films, and another board member exclaimed, "I'd rather see her take her clothes off than hear her use language like 'mother f——r!" Jerald Mast, Editor, *The Movies in Our Midst: Documents in History of Film in America* (Chicago: University of Chicago Press, 1982), 710–11, as found in Boller and Davis, 390. The section, "The Anti-Code" relies in part on Boller and Davis, chapter 30.

15. The section "Pampered to Pieces" relies in part on Charles Fleming, *High Concept* (New York: Doubleday, 1998), 167–71.

Chapter 7

1. Patrick Goldstein, "The Big Picture: Ad Banned but Smoking on Screen Isn't," *Los Angeles Times,* 5 March 2002.

2. John Morgan, "Film Puts Spotlight on Moviemaking," *USA Today,* 30 April 2001.

3. Public Interest Research Group of Massachusetts press release of 29 October 2002.

4. The section "Hand-Me-Down Smoke" relies in part on "Hollywood Defends Smoking on Screen," *BBC News Online,* 6 January 2000.

Chapter 8

1. Patricia Ward Biederman, "Winning the War, One Frame at a Time," *Los Angeles Times,* 30 October 2002, for information on Stanley Frazen and his unit.

2. Interview with Jane Russell, 15 February 2003.

3. Roy Hoopes, *When the Stars Went to War: Hollywood in World War II* (New York: Random House, 1994), 101, 102. See chapter 5 for Pearl Harbor, the aftermath, and pinup quotes.

4. See Hoopes, chapter 6.

5. *Washington Post,* 18 February 2002.

6. *Hollywood Reporter,* 12 December 2002.

Chapter 9

1. See generally Elliott Negin, "The Alar Scare Was for Real: And So Is That 'Veggie Hate Crime' Movement," *Columbia Journalism Review,* 19 September 1996: 13–15.

2. Tom Knudson, "Movement's Prosperity Comes at High Price," *Sacramento Bee,* 22 April 2001, for information on CEO salaries, et cetera.

3. Much of the information on the Environmental Media Association can be found on its Web site, www.ema-online.org.

4. "Mixing Celebrities and Politics," CBSNews.com, 7 June 2002.

5. Daniel B. Wood, "Can't Reach the Beach?: Turf War on Malibu's Coast," *Christian Science Monitor,* 23 September 2002, and James M. Taylor, "Hollywood Hypocrites," *Hartland Institute,* 1 July 2002.

Index